Strategies & Tactics for the MPRE

Multistate Professional Responsibility Exam

Kimm Alayne Walton, J.D.

emanuel®

Also available in the *Strategies & Tactics Series*

- *Strategies & Tactics for the First Year Law Student*
- *Strategies & Tactics for the MBE*
  (Multistate Bar Examination)
- *The Finz Multistate Method*

Other study aid products from Emanuel

- *Emanuel Law Outline series*
- *Law In A Flash* Flashcards
- *Law In A Flash* Interactive Software for Windows & Windows 95
- *The Professor (Smith's Review) Series*
- *Siegel's Essay and Multiple-Choice Q&A series*
- *Steve Emanuel's First Year Questions & Answers*
- *Latin for Lawyers*

ISBN 1-56542-592-8
Printed in Canada

Published by
Emanuel Publishing Corp.
1865 Palmer Avenue, Larchmont, NY 10538
1-800-EMANUEL • http://www.emanuel.com

Table of Contents

Part One
Plan of Attack for the MPRE

A. Introduction

If you think about legal ethics, you will agree it's a pretty bad candidate for a multiple choice exam. The rules are fuzzy and there are a lot of gray areas; there just aren't the bright line distinctions that make for a good, straightforward objective exam. Well if you feel that way, reading this book isn't going to change your mind. If anything, it'll reinforce your feeling that legal ethics shouldn't be the subject of a multiple choice exam. But the fact remains that if you want to practice law in almost any state, you have to take the MPRE, and that's what the MPRE is—a multiple choice exam testing your knowledge of legal ethics.

Ironically enough, the fact that legal ethics is poorly suited to a multiple choice exam actually makes the MPRE a lot easier than it might otherwise be. There's a really sound reason for this: in order for a multiple choice exam to be valid, the answers have to be <u>unquestionably</u> correct. The kiss of death for a multiple choice question is to make you respond "Well, the answer is A if you interpret it this way, and B if you interpret it this other way." That would be called an invalid testing item because it doesn't have only one right answer. This simple idea, that each MPRE question has to have one, indisputably correct answer, means that the questions and answers have to be written in a particularly heavy–handed way. In fact, MPRE questions and answers are written with such broad brush strokes that in a lot of cases, you can actually choose the right answer without even <u>reading</u> the questions themselves at all! I'll show you how that's done a little later in this section. My point right now is just this; the MPRE isn't particularly difficult, and with the advice in this book and a little extra preparation, you should pass it quite easily.

That doesn't mean you can blow off the MPRE entirely, wander in on test day and hope for the best. But it does mean that you'll need to spend far less time studying for it than you would for most exams. Frankly there are only two things that you really need to do: one is to get familiar with the ethics rules, and the other is to get a feel for the kinds of questions that appear on the MPRE.

When it comes to learning the ethics rules, your primary source will be (i) the two codes of lawyer conduct—those are the Model Code of Professional Responsibility and the Model Rules of Professional Conduct—and (ii) the Code of Judicial Conduct. The Bar Examiners claim that the entire MPRE comes from those codes. That's a little disingenuous because the MPRE tests a number of items that you really couldn't answer based just on the ethics codes themselves, like malpractice. Apart from that, the codes are incredibly tedious to read. So you'd be well advised to do a little more substantive preparation than just going over the codes. I recommend the *Law In A Flash* cards on Professional Responsibility and *Siegel's* essay and multiple-choice questions on Professional Responsibility, which you can find at just about any law school bookstore. They cover all three codes to the level of detail tested on the MPRE. The cards take about 8–10 hours to review. They incorporate modern learning techniques which not only teach you the rules, but also how to apply those rules to facts quickly and effectively.

Of course, you can use any source to review the ethics rules—outlines, hornbooks, whatever. The point is, you have to know the rules. Other than that, you ought to get a feel for MPRE questions themselves. And that's what this book will show you. In this first part, I'll show you how to attack MPRE questions, and in Part Two, you'll have a chance to put this plan of attack into practice on some practice MPRE questions. Be careful! I know you'll be tempted to skip this first part and plunge right into the practice questions. I'd strongly discourage that, because if you only spent a half hour preparing for the MPRE, the best way you could possibly spend that time would be to read this first part. If you put my plan of attack to work for you, I think you'd actually have to make an effort to fail the MPRE.

As you'll notice soon if you haven't already, there are only fifty practice questions in this book. If you were expecting to review thousands of questions for the MPRE—relax. The reason there are only fifty review questions here is that you simply don't need any more than that. With the plan of attack I'll lay out for you and these fifty review questions, you really have all the practice you need. You'd be better off spending any additional study time you'd set aside for the MPRE doing substantive review, or chilling out at the beach, for that matter. You just won't need to do any more.

Incidentally, all of the questions in this book—the ones I use for examples in this part, and the practice questions in Part Two—are real MPRE questions. They've all appeared on actual MPREs, and they're in this book courtesy of the National Conference of Bar Examiners. So you don't have to worry about whether the questions in this book resemble the ones you'll see on your MPRE; they're written by the same people who'll write your MPRE!

B. Basic Information About the MPRE

Background – The MPRE is created and administered by the National Conference of Bar Examiners, which is also responsible for the Multistate Bar Examination. It's currently administered in 39 states, as well as the District of Columbia.

When Offered – The MPRE is administered three times a year: in March, August, and November. In many states, you can take the MPRE before you finish law school; most students who do so take the exam in March of their final year of law school.

Format and Length – The MPRE is a 50-question, multiple choice exam which lasts just over two hours. It is similar to the Multistate Bar Examination in the sense that each question includes a fact pattern followed by four answer choices, of which you are supposed to choose the "best" response. Later in Part One I'll give you lots of examples of this question format, and we'll learn to analyze it down to its most essential elements.

Coverage – Officially, the MPRE covers the 1969 Model Code of Professional Responsibility and the 1983 Model Rules of Professional Conduct, as well as the Code of Judicial Conduct, including the 1990 amendments to the Judicial Code. It doesn't cover any individual state's code of ethics, to the extent they disagree with the Model Code and the Model Rules. According to the MPRE information pamphlet issued by the National Conference of Bar Examiners, "[a]all questions should be answered according to the provisions of these codes and rules." As I mentioned earlier, this is a little bit misleading. That's because insofar as they show how ethical rules apply to factual situations, court cases and ABA decisions can be sources of MPRE questions. So you shouldn't think that understanding the codes, without being familiar with how they are applied to facts, is all you can expect to be tested on. Furthermore, malpractice, which isn't mentioned in either code, is tested, which tells you in and of itself that the scope of what's tested goes beyond the codes. In terms of the breakdown of questions, approximately 42–45 cover the two lawyer codes, the Model Rules and the Model Code. The remaining 5–8 questions cover the Code of Judicial Conduct.

4

Scoring – Your MPRE score is determined by how many questions you answer correctly; there's no penalty for incorrect answers. The practical ramification of this is that it pays to answer every question, even if you're not exactly sure what the correct answer is.

Passing Score – This is probably the thing you'd most like to know. Unfortunately there's no single answer for it, because states vary in the passing score they require. To find out the passing score in your state, call your state board of bar examiners.

How to Apply for the MPRE – To apply for the MPRE, write or call:

> National Conference of Bar Examiners
> MPRE Application Department
> Post Office Box 4001
> Iowa City, Iowa 52243
> Phone: 319/337–1287

They'll send you an application form, as well as an information booklet which tells you everything you need to know about the mechanics of sitting for the MPRE.

C. Wrinkles in Studying for the MPRE: How to Reconcile Differences in the Ethics Codes

As I've mentioned before, the MPRE tests three codes of ethics—two lawyer codes and one judicial code. The bulk of the exam covers the two lawyer codes—the 1969 Model Code of Professional Responsibility and the 1983 Model Rules of Professional Conduct.

Now your instinct might be that the MPRE only ought to test the newer, 1983 code. After all, the ABA created the new code because it was better than the old code. The problem is that a lot of states preferred the old code, and some still follow it. So the MPRE tests both codes.

However, this doesn't mean what you might expect—namely, that some of the questions test the Model Code and others test the Model Rules. Instead, one of the most confusing aspects of the MPRE is that the answer to every question must be the same under both lawyer codes. That is, they test both codes at the *same time*. Here in Topic C I'll explain the ramifications of this rather bizarre concept.

I want to get rid of a popular misconception about this idea of "same results" right off the bat. Many students take this to mean that the MPRE can only ask questions in areas where the rule under both codes is the same. This isn't true—the restriction only dictates how questions can be *asked*; it doesn't really cut out any material you have to study. An example is probably the best way to show why this is so.

Suppose you represent a client in a criminal case, who's accused of embezzlement. He tells you that he's going to murder his boss so that the boss can't testify against him. An MPRE question could ask you if it would be proper for you to disclose your client's intent to the police, because under both codes, a lawyer may disclose his client's intent to commit crimes likely to result in imminent death or substantial bodily harm. But say instead that your client tells you that he's going to set up a counterfeiting operation in his basement to support himself once this whole mess is cleared up. You couldn't be asked whether you could disclose his intent on the MPRE, because the result would be different under the two codes. Under the Model Code, you could properly disclose the information, because you can properly disclose a client's intent to commit any crime; however, under the Model Rules, you can only disclose your client's intent to commit crimes likely to result in imminent death or substantial bodily harm. As this example illustrates, the "same result" restriction on the MPRE does eliminate some questions from being asked, but doesn't really cut out any material from your studies.

Having said that the "same result" rule doesn't change what you have to study, there is one exception that you may want to keep in mind: the MPRE won't give you any questions where the result would be unconstitutional. The most common area this is likely to impact is advertising and solicitation. Many of the restrictions on solicitation in the Model Code have since been declared unconstitutional by the Supreme Court. The Model Rules are revised to comport with Supreme Court decisions, but the Model Code isn't. The Bar Examiners say they would not "consciously solicit" an unconstitutional answer, so you can rest assured that much of the Model Code coverage of advertising and solicitation can't be tested.

1. How the Codes Are Organized

NOTE: If you've recently completed a course on Professional Responsibility or are already familiar with the ethics codes, you can skip this topic, and move down to the next one, "Determining where the codes coincide."

It helps, in understanding how the codes are organized, to think of the conduct addressed as fitting a continuum.

Mandatory	Aspirational		Aspirational	Mandatory
Must	Should	**Permissible**	Should not	Must not

| 1. Discipline not to so behave. | 2. Improper not to so behave, but not subject to discipline. | 3. Act/Omission is proper. | 4. Improper to so behave, but not subject to discipline. | 5. Discipline to so behave. |

Let's look at each code separately, to see how each handles conduct along this continuum. Let's start with the Model Code. It has two distinct types of rules: Ethical Considerations and Disciplinary Rules. Ethical Considerations are the aspirational goals of professional conduct. Ethical Considerations cover numbers 2 and 4 on the continuum; they tell a lawyer what he should and shouldn't do. Violating Ethical Considerations, then, means that a lawyer has acted improperly, but he isn't subject to discipline (unless there is a Disciplinary Rule covering the same conduct).

If a goal in the Ethical Considerations is considered sufficiently important (or, and this is just a hunch, sufficiently enforceable), there is a corresponding Disciplinary Rule covering the conduct in question. Conduct covered by the Disciplinary Rules is mandatory; that is, if a lawyer doesn't comport with the Disciplinary Rules, he will be subject to discipline. This conduct is covered on the continuum by numbers 1 and 5.

Now let's turn to the Model Rules. They are organized very differently; there are only Rules, no Ethical Considerations or Disciplinary Rules. Instead, the Rules distinguish between levels of permissibility by using the terms "must" or "shall," "should," "must not" or "shall not," and "should not." If a Model Rule states that a lawyer must or shall act in a specific way, he'll be subject to discipline if he doesn't. This corresponds with #1 on the continuum, and a Disciplinary Rule under the Model Code. If a Model Rule says that a lawyer should perform in a specific way, he acts improperly if he doesn't so behave. This corresponds with #2 on the continuum, and an Ethical Consideration under the Model Code. (The same goes for the other side of the spectrum, with "should not" and "must not" or "shall not.")

The Code of Judicial Conduct ("CJC") doesn't adopt the must/should distinction, nor does it have Ethical Considerations and Disciplinary

Rules; instead, it almost always uses the word "should," but there's an important interpretational difference between this code and the two lawyer codes. When the CJC says "should" or "should not," the conduct is considered mandatory (that is, a judge would be subject to discipline for failure to comply.

Table 1: Differences in Format Between Codes

	MODEL RULES	MODEL CODE	CJC
ASPIRATIONAL	Language used: "Should" "Should not"	Location: Ethical Consideration	
MANDATORY	Language used: "Must," "Shall" "Must not" "Shall not"	Location: Disciplinary Rules	Language used: "Should." All rules are mandatory.

While the two lawyer codes are similar, there are significant differences in some topics between the two. Some areas, like discovery abuses and corporate lawyer problems, simply weren't addressed in the original Model Code; they do appear in the newer Model Rules. The seriousness of some infractions was reconsidered, as well; for instance, the duty of zealous advocacy, mandatory in the Model Code, is only aspirational in the Model Rules. In other instances, the Bar apparently simply reconsidered the desirability of certain conduct (for instance, disclosing client perjury is prohibited under the Model Code, and required under the Model Rules). A complete discussion of the differences between the two codes is beyond the scope of this book, but should form an integral part of your studying for the MPRE. If you use *Law In A Flash* to study for the MPRE, you'll find that the differences between the codes are noted on every applicable card.

2. Determining Where the Codes Coincide

Since you can only be tested on the MPRE on questions where the answer would be the same under both codes, you need to know how to determine what standard applies when the codes disagree. It's easiest to do this by referring back to our continuum of conduct, above. Now I'll warn you up front that this is a little technical, but I'll explain it thoroughly and I think you'll find there's nothing about it that's difficult at all.

As a threshold matter, determining where the codes coincide on any one issue depends on whether the question you're analyzing tells you the lawyer has already done (or not done) something, or whether it asks about the lawyer's future conduct. Simply put, you *have to divide conduct into* past and future conduct. Here are the rules you should remember:

a. MUST/SHOULD: One code says a lawyer <u>must</u> do something; the other says he <u>should</u> do something.

FUTURE – (that is, the conduct hasn't happened yet): If one code tells you a lawyer must do something and the other tells you he *should*, he *should* do it to comply with both codes.

PAST – (that is, the behavior has already occurred): If one code tells you a lawyer must do something and the other tells you he *should*, and he didn't do it, he's acted *improperly* under both codes.

Let's look at an example: the duty of zealous advocacy. Under the Model Code, a lawyer *must* zealously advocate his client's interests; under the Model Rules, a lawyer *should* do so. Thus, in order to comply with both codes, a lawyer *should* zealously advocate his client's interests. This is the "future" possibility. Say instead that a question tells you that a lawyer has already failed to zealously advocate his client's interests. He's acted *improperly* under both codes. Note that he isn't subject to discipline under both codes, since the Model Rules only makes the conduct improper; however, since anything that's disciplinable is inherently improper, he's also acted improperly under the Model Code. This is the "past" possibility.

b. MUST NOT/SHOULD NOT: One code says a lawyer <u>must not</u> do something; the other says he <u>should not</u> do something.

FUTURE – (that is, the conduct hasn't happened yet): If one code tells you a lawyer *must not* do something and the other tells you he *should not*, he *should not* do it to comply with both codes.

PAST – (that is, the behavior has already occurred): If one code tells you a lawyer *must not* do something and the other tells you he *shouldn't*, and he already did it, he acted *improperly* under both codes.

c. SHOULD/MAY: One code says the lawyer <u>should</u> do something, and the other says he <u>may</u> do it.

FUTURE – (that is, the conduct hasn't happened yet): If one code says a lawyer *should* do something and the other says he *may*, he *should* do it in order to act properly.

PAST– (that is, the conduct has already occurred): If one code says a lawyer *should* do something and the other says he *may*, and he doesn't do it, you can only be asked if his failure to so behave is disciplinable. That's because it is not disciplinable under either Code. This chart will make it clearer why this is so. In every case, assume the lawyer didn't do whatever the conduct in question was. So for instance where "Should" and "Discipline" intersect, the question is whether or not the lawyer should be *disciplined* for something he *should* have done, but didn't do. And the answer, as the chart suggests, is "No."

	SHOULD	MAY
DISCIPLINE?	No	No
IMPROPER?	Yes	No
PROPER?	No	Yes

As you can see, the only place where the two codes agree is on discipline, and so that's the only available question.

Say, instead, that the lawyer did the conduct in question. You could be asked if he acted *properly, improperly, or whether he's subject to discipline*, because the answer would be the same under both codes: No. That is, if he did what he should have done or may have done, he's not subject to discipline under both codes, he didn't act improperly under both codes, and he acted properly under both codes.

d. MENTION/SILENT: One code <u>mentions</u> something, and the other <u>doesn't mention</u> it at all.

If one code mentions conduct and the other is silent on the subject, follow the code that mentions it. For instance, corporate lawyer duties are covered in detail under the Model Rules and hardly mentioned under the Model Code. The codes would be *construed* consistently, and so you should follow the one that offers the details.

e. SILENT/SILENT: Neither code mentions something .

If neither code mentions conduct, then a lawyer acts properly whether or not he does it.

3. A Word of Reassurance About Where the Codes Coincide.

If you feel a bit overwhelmed by all these rules, don't be. The MPRE is rarely nit–picky enough to give you a question where the conduct would be subject to discipline under one code and only improper under the other, and ask you whether it would be subject to discipline. Instead, the following are the things you'll most likely see:

a. A question asks you if the Attorney is subject to discipline.

Either both codes will subject the attorney to discipline, in which the answer would be yes, or the conduct is proper under both codes (for instance, because an exception to a rule applies), in which case the answer under both codes is no. You would probably not be asked if conduct was subject to discipline under circumstances where it would be subject to discipline under one code but only improper under the other.

b. A question asks you if the Attorney's conduct was improper.

First, if there are possibilities both codes will subject the attorney to discipline, the answer would be yes. One code will subject him to discipline and the other would consider the conduct improper, in which case the answer would still be yes. Or both codes would consider the conduct improper, in which case the answer would be yes. Or both codes would consider the conduct proper, in which case the answer would be no.

What this tells you is that as long as you can rule out the possibility that the conduct is *proper*, the answer has to reflect the fact that the attorney's conduct was improper.

(Note that you'd use virtually the mirror image of this reasoning if the question asked you if the attorney's conduct was proper.)

c. A question asks you if the attorney is subject to malpractice.

In this case all you need to do is determine if the attorney's conduct was negligent, and whether this negligence continued to a result vastly different and less beneficial to the client than if the attorney had acted properly. As part of the proximate cause element of malpractice, the client would have to show that the result would—not may—have been different had the lawyer acted non–negligently. However, you don't have a problem with rectifying codes in mal-practice, because neither of them mentions it.

D. Attacking the MPRE

1. Getting Familiar with the Question Format.

MPRE questions are arranged this way: They have a fact pattern, which gives you background facts. Those are followed by a specific inquiry, called the "call" of the question. Finally there are four answer choices, of which you are supposed to choose the "best" response. Here's a typical example:

Attorney was retained to represent Client on a contract claim. After a number of attempts at settlement of the case, Attorney concluded that the case could not be settled and would have to be tried. Attorney did not regard himself as a competent trial lawyer and believed that Client's best interests required the association of competent trial counsel.

One week before the trial date, Attorney associated Trier, whom Attorney knew as a competent trial lawyer, to conduct the trial and so informed Client. The total fee charged Client was not increased by the association of Trier.

Was it <u>proper</u> for Attorney to associate Trier?

A. Yes, because Client's best interests required the association of competent trial counsel.

B. Yes, because Client was informed of the association of Trier.

C. No, if Client did not consent to the association of Trier.

D. No, unless Attorney himself attended the trial with Trier.

In this question, the first and second paragraphs are the fact pattern. The final sentence, beginning "Was it proper..." is the "call" of the question—it tells you specifically what you must answer. A through D are "answer options," one of which is the best response, and the other three are "distractors." (Incidentally, the best response is C.) While the question design above is the most common type of MPRE question, there is a variation which you may see, which looks like this:

Client, a new client of Attorney, has asked Attorney to write a letter recommending Client's nephew for admission to the bar. Client has told Attorney that he has no direct contact with nephew, but that Client's sister (nephew's mother) has assured Client that the nephew is industrious and honest.

Which of the following is (are) proper for Attorney?

I. Write the letter on the basis of Client's assurance.

II. Write the letter on the basis of Client's assurance if Attorney has no unfavorable information about the nephew.

III. Make an independent investigation and write the letter only if Attorney is thereafter satisfied that the nephew is qualified.

A. III only

B. I and II, but not III

C. I and III, but not II

D. I, II, and III

As you can see, the difference here is that the answers you have to analyze are really I, II, and III, instead of A, B, C, and D. Otherwise, the question format is the same as the traditional format, and you'll analyze it the same way. (Incidentally, the best response is A.)

2. Reading the Fact Patterns.

On the MPRE, you have approximately two minutes to read a question, answer it, and move on. Not only does this mean that you have to have a ready grasp of the ethics rules, but you also must be able to read quickly and carefully, and you need to know what to look for. That's what we'll discuss here. The most important thing to keep in mind about the MPRE is that it's very constrained in terms of the types of questions that may be raised. I mentioned this point early in the introduction, but I want to flesh it out here because I think it goes a long way toward "defanging" the MPRE.

As with all standardized tests, the MPRE simply cannot test gray areas; the facts must clearly point toward one and only one result in order for the question to be "psychometrically" sound (basically, in order for the question to be a valid measure of competence). What this means in practical terms is best shown by example. Let's say that you and your best friend study for the MPRE together, and you both have an equally detailed knowledge of the rules of ethics; in fact, your knowledge of the rules is identical. In order for any given question on the MPRE to be valid, you would both have to choose the same response; if you *didn't*, this would mean that the question wasn't testing your competence, because you both had the same knowledge of the rules, but, because of the way the question was *presented*, you interpreted the facts differently and arrived at different results. If this one question were the difference between passing and failing the MPRE, one of you would pass and the other would fail, *even though you were equally competent because your knowledge of the codes was identical.* From a testing point of view, this would make the test invalid, because it wouldn't be distinguishing students on the basis of competence.

For instance, say a question involves a lawyer's undertaking representation of multiple parties and there's a conflict of interest involved. The issue is can the lawyer represent all of them in light of this conflict. In order to seek consent from the parties, the lawyer must *reasonably believe* he can represent all parties adequately. "Reasonably" is a word which is totally fact–dependent. Thus, if the Bar Examiner wanted you to decide that the lawyer *could* properly represent all the parties, one of two things would have to be present: 1. the facts would have to make it unmistakably clear that the lawyer's belief is reasonable, or 2. the correct response would have to *condition* the propriety of the representation on reasonability—for instance, by saying, "The representation is proper if the lawyer reasonably believes he can adequately represent the parties and he obtains their fully–informed consent." (We'll cover much more on conditional answers later.) In fact, if, after a question is offered on the MPRE, it doesn't "perform as intended"—a euphemistic term for an ambiguous question sneaking by the drafting committee—it's dropped from the exam.

If this testing validity theory isn't all that clear to you, don't worry. The only thing that really matters is that you appreciate its impact on what you should look for in MPRE fact patterns. Let's look at these individually.

a. Pay special attention to states of mind.

With many ethical rules, conduct is only required or prohibited if the attorney *knows* or *believes* something. Thus, pay special attention to words like "knows," "concludes," "becomes convinced," "believes," "reasonably believes." In fact, for many ethical responsibilities, the attorney's belief is more important than the underlying fact.

For instance, take recommendations for admission to the bar. A lawyer cannot recommend for admission to the bar someone he *knows* to be "unqualified." Note that it doesn't matter whether a person you recommend is a pimp, a drug dealer, or the slimiest form of pond scum ever to crawl the Earth; as long as *you don't know about it*, you're free to recommend that person for admission to the bar.

Take another example, in conflicts of interest. In most conflict cases, the conflict can be remedied by consent of the affected party/parties. However, before the lawyer can even *seek* his client's consent, he must *reasonably believe* he can carry on the representation without adverse effects from the conflict of interest. Here again, it doesn't really matter whether he can or can't do so, as long as he *believes* that he can, and that this belief is reasonable.

We could go on and on with examples, but you get the idea; it's frequently important to pay attention to the attorney's beliefs and knowledge in determining whether or not he's acted ethically.

b. Pay attention to the motivation behind an action or omission.

Just as an attorney's knowledge or beliefs can determine the propriety or impropriety of his behavior, so too can the reason why he undertakes certain conduct. Thus, you should always make special note of why an attorney acts in a particular way in MPRE questions.

In certain areas of ethics, like permissive and mandatory withdrawal from representation, the attorney's motivation in withdrawing is obviously crucial in determining whether or not the withdrawal is ethical. It's not so much that kind of situation we're addressing here, but the more insidious circumstances under which the issue can arise. Take, for instance, calling certain witnesses at trial. Ordinarily, whether or not to call a certain witness is the decision of the attorney, not the client. Thus, if the attorney, in his informed professional judgment, decides *not* to call a certain witness, he's acted perfectly properly. However, say instead that the failure to call the witness was due to laziness. This would not be part of the attorney's professional judgment, but would rather constitute incompetence, and would be unethical on that basis. Thus, where the propriety of behavior can be determined by the attorney's *motivation,* be careful to watch for evidence of that motivation.

c. Ignore "window dressing"—pay attention to the core behavior, and whether or not that behavior (or lack of it) is ethical.

In some MPRE questions, the Bar Examiners test your faith in your knowledge of the ethical rules by taking certain unethical behavior and surrounding it with the "trappings" of propriety, to see if you can be shaken in your belief that the conduct is unethical.

For instance, take competence. You know that lawyers have a duty to provide competent service. A question that asked you whether or not a lawyer would be subject to discipline for providing incompetent service, free of other facts, wouldn't really lure anyone, no matter how little they knew about the rules of ethics, into choosing a wrong answer. As a result it wouldn't make a very good MPRE question. But let's spice it up a bit. Say that the lawyer *tells* the client that he's not competent to handle the matter, but the client insists on the lawyer handling it anyway. Say in addition that the client is the lawyer's biggest client, and that the client says he'll withdraw all his work if the lawyer doesn't accept the matter. Getting more interesting, isn't it? Say that the client even signs an affidavit acknowledging that the lawyer isn't sufficiently skilled in the matter to offer competent service, and promising that the client will not sue for malpractice regardless of the outcome of the case. What you've got now is a situation where the "nut" of the matter is the same: the lawyer is offering incompetent service. But there's a very important addition, namely, the client's insistence on the lawyer handling the work, and his waiver of his right to competent service. What this does is make an easy question into a more challenging one, just by embellishing the facts.

The way to insulate yourself from such a trap is to strip away all the window–dressing, and ask yourself what, in essence, is going on. In our example, the lawyer is offering incompetent service. Then work your way up from there, and see if any of the additional facts—here, client consent—change the nature of that core conduct. In the case of incompetent service, none of the additional facts make the lawyer's conduct ethical. If you maintain your focus this way, you will make it extremely difficult for the bar examiners to undermine your confidence by layering on facts that don't change the nature of the conduct in the question.

3. Reading the Call of the Question

The "call" of the question is where you learn the precise question you have to answer. The facts, up to this point, are no more than background, and they're only important if they impact the call of the question. The call of the question can be general—for instance, asking if Attorney's conduct in the fact pattern was proper, improper, or subject to discipline—or it can be specific, wherein you're asked about a specific aspect of the attorney's conduct. A specific call is far more common than a general one.

a. "General" call.

With a general call, a prevailing issue will probably spring into your mind when you read the fact pattern. Here's an example:

> Attorney is a member of the bar and a salaried employee of the trust department of Bank. As part of his duties, he prepares a monthly newsletter concerning wills, trusts, estates, and taxes which Bank sends to all of its customers. The newsletter contains a recommendation to the customer to review his or her will in light of the information contained and, if the customer has any questions, to bring the will to the bank's trust department where the trust officer will answer any questions without charge. The trust officer is not a lawyer. If the trust officer is unable to answer the customer's questions, the trust officer refers the customer to Attorney.

Is Attorney <u>subject to discipline</u> for the foregoing?

A. Yes, because Attorney is giving legal advice to persons who are not his clients.

B. Yes, because Attorney is aiding Bank in the unauthorized practice of law.

C. No, because no charge is made for Attorney's advice.

D. No, because it is Attorney's duty to present all matters favorable to Client.

When you read the fact pattern, what should have popped out at you is the fact that Attorney is helping a non–lawyer (Bank) practice law. Thus, the issue is the unauthorized practice of law. If, for whatever reason, you have a problem spotting the issue in a "general call" question, try one of the following. Ask yourself the *opposite* question. Here, for instance, you'd ask yourself: Why *shouldn't* Attorney be subject to discipline? Or ask, Why *would* he be? If a question asks you whether certain conduct is unethical, you can be *pretty* sure that the attorney's done something that fits an exception to one of the ethical rules, or that the conduct itself is unethical—otherwise, the question wouldn't be a very good testing item.

b. "Specific call."

A far more likely circumstance is for the call of the question to be *specific:* for instance, "Is it proper for the Attorney to represent both Catco and Ware in the contempt proceedings?" "Is Attorney subject to discipline if he asserts such a defense?" "Is it proper for Attorney Alpha to supply Judge with the requested list of writings on the subject of custody?" Unlike a general call, the specific call will usually give away what the issue is. Let's look at the three just mentioned and a few more to see how this works.

> "Is it proper for the Attorney to represent both Catco and Ware in the contempt proceedings?"

The issue here must be *conflict of interest*, since you're being asked whether it would be proper to represent two people at the same time.

> "Is the attorney subject to discipline if he asserts such a defense?"

The issue here must be one relating to frivolous claims or fraud. For instance, the attorney could only present a defense which is either based on current law or is a good-faith belief that the law should be changed, and he cannot rely on false facts.

> "Is it proper for Attorney Alpha to supply Judge with the requested list of writings on the subject of custody?"

The issue here must be *ex parte* contact with judges.

> "Is it proper for Attorney Alpha to grant the extension of time without consulting Client"?

The issue must be decision–making rights of the attorney and client. The issue is given away by the words "*without consulting Client.*"

If you find this exercise difficult, it's probably because you aren't—yet, anyway—terribly familiar with the codes of ethics. Once you've learned them and how they apply to facts, it will be simple for you to identify the issues presented in questions, especially where the call of the question is specific.

c. Spotting the issue when it's not obvious from the fact pattern.

In either general or specific call questions, if you really can't determine the issue, glance at the answer options. They will give away the issue. That's because not only will the best response address the issue, but in order to be good distractors, at least one or two of the others will, as well. The language will alert you to the issue at hand. Here's an example:

> Attorney Alpha filed an action for damages against Deft on behalf of Client. Attorney Alpha knew that Client disliked both Deft and Deft's lawyer, Attorney Beta. After Deft had been served with process, Beta called Alpha, told Alpha that she thought a settlement could be worked out if she had some time, and asked Alpha for a stipulation extending Deft's time to answer by thirty days. Alpha believes that if he asks Client, Client will instruct him to refuse any extension of time. Alpha grants the extension of time without consulting Client.
>
> Is it proper for Attorney Alpha to grant the extension of time without consulting Client?
>
> **A.** Yes, if Alpha believes Client would refuse the extension of time in order to harass Deft.
>
> **B.** Yes, if granting the extension of time does not substantially prejudice Client's rights.
>
> **C.** No, because Alpha did not first obtain Client's consent.
>
> **D.** No, because Alpha believes Client might instruct him to refuse any extension of time.

Look at the language in the answer options here. "...substantially prejudice Client's rights"; "...Client's consent." this is the language of decision–making, and if you're familiar at all with the rules on decision–making, you'll immediately recognize the issue. (Note, incidentally, that the best response is B.) Once you've got the issue firmly in mind, *immediately summon to mind the rule applicable to it, if you can.* If you can't, you can still choose the best response, because the answers will trigger your memory for it; however, if you can remember the rule before you even *look* at the answer options, you don't have to worry about being misled by tricky wording.

4. **Reading the Answers and Choosing the Best Response.**

As with any standardized test, the best—and sometimes the only—way to arrive at the best response is to eliminate all the ones that are *definitely wrong.*

What this means is that the most important test–taking skill you can develop for the MPRE is deciding when an answer is wrong. There are several elements involved in honing this skill:

• Learning the general principles of eliminating incorrect responses;

• Keeping in mind the substantive rules most likely to trip you up on the MPRE;

• Learning the traps the Bar Examiners expect you to fall into; and

• Learning how to handle *modifiers.*

I'll teach you all four of these skills in the next few pages. But a point you simply can't ignore is that the most important element in your success is your substantive review. Unlike the LSAT and other standardized exams like it, the MPRE is <u>knowledge</u> based. That is, it's supposed to test your knowledge, and you can't expect to pass it without having at least a passing familiarity with the ethics codes. So the advice I'm going to give you on the next few pages assumes that you've already done some substantive review. (If you haven't done any yet, you'll have to take my word for it when I state what the rules are and when I tell you that it's easy to spot how rules apply to facts and answer options.) But there are two things these analysis skills <u>will</u> do for you. First, they'll ensure that you aren't tripped up by the question format on the MPRE, and that you'll get the right answer when you really do know the rule. More importantly, these skills will help you choose the right answer when you're not really sure what that answer ought to be. The bottom line is, if you are pretty familiar with the ethics rules and you apply the principles in this chapter, *the* MPRE *cannot beat you!*

a. General principles of elimination.

We've just stated that the most important skill you can develop for the MPRE is being able to identify when an answer is clearly wrong. What makes this difficult is the *quality* of the wrong answers on the MPRE. Perhaps you've heard it stated that you can tell the quality of a James Bond movie by the bad guy—the better the villain, the better the movie. Well, on standardized exams, the better the wrong answers, the more difficult the exam. The MPRE is only difficult to the extent the Bar Examiners can successfully mask the wrong answers to make them seem right. In this section, we'll show you how to "unmask" those wrong answers and make them easy to spot. Once you can eliminate wrong answers with skill and confidence, you'll be able to choose the *right* answer with great frequency. Here, then, are the rules you need to know.

(1) The first rule is, if you know the answer for sure, ignore these rules.

If there is no question in your mind that an answer is correct, choose it and move on. If you've studied substantively and read and practiced with this book, in all likelihood you will find the MPRE quite easy. Don't make it more difficult than it is. If you spot the right answer right away, keeping in mind all of the rules on modifiers and traps that we're about to discuss, mark your answer sheet and go on to the next question.

(2) Eliminate any answers you know are wrong, and then apply your analysis skills to the remaining answer choices.

In many cases you will immediately recognize that at least one and perhaps two of the answer choices are wrong. If you can spot three, great—you're left with the only option that can possibly be the best response. Don't bother analyzing answer options you can immediately eliminate as wrong; cross them off in your test booklet if necessary to take your mind off them, and concentrate on the remaining possibilities.

(3) Remember that the answer most likely to be correct has a lot in common with the other answers.

This rule isn't set in stone, but the nature of the exam makes it likely that most answers will address the same issue. Remember,

I said that what makes a standardized test difficult is the degree of resemblance between the *wrong* answers and the *right* one. What this boils down to is that, as a *general* rule, if there is a single answer option that's very different from the remaining options, it's probably not the best response.

(4) Remember the way in which an option can be wrong.

There is a limited universe of ways in which MPRE answers can be wrong. They can basically do one of the following:

(a) They can misapply a rule of ethics to the facts. This is far and away the most common type of distractor; we discuss this in detail under "Traps Set by the Bar Examiners."

(b) They can misstate the ethics rules. This is relatively common.

(c) They can misstate the facts. Because such answers are generally clearly wrong, this is an unusual type of distractor, since it fools only the least prepared examinees.

b. Substantive rules to remember.

Here are a few general rules you should keep in mind, they will save you a lot of time in eliminating wrong responses on the MPRE.

(1) Don't get hung up on results.

This is a very common MPRE trap: the lawyer does something wrong, but this doesn't adversely impact his client in any way. When this happens in an MPRE question, you can bet your bottom dollar that at least one of the distractors will say that the lawyer's conduct was proper because his client wasn't "prejudiced," or "adversely effected," or the like. As a result, it's important to keep the following rule in mind: Even if things work out all right for the client, if the lawyer has violated the ethics rules, that's all that counts–*except for malpractice, which requires prejudice to the client.*

Let's look at an example. Say a lawyer allows a paralegal in his office to practice law. The lawyer will be subject to discipline for unauthorized practice *even if* the paralegal renders competent service. Try another one. If the lawyer neglects the client's work, he'll be subject to discipline *even if* the client's claim is filed before the Statute of Limitations runs out. See what I mean? This

kind of behavior is analogous to crimes like burglary, where
once a person's broken into a dwelling at night with the intent to
commit a felony, it doesn't matter what happens after that—
changing his mind, leaving, or returning the booty—he'll still be
guilty of burglary. It's the same here. Once a lawyer has undertaken unethical conduct, it doesn't really matter what the upshot
of that conduct is; he's violated the ethics rules.

(2) When it comes to fees, less is better.

Occasionally on the MPRE, you'll be asked about the propriety
of the lawyer's keeping a fee which is in dispute. Remember that
the ethics rules are concerned with lawyers charging *too much*
for their services; it will always be proper for a lawyer to charge
less, or nothing at all, for his services. Thus, when a question
asks you how much of a fee it's proper for a lawyer to keep,
you'd almost always be safe opting for the choice that leaves the
lawyer with the lowest fee. Here's an example:

> Deft retained Attorney to appeal Deft's criminal conviction
> and to seek bail pending appeal. The agreed fee for the ap-
> pearance on the bail hearing was $50 per hour. Attorney re-
> ceived $800 from Deft of which $300 was a deposit to secure
> Attorney's fee and $500 was for bail costs in the event that
> bail was obtained. Attorney maintained two office bank ac-
> counts: a "Fee Account," in which all fees were deposited and
> from which all office expenses were paid, and a "Client Fund
> Account." Attorney deposited the $800 in the "Client Fund
> Account" and expended six hours of time on the bail hearing.
> The effort to obtain bail was unsuccessful. Dissatisfied, Deft
> immediately demanded return of the $800.

It is now <u>proper</u> for Attorney to:

A. transfer the $800 to the "Fee Account."

B. transfer $300 to the "Fee Account" and leave $500 in the
"Client Fund Account" until Attorney's fee for the final
appeal is determined.

C. transfer $300 to the "Fee Account" and send Deft a $500
check on the "Client Fund Account."

D. send Deft a $500 check and leave $300 in the "Client
Fund Account" until the matter is resolved with Deft.

With nothing else in mind apart from our rule "less is better," you can see that the best response would have to be D, because it's the one wherein Attorney gets to keep less than he does in any other response.

(3) Remember that if a rule prevents a certain kind of communication, it doesn't matter who initiates it.

There are many cases in the ethics codes where a lawyer isn't permitted to communicate with someone. For instance, contact with a person represented by another attorney is banned without that person's counsel's consent; a judge's *ex parte* contact with a lawyer is generally banned, as is *ex parte* contact with jurors.

The thing to keep in mind is that when such communications are banned, they're banned regardless of who contacts whom first. For instance, if a juror tries to strike up a conversation about the case with one of the lawyers, the lawyer has to politely, but firmly, terminate the conversation. It's quite common on the MPRE for a distractor to suggest that a communication is proper because someone other than the lawyer in question started it. Don't be fooled by this!

(4) Remember that an attorney can't help a judge do anything that would violate the Code of Judicial Conduct.

Sometimes on the MPRE you'll see a judge violating the Code of Judicial Conduct, with a lawyer's help. A common example is a judge's contacting a lawyer who's an expert in a particular area, instead of relying on the briefs of counsel in a case. While there's nothing in the lawyers' codes of ethics that would stop a lawyer from advising a judge on the law in a given area, such conduct does violate the CJC, unless the judge sends a copy of the advice to the lawyers in the case and gives them a chance to respond. *However,* don't be misled into thinking that just because the lawyers' codes don't prohibit something, a lawyer can help a judge violate the CJC. On the contrary, under MR 8.4(f), a lawyer can't knowingly aid a judge in violating the law or the CJC. Thus, if conduct violates the CJC, and a lawyer helps a judge do that, the lawyer has violated the ethics rules.

(5) A client's insistence on a course of conduct doesn't, as a general rule, make it ethical.

Sometimes on the MPRE you'll encounter fact patterns where the attorney is doing something unethical, and the client *insists* on the unethical conduct (like filing a baseless, harassing lawsuit, or undertaking work for which the lawyer isn't competent). Remember that unless the unethical nature of the conduct can be remedied by client consent (e.g., most conflicts of interest), the fact that the client insists on the conduct doesn't make it ethical.

c. Traps set by the Bar Examiners.

Knowing how the Bar Examiners try to lure you into choosing the wrong answer can stop you from yielding to their temptations. When the Bar Examiners create the MPRE, the central concern they have is the integrity of the exam. They want people who know legal ethics to pass the exam, and people who don't know the rules, to fail. (In fact this is the only way they can convince states to include the exam as part of their licensing requirements.) What they do is to set "traps" for the unwary.

It's almost as though they have a list of mistakes they expect you to make, if you're less than sure of an answer, and they key "distractors"—wrong answers—to lure you into making mistakes.

(1) The "Hmmm, that sounds familiar" trap.

This is the most common—and most insidious—trap on the MPRE. It's a well known learning principal that students have a tendency to review material only until it looks familiar, not to the point of understanding it and applying it to facts. Perhaps because of this, most good distractors on the MPRE rely on the reasoning of a rule that doesn't apply to the issue at hand. Let's look at an example:

> Attorney is in the private practice of law, conducting a general practice. Psy is licensed by the state as a clinical psychologist and maintains a private practice as a marriage counselor. In his practice, Psy sees many individuals whose marriages are, in Psy's judgment, irretrievably broken. Psy has many clients who are unable to pay any fee. Psy has been represented by Attorney in both his business and personal affairs, and Psy has confidence in Attorney's ability.

Attorney proposed to Psy that Psy refer all of his clients who want a divorce to Attorney and Attorney will represent them for a reasonable hourly rate.

Is Attorney <u>subject to discipline</u> if Attorney enters into this agreement?

  A. Yes, because Attorney requested that Psy recommend the use of Attorney's legal services.

  B. Yes, unless Psy agrees not to attempt to influence the exercise of Attorney's independent professional judgment.

  C. No, if Psy is not compensated in any way for referring cases to Attorney.

  D. No, if Psy's clients are fully informed of Psy's arrangements with Attorney and are given an opportunity to consult with other lawyers.

Look at option D. This is a tempting choice because it sounds familiar; you may even say to yourself, "I've seen this in the code, so it must be right." The problem is, the language used—the right to consult other lawyers—is one of the requirements of a prepaid legal services plan, under DR 2103(D)(4)(e). It doesn't have anything to do with referrals, which is what's at issue here.

Option B does the same thing, with a different rule. The "influence the exercise of Attorney's independent professional judgment" language is reminiscent of the rule on third parties paying attorney fees for a client. Under MR 1.8(f) and DR 5–107(A)(1), a lawyer cannot let someone other than his client pay his bill if there's interference with the lawyer's independent professional judgment. See how tempting it is to apply this rule to the facts here? You do have a third party involved—Psy—and the language is familiar to you. Unless you knew for a fact that the issue here was the improper referral agreement, you might be tempted to choose B—a rule of conflicts of interest. Don't think the Bar Examiners don't realize this when they create answer options like this! (Incidentally, the best response is A.)

The only way to insulate yourself from this trap is adequate substantive review. If you are sufficiently familiar with the ethics rules, you'll be able to differentiate between rules easily. As I've mentioned earlier, the easiest way to gain this mastery of the ethics rules is with *Law In A Flash*; however, if you use anything else, make sure your method makes you familiar enough with the rules to overcome the "Hmm, that sounds familiar" trap.

(2) Stating part of a rule, and ignoring a part that would change the result.

A frequent basis for distractors is a partial rule, or stating a rule without an applicable exception. Let's look at an example.

> The three members of the law firm of Alpha, Beta, and Gamma entered into a partnership agreement which provided that, upon the death of a partner, the remaining partners would pay to the estate of the deceased partner 20% of the profits from the firm each year for a period of five years.
>
> Is such an agreement proper?
>
> **A.** Yes, because the agreement provides for payment to the estate of the deceased partner and not to an individual non-lawyer.
>
> **B.** Yes, if the amount of the payments represents the reasonable value of the interest of the deceased partner in unfinished business and partnership assets.
>
> **C.** No, because the agreement provides for fee sharing with a person who is not a lawyer or member of the law firm.
>
> **D.** No, unless the payments are limited to fees earned on cases completed at the date of the partner's death.

Look at option C. What it does is to address the *general* rule on splitting fees with non–lawyers, without taking into account that one of the *exceptions* to the rule is buried in these facts. That exception is that payments to a deceased lawyer's estate by surviving members of his firm, for a reasonable time after his death, *are* permissible. DR 3–102(A)(1), MR 5.4(a)(1). Thus, *whenever* a rule seems to be stated in an option, don't assume the statement at face value—scan your memory to see if the rule is stated either completely or in *pertinent* part, and pay special attention to the existence of any exceptions.

(3) Focusing on an issue that wasn't addressed in the "call" of the question.

Sometimes when you read a fact pattern on the MPRE, there will be an issue that jumps off the page at you. It's *very* important to focus *only* on what's asked in the *call* of the question. If it's a specific call, and it doesn't address the issue that you spotted, you can be sure that one of the distractors will focus on your "red herring." (Remember, this rule only applies to a question with a <u>specific</u> call. If the call of the question is general—e.g., "Is Attorney subject to discipline for his conduct?"—then the issue you spotted may be the focus of the best response.)

d. How modifiers can determine the best response.

Remember the basic format of MPRE answer options looks like this: "No, if Psy is not compensated in any way for referring cases to Attorney." The first word, the "Yes" or "No," is the <u>result</u>. The word immediately after the comma is the <u>modifier</u>. And the remainder of the answer is the <u>reasoning</u>. Your instinct will tell you that the reasoning is the most important part of the answer option. But frequently that one word modifier—the "if," "unless," or "because" immediately after the comma—is even <u>more</u> important than the reasoning itself! Learning how to analyze answers based on their modifiers will dramatically improve your chances of answering any MPRE question correctly. And that's what I'll explain to you here.

There are three kinds of modifiers you will find on the MPRE—"because," "if," and "unless." Let's look at how each one affects the meaning of the answer.

(1) The definite modifier—"because."

"Because" is a *definite*, as opposed to a *conditional*, modifier. Simply put, when "because" is the modifier, it must *necessarily* be true that this reasoning creates this result. In order for this to happen, the following three elements must be satisfied.

(a) Resolve central issue.

The reasoning must address and resolve an issue central to the call of the question (or, at least, an issue more central than any other response);

(b) Unequivocally reflect facts.

The facts in the reasoning must *completely* and *unequivocally* reflect the facts (for instance, if an option states, "because there was a conflict between two of his clients, Alpha and Beta," the facts must *clearly* show a conflict between Alpha and Beta); and

(c) Agreement between result and reasoning.

The result must be consistent with the reasoning. For instance, if the reasoning tells you, "because the representation was competent," the result must be that the representation is proper (although keep in mind that if competence isn't the central issue, this element *alone* will not make the option the best response).

This is pretty technical stuff. Let's look at an example to illustrate what I'm talking about.

> Four years ago, Alpha was a judge in a state court of general jurisdiction and heard the civil case of Plaintiff against Defendant in which Plaintiff prevailed and secured a judgment for $50,000 which was sustained on appeal. Since then Alpha has resigned from the bench and returned to private practice. Defendant has filed suit to enjoin enforcement of the judgment on the grounds of extrinsic fraud in its procurement. Plaintiff has now asked Alpha to represent plaintiff in defending the suit to enjoin enforcement.
>
> Is it <u>proper</u> for Alpha to accept the representation of Plaintiff in this matter?
>
> **A.** Yes, because Alpha would be upholding the decision of the court.
> **B.** Yes, if Alpha's conduct of the first trial will not be in issue.
> **C.** No, unless Alpha believes the present suit is brought in bad faith.
> **D.** No, because Alpha had acted in a judicial capacity on the merits of the original case.

Let's look at option D, a "because" answer option. By the time you read option D, you have already determined that the *problem* here is a conflict of interest based on lawyer's movement from the judiciary to private practice. The rule is that a lawyer can't accept private employment in a matter when, in a judicial capacity, he previously acted on the merits of the matter. DR 9–101(A)(MR 1.12(a) essentially agrees, but allows all parties a chance at informed consent to waive the conflict).

Now, let's go through the three elements for the "because" modifier to see if D is correct. Remember, our shorthand for those three elements was: resolve a central issue, unequivocally reflect facts, and consistency between result and reasoning.

First, does option D address and resolve a central issue? Yes, it does; the issue is whether Alpha can properly represent Plaintiff, and this turns on whether his conflict of interest prevents him from doing so. D cites the rule on conflicts of interest for former judges, the central issue, so D passes the first hurdle.

The second hurdle is determining whether the reasoning unequivocally reflects the facts. It does. You're told that Alpha was the judge in Plaintiff v. Defendant, and the new suit addresses the enforceability of that judgment. Thus, as option D states, Alpha did in fact act as judge for the original case.

Finally, the result and the reasoning must agree. Given that the reasoning in D is true, then a conflict of interest exists which would prevent Alpha from representing Plaintiff. Option D tells you that it would not be proper for Alpha to represent Plaintiff. Thus, its result and its reasoning agree. (Note, incidentally, that not only would representing Plaintiff be improper, but it would subject Alpha to discipline; but since every disciplinable act or omission is also improper, this isn't a problem.)

Now that you see how a "because" option can be correct, let's see how a "because" answer can be *incorrect.* Look at option A. You already have the rule in mind, so let's look directly at the "hurdles." First, does the reasoning address and resolve a central issue? *No.* It doesn't matter if Alpha is upholding the decision or not; what matters here is that it was his decision which creates a conflict. Because option A fails to clear the first hurdle, you can move on, since it can't be the best response.

If, during the MPRE, you have difficulty determining whether a "because" option is correct, there is a way you can quickly make it easier to visualize the rule. What you can do is combine the reasoning with the call of the question into an "if–then" statement, which must be true in order for the option to be correct. Doing this with option A, you wind up with the following statement: "If Alpha is upholding the decision of the court, then it would be proper for Alpha to represent Plaintiff." As you can see, the "if" clause is the reasoning of the option, and the "then" statement is the call of the question. In order for this to be true, the "if" clause must provide the reason why the "then" part should occur. For option A, it doesn't; the fact that Alpha isn't challenging the judgment doesn't resolve his conflict of interest in favor of representing Plaintiff. If you're stuck on a "because" option, try rewording it like this to help clarify whether or not it's correct.

Incidentally, did you notice what kind of a "distractor" option A is? It's one of those where the reasoning implies a rule that *doesn't apply* to these facts. Option A refers to the lawyer's duty of loyalty to former clients; that is, a lawyer can't challenge work he previously did for another client, on behalf of a new client. MR 1.9(a), DR 5–105. For instance, a lawyer can't seek to rescind on behalf of a new client a contract he drafted for an old client, or challenge the validity of a will he prepared and witnessed. Option A suggests that because Alpha isn't challenging his own judgment, representing Plaintiff is proper. Of course, the reason this is wrong is that the conflict exists *independently* of whether Alpha challenged his own work. Nonetheless, you can see why implying the application of another rule makes A a good distractor.

(2) The conditional modifiers: "if" and "unless."

These are called conditional responses, because the result is conditional on the reasoning. Unlike the MBE—where "if" and "unless" responses are rare—these are very common on the MPRE, because the nature of the rules is more fact–dependent than are the more concrete rules tested by the MBE.

When you see "if" or "unless" as a modifier in an answer option, the reasoning will do one of two things:

–It will clarify ambiguous facts in the fact pattern, or

–It will add facts which resolve a central issue.

Let's look at each modifier separately to see how you should analyze it.

(a) When "if" is the modifier.

In order for "if" to be the best response, it must overcome these three hurdles:

(1) Plausibility – The reasoning must be *plausible* on the facts; that is, there can't be anything in the facts to suggest it *couldn't* be true. Of course, this also means that the reasoning couldn't be *unequivocally* proven in the facts, either. For instance, let's say you have an MPRE question where the issue is incompetence, and you're told that Attorney went on a three–month drunken binge and forgot to file his client's complaint before the Statute of Limitations ran out. If the call of the question asked you whether Attorney was subject to discipline, a response would not be correct if it said, "Yes, *if* he rendered incompetent representation," because Attorney *unquestionably* did so; there's no realistic way Attorney didn't offer incompetent service, so this fact couldn't be considered merely plausible instead of definite. As a result it couldn't be part of a conditional response.

(2) Central issue – It must address a *central issue.* In order for an "if" option to be correct, it must either add or clarify facts in such a way as to resolve a central issue. The easiest way to show what this means is with an example.

Attorney is admitted to the bar in State First, but does not engage in the practice of law. In association with a nonlawyer, Attorney engaged in a real estate investment business in State Second. Attorney was sued in

State Second in a civil action that alleged fraud in a matter connected with Attorney's real estate investment business. Judgment was rendered against Attorney and that judgment is now final.

Is Attorney <u>subject to discipline</u> in State First?

A. Yes, if Attorney's conduct involved fraud.

B. Yes, because Attorney was the defendant in a civil action alleging fraud.

C. No, because Attorney's conduct did not involve the practice of law.

D. No, because Attorney's conduct, involved in the civil action, took place outside State First;

Let's look at option A. Remember our first two hurdles: Plausibility and central issue. So the first hurdle option A must clear in order to be the best response is to be *plausible* under the facts. The facts here tell you that Attorney was sued for fraud. Thus, it's plausible—neither definite nor impossible—that his conduct actually did involve fraud, so option A clears the first hurdle.

Now we have to see if it clears the second hurdle—namely, does option A address a *central issue?* To do that, we have to step back a minute, and think about the rule that applies to these facts. When you read the call of the question, you come up with two issues: First, the fraud, if it existed, didn't take place in State First, which is trying to discipline Attorney. And second, the fraud didn't have anything to do with practicing law. But neither of these matters because the rule is that an attorney is disciplinable anywhere he is licensed to practice and anywhere he violates the ethics codes. MR 8.5. Furthermore, a licensed attorney can be subject to discipline for misconduct even if he isn't practicing law and the misconduct has nothing to do with the practice of law. MR 8.4(c), DR 1–102(A)(4). When you look at these facts in light of these rules, you can see that the only <u>relevant</u> fact is whether or not Attorney actually committed the fraud, which would be disciplinable misconduct. If he didn't, he isn't subject to discipline, and if he did, he is. Option A conveniently solves this problem for you by conditioning Attorney's discipline on his having committed a fraud; in other words, it adds a fact—that Attorney committed a fraud. In doing so, it resolves a central issue.

(3) Agreement between result and reasoning.

The result and the reasoning must agree. Given that an "if" option is plausible under the facts and it resolves a central issue, it has just one last hurdle to clear: The result—before the comma—and the reasoning—after the comma—must agree. In our sample problem, if Attorney committed a fraud, he'll be subject to discipline. Since the call of the question asks you if he'll be subject to discipline, the result would have to be "yes." Since it is, option A must be the best response—and it is.

Note that if the reasoning provided the opposite fact, the result would have to be opposite in order for option A to be correct. That is, if the reasoning had been "Attorney's conduct didn't involve fraud," then the result would have to have been "No" in order for the option to be correct. So if you reversed both the result and the reasoning in option A, it would say, "No, if Attorney's conduct didn't involve fraud." Incidentally, note that with this reversal option A *still* would have been correct, because it would be plausible under the facts, it would resolve a central issue, and its result and reasoning would agree.

(b) Where "unless" is the modifier.

Like "if," "unless" is conditional. In fact, "if" and "unless" are almost mirror images—however, though a correct "if" response provides circumstances under which the result would occur, when "unless" is the modifier, the *reasoning must provide the only circumstances under which the result would not occur* to make the option the best response. For instance, if the call of the question asks you whether an attorney's conduct is proper, and an answer option begins "No, unless." the reasoning must provide the only way that the attorney's conduct *would* be proper. If instead the call of the question asks you whether an attorney is subject to discipline, and an answer option begins, "Yes, unless." the reasoning must provide the only way that attorney could *avoid* discipline. If you can think of even *one other way* in which the result could occur, the option *cannot* be the best response.

As with "if" answers, the reasoning in a correct "unless" response will either clarify facts, or provide an additional fact that resolves a central issue. Let's look at an example:

> Attorney represents Client, the defendant in an action for damages in a state that has adopted comparative negligence, but has retained assumption of risk as a complete defense.
>
> Attorney believes that, while Client was negligent, Plaintiff was partially at fault and may even have voluntarily assumed the risk involved. However, Attorney believes that to assert the defense of assumption of risk would be bad trial tactics in that, if the jury did not accept it, they might also hold that Plaintiff was free from fault and therefore render a much larger verdict than they would if they found some negligence on Plaintiff's part.
>
> Is it <u>proper</u> for Attorney not to plead assumption of the risk as a defense?
>
> **A.** Yes, if Attorney determines that it is in Client's best interests not to plead that defense.
>
> **B.** Yes, because Attorney is responsible for the determination of the tactics to be employed at the trial.
>
> **C.** No, unless Client, after being fully advised, concurs in Attorney's decision.
>
> **D.** No, if a good faith argument can be made that, under the facts, the defense is applicable.

Look at option C. For this question, when you read the call of the question, you recognized that the issue was whether or not it was proper for Attorney to fail to plead assumption of the risk, without Client's consent. You also summoned to mind the rule on decision–making allocation between attorney and client. That is, the client makes *major* decisions concerning the objectives of the representation, affecting the merits of the case, and substantially prejudicing his own rights. On the other hand, the attorney makes procedural and strategic decisions, which are the means of effectuating the client's objectives, except that the client makes these decisions when they relate to costs incurred and concerns about the adverse affect of certain tactics on third parties. MR 1.2, EC 7–7 (OK, maybe you didn't summon this rule to mind in this much detail; but you hopefully remembered that it's the client's decision whether or not to plead affirmative defenses like assumption of the risk).

Looking at the facts in this problem, you can see that there's one significant fact missing; namely, whether or not Attorney consulted Client and got his consent on leaving out the assumption of the risk defense. If Attorney got the consent, his conduct was proper; if he didn't, it's not. Thus, any correct response to this question would *have* to resolve this ambiguity! And that's what option C does—it conditions the propriety of Attorney's conduct on his obtaining Client's consent. That is, option C tells you that the only way Attorney could behave properly was to get Client's consent.

Remember how a couple of paragraphs back, I said, that "unless" and "if" were *almost* mirror images? Let's change option C a little bit to see how this works. Say option C, instead of "No, unless..." said "Yes, if Client, after being fully advised, concurs in Attorney's decision." Note that the reasoning is plausible, it addresses and resolves a central issue, and the reasoning and the result agree. Thus, it's just as correct as option C is as it now stands. Keep in mind, however, that "if" and "unless" aren't perfect mirror images, because "unless" is exclusive, and "if" isn't. Looking at our modified option C, with "if" as the modifier, you can see that what it's saying is that assuming Client consents to Attorney's action, the action is proper—but it doesn't exclude other ways that Attorney's action might be proper, as well. When "No, unless..." begins the option, it's telling you that the only way for this result to occur is if this reasoning doesn't apply; in other words, there isn't any other way for Attorney to avoid discipline. A perfect mirror image of unless, then, would be "if and only if."

This whole argument of modifiers, and exactly what they mean, may strike you as overly technical for such simple words. However, if you're thoroughly familiar with the way to analyze modifiers, you'll frequently be able to save yourself from picking a wrong answer.

E. How to Pick the Right Answer Without Reading the Question.

Learning how to analyze answers can frequently do more than simply help you avoid pitfalls in the facts. If you put to work all of the principles I've discussed here, you'll frequently be able to pick the right answer to MPRE questions without reading the facts at all! Of course, you shouldn't do this on the MPRE, but in many cases, you could do it. The fact is, your ability to do this harkens back to something I've mentioned before—namely, the tension between the vague nature of the ethics rules and the necessity for concrete answers on standardized exams. Because of this, the answers themselves will frequently have to give away so much qualifying information that they give away what the correct response must be. Let's look at a few examples of how this works. Here are the four answer options to a past MPRE question:

    A. Yes, because it involves a legal doctrine that is directly contrary to decisions of the state's highest court.

    B. Yes, unless Attorney can distinguish the contrary decisions of the state's highest court.

    C. No, because it is Attorney's duty to present all matters favorable to the client.

    D. No, if Attorney believes in good faith that the defense has merit.

Without knowing any of the facts, you ought to be able to pick out the best response. First, a quick glance at each of the options tells you that the lawyer in question must be arguing a defense that is contrary to a state supreme court case, because good distractors focus on the same issue as the best response. This means the issue must be whether or not the argument is frivolous, since a lawyer may only make meritorious arguments; that is, based on the law as it stands or a good–faith belief that the law ought to be changed. With this rule in mind, you can see that the best response is almost definitely option D, regardless of the facts, because it conditions the propriety of Attorney's conduct on whether or not the defense is meritorious. In addition, the call of the question must be asking whether Attorney would be acting unethically (either improperly or subject to discipline), for the answer to be "No." Bolstering the argument that D is the correct option is the fact that all of the other options are incorrect statements of the ethics rules. In case you're curious, here are the facts to this question:

> Attorney is representing Client, the defendant in the trial of a civil case in the state trial court. Plaintiff is relying on certain decisions of the state's highest court. One defense that Attorney intends to assert is a legal doctrine that is directly contrary to those decisions.
>
> Is Attorney subject to discipline if he asserts such a defense?

As you can see, the facts just reinforce the fact that D is the best response, which you might have deduced without even reading the fact pattern. Let's try another one.

A. Yes, if Alpha lists both articles that are favorable and articles that are unfavorable to Mother's position.

B. Yes, because the matter has not yet been assigned to Judge for hearing.

C. No, unless Alpha sends Father's lawyer of record a copy of the list and the cover letter to Judge.

D. No, because Alpha is not a disinterested expert.

From these answers, what must be going on in the question? Judge must have asked Alpha for a list of readings on the law on a certain issue. That's implied by all of the answer options, and as you know by now, distractors are only effective if they approximate the correct answer. The rule on *ex parte* contact with a judge is that the only way such *ex parte* contact is appropriate is if the opposing party also receives a copy of the communication. (You can assume that Alpha is involved in the trial, since option D tells you he's not disinterested.) What this tells you is that option C must be the best response. Let's look at the facts to see whether this is true.

> Three years ago, in a contested marriage dissolution proceeding, Father was awarded custody of the parties' child. Mother has recently remarried. On Mother's behalf, Attorney Alpha has filed a motion requesting that the decree be modified and Mother be awarded custody of the child. A copy of the motion has been served on Father's lawyer of record.
>
> Judge is a newly appointed judge sitting in Domestic Relations Court to whom Mother's motion will be assigned for hearing. Attorney Alpha met Judge at a bar association meeting. Judge said to Alpha, "You have practiced heavily in the family law area for a long time. I want to do

some reading in the custody area. Would you be willing to give me a list of the best writings on the subject?"

Is it proper for Attorney Alpha to supply Judge with the requested list of writings on the subject of custody?

As you can see, reading the facts, as in our last example, only reinforces the correctness of option C. Let's try one more.

A. Yes, if Alpha believes Client would refuse the extension of time in order to harass Deft.

B. Yes, if granting the extension of time does not substantially prejudice Client's rights.

C. No, because Alpha did not first obtain Client's consent.

D. No, because Alpha believes Client might instruct him to refuse any extension of time.

Looking at these options, you can see that what Attorney must have done was approve an extension without consulting Client. Thus, the issue must be how decision–making responsibility is split between a lawyer and his client. The rule on this is that the client makes all major decisions concerning the objectives of the representation, affecting the merits of the case, and substantially prejudicing the client's rights, and the attorney makes strategic decisions, except that he must defer to the client regarding costs incurred and concerns about the adverse affect of certain tactics on third parties. With this in mind, options A and D can't be correct, because whether or not Attorney gets to make a decision doesn't depend on what Client's decision might be; if it's within Client's sphere of authority, then Client gets to make the decision regardless of what he decides. That leaves you with B and C. C isn't a good choice, because keeping in mind the rule on decision–making, option C definitively states that granting the extension is within Client's rights; in fact, unless it substantially prejudices Client's rights, it's not Client's decision at all, but Attorney's. That leaves B, which comports with the rule on decision–making, since it conditions Attorney's having to defer to Client on whether or not granting the extension will substantially prejudice Client's rights. As a result, you know that B is the best response even without reading the question!

The facts to this question bear this out:

Attorney Alpha filed an action for damages against Deft on behalf of Client. Attorney Alpha knew that Client disliked both Deft and Deft's lawyer, Attorney Beta. After Deft had been served with process, Beta called Alpha, and told Alpha that she thought a settlement could be worked out if she had some time, and asked Alpha for a stipulation extending Deft's time to answer by thirty days. Alpha believes that if he asks Client, Client might instruct him to refuse any extension of time. Alpha grants the extension of time without consulting Client.

Is it proper for Attorney Alpha to grant the extension of time without consulting Client?

We could go on like this, but you've got the point by now—if you are sufficiently well–versed in analyzing answer options to MPRE questions, you'll be so well prepared for the MPRE that you could well pass the exam, without reading any questions! But don't get the wrong idea. We're emphasizing the skills you will need, but we don't recommend that you skip the facts.

Part Two

Practice Questions and Answers

In Part One, I did all the work. Here in Part Two, it's your turn. With these practice questions, you should put into practice the plan of attack you learned in Part One. There are fifty practice questions, followed by a complete explanation of every answer option. The answers begin on page 71.

A couple of brief words of advice before you get started. First of all, don't pay attention to timing as you practice. On the real MPRE, you'll have about two minutes, on average, for each question. Put that out of your mind for now. When you practice here, it's much more important to pay attention to applying the analysis principles from Part One than to beat the clock. Speed will come naturally as you become more proficient at answering the questions.

Also, don't just read the correct response to any question you miss; also read the explanation for the option you chose, and any other responses you were seriously considering (it's a good idea to make note of these "near–misses" as you answer the questions). Each response is designed to teach you not just the correct rule of ethics, but far more importantly the mistake you made if you chose that response. Thus, you'll learn far more from reading the wrong answer you chose than from reviewing the right answer!

Now in terms of breaking up the questions, you can do whatever makes you feel comfortable. My guess would be that you'd be wise to do ten or so practice questions, check your results, and then proceed. Breaking your review down into small chunks like this, and reviewing answers as you go, gives you a chance to identify and correct any test–taking flaws you have before they become habits. But if you feel very confident from the start, there's no reason why you can't just do all fifty questions at once, and then review the answers.

With that in mind—let's get started.

A. Practice Questions

Question 1.

Attorney, while working in her office, overheard a conversation between two law students, who were summer interns, about a third intern, Stu. At the time, all three students were about to enter their last year of law study. The conversation indicated that Stu had used some law school student bar association funds for his own purposes. Attorney later discussed the matter with Stu, who admitted having used the funds but explained that he did so because of an emergency illness. Stu indicated that he had repaid the student bar association in full. Stu is now applying for admission to the bar. The admitting authority has asked Attorney for an evaluation of Stu's fitness for admission to the bar, including any knowledge of facts material to his moral character.

Which of the following correctly states Attorney's professional responsibility?

A. Attorney *should* inform the bar admission authority about Stu's past conduct and may make whatever recommendation Attorney believes is justified.

B. Attorney should recommend Stu for admission without disclosing Attorney's knowledge of Stu's past conduct if Attorney believes Stu is of good moral character.

C. Attorney should decline to reply because Attorney acquired some of her information in a discussion with Stu.

D. Attorney should decline to reply because Stu has not asked her for a recommendation.

Question 2.

Attorney is representing Seller in a civil suit for breach of a contract in which Seller agreed to sell a racehorse to Buyer for $25,000. Buyer refused to accept the horse when it was delivered after a three–hour trip because the horse had a condition that made it unfit for racing. The horse had been placed in Buyer's trailer by Seller. If the horse was injured during transit in the trailer, Seller will recover.

Seller asserts that the horse was in good condition and fit for racing when placed in the trailer and insists that Attorney file a motion for summary judgment supported by Seller's affidavit to that effect. Attorney's investigation has disclosed that the horse's condition is one that ordinarily is caused by prolonged neglect. Attorney has advised Seller that there is a disputed issue of fact, and, therefore, the motion will almost certainly be denied.

Is Attorney <u>subject to discipline</u> if Attorney does not withdraw from the case?

A. Yes, if Attorney believes the motion for summary judgment will be denied.

B. Yes, because Seller refuses to follow Attorney's advice.

C. No, because Attorney must accept Seller's version of the facts.

D. No, unless Attorney knows that Seller's affidavit will contain false statements.

Question 3.

Attorney employs Baker as an office assistant. Baker has studied law extensively but has never been admitted to practice. Attorney has several corporations as clients. If a corporate client is sued and the matter involves more than the jurisdictional limit of the small claims court but is less than $10,000, Attorney has the corporate client execute a power of attorney authorizing Baker to act on its behalf. Baker then represents the corporate client in the trial of the matter.

Is Attorney <u>subject to discipline</u>?

A. Yes, because Attorney is employing Baker in the unauthorized practice of law.

B. Yes, because a corporation may not confer a power of attorney on a person who is not an officer or employee.

C. No, if, in each matter, Attorney obtains the client's informed consent to representation by Baker.

D. No, if Baker competently represents the client.

Question 4.

Four years ago, Mafco, represented by Attorney, purchased a parcel of land and took title in the name of Trust Company. Mafco's president had informed Attorney that Mafco intended to build a large manufacturing plant on the property but did not wish its ownership of the land or its building plans to be public. After the purchase was completed, Attorney did not represent Mafco in any other matter. Because of financial problems, Mafco postponed construction of the plant.

One year ago, Investor, a client of Attorney, consulted Attorney about the tax consequences of acquiring the local electric utility company. Attorney, without revealing the name of Mafco, told Investor that a company was planning to build a large manufacturing plant in the area and that if the company went ahead with its plans, Investor's investment in the electric utility should be very profitable. Investor acquired the utility company.

Mafco is now building the manufacturing plant.

Is Attorney <u>subject to discipline</u>?

A. Yes, because Attorney accepted representation of Investor, knowing that Investor's financial interests might be adverse to those of Mafco.

B. Yes, because Attorney revealed to Investor information Attorney acquired during the representation of Mafco.

C. No, because Attorney did not personally profit from Investor's acquisition of the utility company.

D. No, because Investor initiated the discussion with Attorney with regard to acquiring the utility company.

Question 5.

Attorney, an experienced trademark litigator, represents Publisher in an action seeking damages from Bookco for an alleged trademark violation. Attorney believes the services of an expert witness are essential to proper presentation of the case.

Wit, a competent expert witness, was available to testify on Publisher's behalf, but Wit demanded a fee of $8,000. Publisher was unable to pay a fee of that size. Expert, an equally competent expert witness, offered to testify for Publisher for a fee of $1,000 plus 10% of any damages recovered. Publisher is willing to agree to Expert's requested fee.

Which of the following would be <u>proper</u> for Attorney?

I. Withdraw from representation of Publisher if the inability to obtain an expert witness will make the suit difficult to win.

II. Guarantee to Wit the requested fee of $8,000 upon Publisher's agreeing to reimburse Attorney when Publisher is able to do so.

III. Employ Expert on the terms requested by Expert.

A. I only.

B. II only.

C. I and II, but not III.

D. II and III, but not I.

Question 6.

Attorney Alpha was retained by Passenger, a passenger on a bus, who had been injured in a collision between the bus and a truck. Passenger paid Alpha a retainer of $1,000 and agreed further that Alpha should have a fee of 25% of any recovery before filing suit, 30% of any recovery after suit was filed but before judgment, and 35% of any recovery after trial and judgment. Alpha promptly called the lawyer for the bus company and told him she was representing Passenger and would like to talk about a settlement. Alpha made an appointment to talk to the lawyer for the bus company but did not keep the appointment. Alpha continued to put off talking to the lawyer for the bus company. Meanwhile, Passenger became concerned because she had heard nothing from Alpha. Passenger called Alpha's office but was told Alpha was not in and would not call back. Passenger was told not to worry because Alpha would look after her interests. After ten months had passed, Passenger went to Attorney Beta for advice. Beta advised Passenger that the statute of limitations would run out in one week and immediately filed suit for Passenger. Alpha, upon Passenger's demand, refunded the $1,000 Passenger had paid.

Is Alpha <u>subject to discipline</u>?

A. Yes, unless Alpha's time was completely occupied with work for other clients.

B. Yes, because Alpha neglected the representation of Passenger.

C. No, because Passenger's suit was filed before the statute of limitations ran.

D. No, because Alpha returned the $1,000 retainer to Passenger.

Question 7.

Attorney Alpha filed a personal injury suit on behalf of Plaintiff against Defendant. Defendant was personally served with process. Alpha knows that Defendant is insured by Insco and that Attorney Beta has been retained by Insco to represent Defendant. No responsive pleading has been filed on behalf of Defendant, and the time for filing expired over ten days ago.

Is Alpha subject to discipline if Alpha proceeds to have a default judgment entered?

A. Yes, because Alpha knew that Beta had been retained by Insco to represent Defendant.

B. Yes, because Alpha failed to extend professional courtesy to another lawyer.

C. No, because Alpha is properly representing her client's interests.

D. No, because any judgment will be satisfied by Insco.

Question 8.

Attorney is a candidate in a contested election for judicial office. Her opponent, Judge, is the incumbent and has occupied the bench for many years. The director of the state commission on judicial conduct, upon inquiry by Attorney, erroneously told Attorney that Judge had been reprimanded by the commission for misconduct in office. Attorney, who had confidence in the director, believed him. In fact, Judge had not been reprimanded by the commission; the commission had conducted hearings on Judge's alleged misconduct in office and, by a three to two vote, declined to reprimand Judge.

Decisions of the commission, including reprimands, are not confidential.

Is Attorney subject to discipline for publicly stating that Judge had been reprimanded for misconduct?

A. Yes, because the official records of the commission would have disclosed the truth.

B. Yes, because Judge had not been reprimanded.

C. No, if Attorney reasonably relied on the director's information.

D. No, because Judge was a candidate in a contested election.

Question 9.

Attorney is a well–known, highly skilled litigator. Attorney's practice is in an area of law in which the trial proceedings are heard by the court without a jury.

In an interview with a prospective client, Attorney said, "I make certain that I give the campaign committee of every candidate for elective judicial office more money than any other lawyer gives, whether it's $500 or

$5,000. Judges know who help them get elected." The prospective client did not retain Attorney.

Is Attorney <u>subject to discipline</u>?

A. Yes, if Attorney's contributions are made without consideration of candidates' merits.

B. Yes, because Attorney implied that Attorney receives favored treatment by judges.

C. No, if Attorney's statements were true.

D. No, because the prospective client did not retain Attorney.

Questions 10–11 are based on the following fact situation.

Judge is presiding in a case that has, as its main issue, a complicated point of commercial law. The lawyers have not presented the case to Judge's satisfaction, and Judge believes she needs additional legal advice. Judge's former partner in law practice, Attorney, is an expert in the field of law that is at issue. Attorney has no interest in the case.

Question 10.

Is it <u>proper</u> for Attorney to advise Judge in the matter?

A. Yes, because Judge was not satisfied with the presentation by the lawyers in the case.

B. Yes, if Judge requests Attorney's legal advice.

C. No, because Attorney may not participate in the case unless retained by a party to the proceeding.

D. No, unless Attorney first gives notice to the parties of the intent to advise Judge.

Question 11.

Is it <u>proper</u> for Judge to consult Attorney?

A. Yes, because Attorney has no interest in the case.

B. Yes, if Judge believes that Attorney's advice is needed to serve the interests of justice.

C. No, unless all parties in the case first give their written consent to Judge's consultation with Attorney.

D. No, unless Judge informs the parties of Attorney's identity and the substance of A.

Question 12.

Attorney is a lawyer employed by State's Industrial Safety Agency (ISA). ISA is authorized, after investigation and hearing, to make administrative determinations requiring employers to install industrial safety devices. Attorney is considering a career change and has submitted his application for employment as chief counsel of Union, a large industrial labor union. Attorney has directed ISA's investigation of the need for smoke and toxic fume detectors at Giant's steel mill. Giant is State's largest private employer.

At a public hearing conducted by ISA pursuant to statute, Attorney presented the case for ISA. Attorney made an opening statement in which he said that the evidence to be produced would show that Giant had failed to install safety devices "in callous, willful, and total disregard for the safety and welfare of Giant's employees." Attorney made his opening statement with knowledge that members of Union's Executive Committee, to whom his application for employment with Union had been sent, were in attendance at the hearing.

Was it proper for Attorney to make the quoted statement?

A. Yes, because opening statements are not evidence

B. Yes, if Attorney believed the statement would be supported by the evidence.

C. No, because the statement was made in the presence of representatives of Attorney's prospective employer.

D. No, because the statement exceeded the bounds of justifiable advocacy.

Question 13.

Attorney's advertisement in the local newspaper includes the following information, all of which is true:

I. Attorney, B.A., magna cum laude, Eastern College; J.D., summa cum laude, State Law School; LL.M., Eastern Law School.

II. My offices are open Monday through Friday from 9:00 a.m. to 5:00 p.m., but you may call my answering service twenty–four hours a day, seven days a week.

III. I speak modern Greek fluently.

For which, if any, of these statements is Attorney <u>subject to discipline</u>?

A. III only

B. I and II, but not III

C. I, II, and III

D. Neither I, nor II, nor III

Question 14.

Trustco, a trust company, entered into the following arrangement with Attorney, a lawyer newly admitted to the bar.

Trustco would provide Attorney with free office space in the building in which Trustco had its offices. If a customer of Trustco contacted Trustco about a trust or will, an officer of Trustco, who is not a lawyer, would advise the customer and help the customer work out the details of the trust or will. The customer would be informed that the necessary documents would be prepared by Trustco's staff. The completed documents would be submitted by an officer of Trustco to the customer for execution.

Attorney, in accordance with a memorandum from Trustco's trust officer detailing the plan, would prepare the necessary documents. Attorney would never meet with the customer and would not charge the customer for these services. Attorney would be free to engage in private practice, subject only to the limitation that Attorney could not accept employment adverse to Trustco.

Is Attorney <u>subject to discipline</u> for entering into the arrangement with Trustco?

A. Yes, because Attorney is restricting his right to practice.

B. Yes, because Attorney is aiding Trustco in the practice of law.

C. No, because Attorney is not charging the customer for his services.

D. No, because Attorney is not giving advice to Trustco's customers.

Question 15.

Attorney represented Husband and Wife in the purchase of a business financed by contributions from their respective separate funds. The business was jointly operated by Husband and Wife after acquisition. After several years, a dispute arose over the management of the business. Husband and Wife sought Attorney's advice, and the matter was settled on the basis of an agreement drawn by Attorney and signed by Husband and Wife. Later, Wife asked Attorney to represent her in litigation against Husband based on the claim that Husband was guilty of fraud and misrepresentation in the negotiations for the prior settlement agreement.

Is it <u>proper</u> for Attorney to represent Wife in this matter?

A. Yes if all information relevant to the litigation was received by Attorney in the presence of both Husband and Wife.

B. Yes, if there is reason to believe Husband misled both Wife and Attorney at the time of the prior agreement.

C. No, because Attorney had previously acted for both parties in reaching the agreement now in dispute.

D. No, unless Husband is now represented by independent counsel.

Question 16.

Attorney represents Deft, the defendant in a criminal prosecution that has attracted widespread publicity. After the indictment was returned, but before arraignment, Attorney was interviewed and, in response to reporters' questions, stated:

I.   Where Deft was arrested.

II. The nature of the specific charges contained in the indictment.

III. That Deft denied the charges against him and would plead not guilty at his arraignment.

Is Attorney <u>subject to discipline</u> for making any of the above statements?

A. No.

B. Yes, for statement III only.

C. Yes, for statements I and II, but not III.

D. Yes, for statements II and III, but not I.

Question 17.

Alpha and Beta are members of the bar in the same community but have never practiced together. Beta is a candidate in a contested election for judicial office. Beta is opposed by Delta, another lawyer in the community. Alpha believes Beta is better qualified than Delta for the judiciary and is supporting Beta's candidacy.

Which of the following would be proper for Alpha?

I.   Solicit public endorsements for Beta's candidacy by other attorneys in the community who know Beta and are likely to appear before Beta if Beta becomes a judge
II. Solicit contributions to Beta's campaign committee from other attorneys in the community who are likely to appear before Beta if Beta becomes a judge
III. Publicly oppose the candidacy of Delta

A. I only
B. I and II, but not III
C. I and III, but not II
D. I, II, and III

Question 18.

Attorney advertises on the local television station. In the advertisements, a professional actor says:

> "Do you need a lawyer? Call Attorney—her telephone number is area code 555–555–5555. Her fees might be lower than you think."

Attorney approved the prerecorded advertisement and is keeping in her office files a copy of the recording of the actual transmission and a record of when each transmission was made.

Is the advertisement proper?

A. Yes.
B. No, unless Attorney's fees are lower than those generally charged in the area where she practices.
C. No, because she used a professional actor for the television advertisement.
D. No, if she makes a charge for the initial consultation.

Questions 19–20 are based on the following fact situation.

Deft, who has been indicted for auto theft, is represented by Attorney. Prosecutor reasonably believes that Deft committed the offense, but, because of Deft's youth, it is in the interest of justice to permit Deft to plead guilty to the lesser offense of "joy–riding" in return for an agreement by Prosecutor to recommend probation. Prosecutor has so advised Attorney, but Attorney told Prosecutor she would not plea bargain and would insist on a jury trial. Attorney informed Deft of Prosecutor's offer and advised Deft not to accept it. Deft followed Attorney's advice. Attorney is a candidate for public office, and Prosecutor suspects that Attorney is insisting on a trial of the case to secure publicity for herself.

Question 19.

Which of the following would be <u>proper</u> for Prosecutor?

I.   Send a member of his staff who is not a lawyer to consult with Deft.

II. Move the trial court to dismiss the indictment and accept a new complaint charging the offense of "joy–riding."

III. Proceed to trial on the indictment and prosecute the case vigorously.

A. II only

B. III only

C. I and II, but not III

D. II and III, but not I

Question 20.

Assume for the purposes of this question ONLY that Deft was tried, convicted, and sentenced to prison for two years.

<u>Should</u> Prosecutor report to the disciplinary authority his suspicions about Attorney's conduct of the case?

A. Yes, because Deft suffered a detriment from Attorney's refusal to plea bargain.

B. Yes, if Attorney in fact received widespread publicity as a result of the trial.

C. No, unless Prosecutor has knowledge that Attorney's refusal to plea bargain was due to personal motives.

D. No, if Attorney zealously and competently represented Deft at the trial.

Question 21.

Driver consulted Attorney and asked Attorney to represent Driver, who was being prosecuted for driving while intoxicated in a jurisdiction in which there is an increased penalty for a second offense. Driver told Attorney that his driver's license had been obtained under an assumed name because his prior license had been suspended for driving while under the influence of alcohol. Driver asked Attorney not to disclose Driver's true name during the course of the representation and told Attorney that, if called as a witness, he would give his assumed name. Attorney informed Driver that, in order to defend the case properly, Attorney must call Driver as a witness.

Attorney called Driver as a witness and, in response to Attorney's question "What is your name?," Driver gave his assumed name and not his true name.

Is Attorney <u>subject to discipline</u>?

A. Yes, because Attorney knowingly used false testimony.

B. Yes, if Driver committed a felony when he obtained the driver's license under an assumed name.

C. No, because Attorney's knowledge of Driver's true name was obtained during the course of representation.

D. No, unless Driver's true name is an issue in the proceeding.

Question 22.

Attorney represents Client, a plaintiff in a personal injury action. Wit was an eyewitness to the accident. Wit lives about 500 miles distant from the city where the case will be tried. Attorney interviewed Wit and determined that Wit's testimony would be favorable for Client. Wit asked Attorney to pay Wit, in addition to the statutory witness fees while attending the trial, the following:

I. Reimbursement for actual travel expenses while attending the trial

II. Reimbursement for lost wages while present at the trial

III. An amount equal to 5% of any recovery in the matter

If Attorney agrees to pay Wit the above, for which, if any, is Attorney subject to discipline?

A. III only

B. II and III, but not I

C. I, II, and III

D. Neither I, nor II, nor III

Question 23.

Judge is a judge of the trial court in City. Judge has served for many years as a director of a charitable organization that maintains a camp for disadvantaged children. The organization has never been involved in litigation. Judge has not received any compensation for her services. The charity has decided to sponsor a public testimonial dinner in Judge's honor. As part of the occasion, the local bar association intends to commission and present to Judge her portrait at a cost of $4,000. The money to pay for the portrait will come from a "public testimonial fund" that will be raised by the City Bar Association from contributions of lawyers who are members of the association and who practice in the courts of City.

Is it proper for Judge to accept the gift of the portrait?

A. Yes, because the gift is incident to a public testimonial for Judge.

B. Yes, because Judge did not receive compensation for her services to the charitable organization.

C. No, because the cost of the gift exceeds $1,000.

D. No, because the funds for the gift are contributed by lawyers who practice in the courts of City.

Question 24.

Three lawyers, Alpha, Beta, and Delta, formed a partnership to practice law with offices in both State First and State Second. Alpha is admitted to practice only in State First, Beta is admitted to practice only in State Second, and Delta is admitted to practice in both States First and Second. The following letterhead is on stationery used by their offices in both states:

Alpha, Beta, and Delta
Attorneys at Law

100 State Street
City, State First
(200) 555–5555

200 Bank Building
City, State Second
(202) 555-5555

Attorney Alpha
Admitted to practice only
in State First

Attorney Beta
Admitted to practice only
in State Second

Attorney Delta
Admitted to practice
in States First and Second

Are the members of the partnership <u>subject to discipline</u>?

A. No, because the letterhead states the jurisdictions in which each
partner is admitted.

B. Yes, because there is no jurisdiction in which both Alpha and Beta are
admitted to practice.

C. Yes, because the firm name used by each office contains the name of a
lawyer not admitted to practice in that jurisdiction.

D. Yes, unless Delta actively practices law in both States First and Second.

Question 25.

Attorney, who had represented Testator for many years, prepared Testator's will and acted as one of the two subscribing witnesses to its execution. The will gave 90% of Testator's estate to Testator's housekeeper and 10% to Testator's son and sole heir, Son. Upon Testator's death one year later, Executor, the executor named in the will, asked Attorney to represent him in probating the will and administering the estate. At that time Executor informed Attorney that Son had notified him that he would contest the probate of the will on the grounds that Testator lacked the required mental capacity at the time the will was executed. Attorney believes that Testator was fully competent at all times and will so testify, if called as a witness. The other subscribing witness to Testator's will predeceased Testator.

Is it <u>proper</u> for Attorney to represent Executor in the probate of the will?

A. Yes, because Attorney is the sole surviving witness to the execution of the will.

B. Yes, because Attorney's testimony will support the validity of the will.

C. No, because Attorney will be called to testify on a contested issue of fact.

D. No, because Attorney will be representing an interest adverse to Testator's heir at law.

Question 26.

Attorney, after being sued groundlessly for malpractice by a disgruntled former client, instituted the practice of conducting a final interview with each client whose work Attorney had completed. Attorney informed the client that the purpose of the interview was to explain to the client's satisfaction all action taken on the client's behalf. After Attorney obtained the client's consent to do so, the interview was recorded on tape, and the tape was placed in the client's closed file. At the interview, Attorney reviewed all matters in the client's file, explained each item, answered the client's questions, and described the choices Attorney had made in the case and the reasons for each of the decisions. At the end of the interview, Attorney asked these questions: "Do you fully understand the work I have done for you? Do you have any questions you want to ask me?"

Is Attorney <u>subject to discipline</u> for this practice?

A. Yes, if Attorney is attempting to preserve evidence relevant to a possible malpractice claim.

B. Yes, because Attorney is acting adversely to the client before the lawyer–client relationship has been terminated.

C. No, because the interview was conducted after Attorney had completed the client's work.

D. No, if Attorney fully explained in good faith all items in the file.

Question 27.

Plaintiff and Defendant are next–door neighbors and bitter personal enemies. Plaintiff is suing Defendant over an alleged trespass. Each party believes, in good faith, in the correctness of his position. Plaintiff is represented by Attorney Alpha, and Defendant is represented by Attorney Beta. After Plaintiff had retained Alpha, he told Alpha: "I do not want you to grant any delays or courtesies to Defendant or his lawyer. I want you to insist on every technicality."

Alpha has served Beta with a demand to answer written interrogatories. Beta, because of the illness of his secretary, has asked Alpha for a five–day extension of time within which to answer them.

Is Alpha <u>subject to discipline</u> if she grants Beta's request for a five–day extension?

A. Yes, because Alpha is acting contrary to her client's instructions.

B. Yes, unless Alpha first informs Plaintiff of the request and obtains Plaintiff's consent to grant it.

C. No, unless granting the extension would prejudice Plaintiff's rights.

D. No, because Beta was not at fault in causing the delay.

Question 28.

Attorneys Alpha and Beta had been political opponents. Alpha was elected to the state legislature after a bitter race in which Beta had managed the campaign of Alpha's opponent. Alpha had publicly blamed Beta at that time for what Alpha reasonably believed were illegal and unethical campaign practices and later had publicly objected to Beta's appointment as a judge.

Alpha represented Client in a widely publicized case tried in Judge Beta's court. At the conclusion of the trial, Beta ruled against Alpha's client. Alpha then held a press conference and said: "All that you reporters have to do is check your files and you will know what I think about Judge Beta's character and fitness."

Is Alpha *subject to discipline* for making this statement?

A. Yes, if Alpha's statement might lessen confidence in the legal system.

B. Yes, because Alpha's past accusations were unrelated to Beta's legal knowledge.

C. No, because Alpha reasonably believed that the statements about Beta were true.

D. No, if Beta had equal access to the press.

Question 29.

Judge and Attorney were formerly law partners and during their partnership acquired several parcels of real property as co–tenants. After Judge was elected to the trial court in County, she remained a co–tenant with Attorney, but left the management of the properties to Attorney.

Judge's term of office will expire soon and she is opposed for re–election by two members of the bar. Attorney, who has not discussed the matter with Judge, intends to make a substantial contribution to Judge's campaign for re–election.

Judge is one of fifteen judges sitting as trial court judges in County.

Is Attorney <u>subject to discipline</u> if Attorney contributes $10,000 to Judge's re–election campaign?

A. Yes, if Attorney frequently represents clients in cases tried in the trial court of County.

B. Yes, because Judge and Attorney have not discussed the matter of a campaign contribution.

C. No, if the contribution is made to a campaign committee organized to support Judge's re–election.

D. No, because Attorney and Judge have a longstanding personal and business relationship.

Question 30.

Alpha, a member of the bar, placed a printed flyer in the booth of each artist exhibiting works at a county fair. The face of the flyer contained the following information:

"I, Alpha, am an attorney, with offices in 800 Bank Building, telephone (555) 555–5555. I have a J.D. degree from State Law School and an M.A. degree in fine arts from State University. My practice includes representing artists in negotiating contracts between artists and dealers and protecting artists' interests. You can find me in the van parked at the fair entrance."

All factual information on the face of the flyer was correct. There was a retainer agreement on the back of the flyer. At the entrance to the fair, Alpha parked a van with a sign that read "Alpha—Attorney at Law."

For which, if any, of the following is Alpha <u>subject to discipline</u>?

I. Placing copies of the flyer in the booth of each artist
II. Including a retainer agreement on the back of the flyer
III. Parking the van with the sign on it at the fair entrance

A. III only
B. I and II, but not III
C. I, II, and III
D. Neither I, nor II, nor III

Question 31.

Witness was subpoenaed to appear and testify at a state legislative committee hearing. Witness retained Attorney to represent her at the hearing. During the hearing, Attorney, reasonably believing that it was in Witness's best interest not to answer, advised Witness not to answer certain questions on the grounds that Witness had a constitutional right not to answer. The committee chairperson directed Witness to answer and cautioned her that refusal to answer was a misdemeanor and that criminal prosecution would be instituted if she did not answer.

Upon Attorney's advice, Witness persisted in her refusal to answer. Witness was subsequently convicted for her refusal to answer.

Is Attorney subject to discipline?

A. Yes, because his advice to Witness was not legally sound.
B. Yes, because Witness, in acting on Attorney's advice, committed a crime.
C. No, if the offense Witness committed did not involve moral turpitude.
D. No, if Attorney reasonably believed Witness had a legal right to refuse to answer the questions.

Question 32.

Attorney had been representing Client for several months in a matter involving the ownership of some antique jewelry. Client claimed he purchased the jewelry for his wife with his own funds. Partner, Client's business partner, claimed the jewelry was a partnership purchase in which he, Partner, had a one-half interest. While the matter was pending, Client brought a valuable antique jewelry box to Attorney's office and said:

"Keep this in your vault for me. I bought it before I went into business with Partner. Don't tell him or anyone else about it until my matter with Partner is settled."

Later that same day, a police officer, who was in Attorney's office on another matter, saw the jewelry box when a clerk opened the vault to put in some papers. The police officer recognized it as one that had recently been stolen from a collector. Attorney was arrested and later charged with receiving stolen property.

Is Attorney <u>subject to discipline</u> if Attorney reveals that Client brought the box to her office?

A. Yes, because Client instructed Attorney not to tell anyone about the jewelry box.

B. Yes, if the disclosure would be detrimental to Client's interests.

C. No, because the jewelry box was not involved in the dispute between Client and Partner.

D. No, if the disclosure is necessary to enable Attorney to defend against a criminal charge.

Question 33.

Attorney Alpha currently represents Builder, a building contractor and the plaintiff in a suit to recover for breach of a contract to build a house. Builder also has pending before the zoning commission a petition to rezone property that Builder owns. Builder is represented by Attorney Beta in the zoning matter.

Neighbor, who owns property adjoining that of Builder, has asked Alpha to represent Neighbor in opposing Builder's petition for rezoning. Neighbor knows that Alpha represents Builder in the contract action.

Is it <u>proper</u> for Alpha to represent Neighbor in the zoning matter?

A. Yes, if there is no common issue of law or fact between the two matters.

B. Yes, because one matter is a judicial proceeding and the other is an administrative proceeding.

C. No, because Alpha is currently representing Builder in the contract action.

D. No, if there is a possibility that both matters will be appealed to the same court.

Question 34.

Attorney represented Plaintiff, the plaintiff in an automobile accident case against Defendant. The accident occurred at the intersection of two rural roads; the intersection was marked by four–way stop signs. Plaintiff had told Attorney that he arrived at the intersection before Defendant and that Plaintiff came to a full stop before entering the intersection. Plaintiff said that Defendant did not slow down but proceeded into the intersection without stopping and hit the side of Plaintiff's car.

Attorney learned from highway patrol records that Wit, who was a disinterested witness, had called the patrol and reported that she had seen the collision between Plaintiff and Defendant. The highway patrol records did not disclose the substance of Wit's observations. In fact, Wit's testimony would support Plaintiff's version of the accident.

Attorney believed that Plaintiff's testimony would be persuasive and did not interview Wit. At the trial, Defendant testified that he had entered the intersection first and that Plaintiff ran the stop sign. The jury believed Defendant and returned a verdict in his favor.

Is Attorney <u>subject to discipline</u>?

A. Yes, because Attorney's preparation for trial was inadequate.

B. Yes, unless Wit was not subject to subpoena.

C. No, because the highway patrol records did not disclose the substance of Wit's testimony.

D. No, if Attorney believed that Plaintiff's testimony would be sufficient to establish Plaintiff's case.

Question 35.

Client consulted Attorney and asked Attorney to represent him on a claim for damages for personal injuries. Attorney told Client that she would not accept employment unless Client executed a retainer agreement containing the following provision:

"Attorney has full authority to reject any settlement offer if, in Attorney's opinion, it is inadequate and to accept a settlement offer, provided the net recovery to Client, after payment of Attorney's fee and all costs and expenses of litigation, appears reasonable to Attorney."

Was it <u>proper</u> for Attorney to require execution of the retainer agreement as a condition to employment?

A. Yes, if Client was fully advised of the effect of the provision.

B. Yes, because Attorney is in a better position than Client to evaluate a settlement offer.

C. No, because Client was asked to surrender his right to accept or reject the settlement offer.

D. No, unless Attorney's fee is a determined amount and not contingent on the amount of recovery.

Question 36.

Alpha and Beta practiced law under the firm name of Alpha and Beta. When Beta died, Alpha did not change the firm name. Thereafter, Alpha entered into an arrangement with another attorney, Gamma. Gamma pays Alpha a certain sum each month for office space and use of Alpha's law library and for secretarial services, but Alpha and Gamma each has his own clients, and neither participates in the representation of the other's clients or shares in fees paid. On the entrance to the suite of offices shared by Alpha and Gamma are the words "Law Firm of Alpha, Beta, and Gamma."

Is Alpha subject to discipline?

A. Yes, because Beta was deceased when Alpha made the arrangement with Gamma.

B. Yes, because Gamma is not a partner of Alpha.

C. No, because Alpha and Beta were partners at the time of Beta's death.

D. No, because Gamma is paying a share of the rent and office expenses.

Question 37.

Attorney was employed as a lawyer by the state Environmental Control Commission (ECC) for ten years. During the last two years of her employment, Attorney spent most of her time in the preparation, trial, and appeal of a case involving the discharge by Deftco of industrial effluent into a river in the state. The judgment in the case, which is now final, contained a finding of a continuing and knowing discharge of a dangerous substance into a major stream by Deftco and assessed a penalty of $25,000.

The governing statute also provides for private actions for damages by persons injured by the discharge of the effluent.

Attorney recently left the employment of ECC and went into private practice. Three landowners have brought private damage actions against Deftco. They claim their truck farms were contaminated because they irrigated them with water that contained effluent from dangerous chemicals discharged by Deftco. Deftco has asked Attorney to represent it in defense of the three pending actions.

Is Attorney <u>subject to discipline</u> if she represents Deftco in these actions?

A. Yes, unless the judgment in the prior case is determinative of Deftco's liability.

B. Yes, because Attorney had substantial responsibility in the matter while employed by ECC.

C. No, because Attorney has acquired special competence in the matter.

D. No, if all information acquired by Attorney while representing ECC is now a matter of public record.

Question 38.

Attorney Alpha is skilled in trying personal injury cases. Alpha accepted the representation of Plaintiff in a personal injury case on a contingent fee basis. While preparing the case for trial, Alpha realized that the direct examination and cross–examination of the medical experts would involve medical issues with which Alpha was not familiar and, as a consequence, Alpha might not be able to represent Plaintiff competently.

Without informing Plaintiff, Alpha consulted Beta, who is both a lawyer and a medical doctor and who is a recognized specialist in the care and treatment of injuries of the type sustained by Plaintiff. Alpha and Beta agreed that Beta would participate in the trial to the limited extent of conducting the direct examination and cross–examination of the medical experts and that Alpha would divide the fee in proportion to the services performed and the responsibility assumed by each.

Was the arrangement between Alpha and Beta <u>proper</u>?

A. Yes, because the fee to be paid by Plaintiff was not increased by reason of Beta's association.

B. Yes, because the fee would be divided in proportion to the services performed and the responsibility assumed by each.

C. No, because Plaintiff was not informed of the association of Beta.

D. No, unless, upon conclusion of the matter, Alpha provides Plaintiff with a written statement setting forth the method of determining both the fee and the division of the fee with Beta.

Question 39.

Attorney was retained by Defendant to represent him in a paternity suit. Aunt, Defendant's aunt, believed the suit was unfounded and motivated by malice. Aunt sent Attorney a check for $1,000 and asked Attorney to apply it to the payment of Defendant's fee. Aunt told Attorney not to tell Defendant of the payment because "Defendant is too proud to accept gifts, but I know he really needs the money."

Is it <u>proper</u> for Attorney to accept Aunt's check?

A. Yes, if Aunt does not attempt to influence Attorney' s conduct of the case.

B. Yes, if Attorney's charges to Defendant are reduced accordingly.

C. No, because Aunt is attempting to finance litigation to which she is not a party.

D. No, unless Attorney first informs Defendant and obtains Defendant's consent to retain the payment.

Question 40.

Attorney represents Client, a famous politician, in an action against Newspaper for libel. The case has attracted much publicity, and a jury trial has been demanded. After one of the pretrial hearings, as Attorney left the courthouse, news reporters interviewed Attorney. In responding to questions, Attorney truthfully stated:

"The judge has upheld our right to subpoena the reporter involved, identified in our motion as Repo, and question her on her mental impressions when she prepared the article."

Is Attorney <u>subject to discipline</u> for making this statement?

A. Yes, because Attorney identified a prospective witness in the case.

B. Yes, because prospective jurors might learn of Attorney's remarks.

C. No, because the statement relates to a matter of public record.

D. No, because the trial has not commenced.

Question 41.

Attorney Alpha has been employed as an assistant prosecutor in the district attorney's office during the time that an investigation of Deft was being conducted by that office. Alpha took no part in the investigation and had no knowledge of the facts other than those disclosed in the press. Two months ago, Alpha left the district attorney's office and formed a partnership with Attorney Beta.

Last week, Deft was indicted for offenses allegedly disclosed by the prior investigation. Deft asked Alpha to represent him. Alpha declined to do so, but suggested Beta.

Is Beta subject to discipline if Beta represents Deft?

A. Yes, because Alpha was employed in the district attorney's office while the investigation of Deft was being conducted.

B. Yes, unless the district attorney's office is promptly notified and consents to the representation.

C. No, unless Alpha participates in the representation or shares in the fee.

D. No, because Alpha had no responsibility for or knowledge of the facts of the investigation of Deft.

Question 42.

The following advertisement appeared in daily newspapers published in City, where Legal Associates Group (LAG) maintains its offices. The use of the trade name Legal Associates Group is permitted in the jurisdiction. City is located in a jurisdiction that certifies legal specialists.

"Do you need a lawyer who specializes in handling the kind of problem you face?

"Legal Associates Group (LAG) will put you in touch with the right lawyer. We can furnish you with a lawyer on our staff who is a specialist in your kind of legal problem. And, the fee for our first consultation is only $15.

Consumer Law	Negligence
Criminal	Wills
Family	Real Estate

LAG
Telephone: 555–5555 (24 hours–day or night)"

Is this advertisement proper?

A. Yes, if each of the lawyers on the staff of LAG limits his or her practice to one of the named areas of law.

B. Yes, if a prospective client, during the first consultation, is given an estimate of the fee to be charged.

C. No, because the advertisement does not contain any fee schedule for services rendered after the first consultation.

D. No, unless there are lawyers on the staff of LAG who are certified as specialists in the listed areas by the appropriate authority in the jurisdiction.

Question 43.

Attorney limits her practice to criminal defense. When she is consulted by a prospective client who is not indigent, Attorney informs the prospective client, in advance of accepting employment, of the amount of her fee. Her fee is fixed and is based on the difficulty of the case and a reasonable hourly charge for the estimated time that she will spend in the preparation for trial and actual trial of the case. Attorney will not accept the employment unless the prospective client agrees to the fee set by Attorney, pays at least 50% of the fee in advance, and gives a negotiable promissory note with full collateral to secure payment of the balance of the fee.

Is Attorney's conduct proper?

A. Yes, because there is no attorney–client relationship at the time Attorney sets her fee.

B. Yes, if the amount of the fee fixed by Attorney is reasonable.

C. No, because Attorney required at least 50% of the fee in advance of rendering service.

D. No, because Attorney will be acquiring a security interest in the property of a client in a criminal matter.

Question 44.

Deft was on trial for the murder of Victim, who was killed during a barroom brawl. In the course of closing arguments to the jury, Prosecutor said, "Deft's whole defense is based on the testimony of Wit, who said that Victim attacked Deft with a knife before Deft struck him. No other witness testified to such an attack by Victim. I don't believe Wit was telling the truth, and I don't think you believe him either."

Was Prosecutor's statement proper?

A. Yes, if Prosecutor accurately stated the testimony in the case.

B. Yes, if Prosecutor, in fact, believed Wit was lying.

C. No, because Prosecutor alluded to the beliefs of the jurors.

D. No, because Prosecutor asserted his personal opinion about Wit's credibility.

Question 45.

Attorney, representing Plaintiff, failed to appear at the hearing of a motion to set the case for trial. At the request of Defendant's lawyer, Judge dismissed the case for failure to proceed in a timely manner. Six months later, Attorney filed a motion to set aside the dismissal, which was denied.

<u>Should</u> Judge report to the disciplinary authority Attorney's failure to appear at the motion to set the case for trial?

A. Yes, if Judge believes that Attorney's failure to appear was due to incompetence.

B. Yes, because Attorney's failure to appear resulted in Plaintiff's case being dismissed.

C. No, unless Judge is reasonably certain Plaintiff would have prevailed at trial.

D. No, unless Attorney's conduct was a contempt of court.

Question 46.

Commission, the State Waterways Commission, announced that it would conduct a hearing to consider a proposed plan for straightening a small river. Several landowners, whose lands abut the river, objected to the plan. At a meeting of the landowners, Baker, one of the landowners, offered to have her lawyer, Attorney, appear on behalf of all the landowners and agreed to pay Attorney's fee. All the landowners present agreed to Baker's proposal.

Attorney appeared at the hearing. At that time, Commission proposed a modification in the plan. This modification would reduce the risk of flooding Baker's land, while increasing the risk for the other landowners who had been present at the previous meeting. Attorney supported the modified plan, and it was approved by Commission.

Was Attorney's conduct <u>proper</u>?

A. Yes, if, in Attorney's professional judgment, the modified plan was in the public interest.

B. Yes, because the modified plan was proposed by Commission and not by Attorney.

C. No, because Attorney did not adequately represent the interests of all the landowners.

D. No, unless failure to support the modified plan would cause Baker substantial hardship.

Question 47.

Attorney represented Deft, who was charged with arson, at Deft's trial. Deft was convicted. Thereafter, Attorney received information which, if true, established that the key prosecution witness had given perjured testimony. Attorney, with Deft's knowledge but using Attorney's own funds, employed a private investigator. Attorney instructed the investigator to gain the confidence of the prosecution witness in an attempt to get that witness to admit that he had given perjured testimony at Deft's trial.

Is Attorney <u>subject to discipline</u> for so employing and instructing the investigator?

A. Yes, unless Attorney first advises the court of the information received.

B. Yes, because Attorney is arranging to have a prosecution witness interviewed.

C. No, because Attorney is properly representing the interests of his client.

D. No, unless Attorney personally communicated with the witness.

Question 48.

Attorney represents Client, plaintiff in a civil action that was filed a year ago and is about to be set for trial. Client informed Attorney that he could be available at any time during the months of October, November, and December. In discussing possible trial dates with opposing counsel and the court clerk, Attorney was advised that a trial date on October 5 was available and that the next available trial date would be December 10. Without first consulting Client, Attorney requested the December 10 trial date because she was representing Deft, the defendant in a felony criminal trial that was set for October 20 and she wanted as much time as possible to prepare for that trial.

Was it <u>proper</u> for Attorney to agree to the December trial date without obtaining Client's consent?

A. Yes, unless Client will be prejudiced by the delay.

B. Yes, because a criminal trial takes precedence over a civil trial.

C. No, because Attorney should manage her calendar so that her cases can be tried promptly.

D. No, unless Attorney was court–appointed counsel in the criminal case.

Question 49.

Able, Baker, and Carter had been indicted for the armed robbery of the cashier of a grocery store. Together, Able and Baker met with Attorney and asked Attorney to represent them. Attorney then interviewed Able and Baker separately. Each told Attorney that the robbery had been committed by Carter while Able and Baker sat in Carter's car outside the store, that Carter had said he needed some cigarettes, and that each knew nothing of Carter's plan to rob the cashier. Attorney agreed to represent both Able and Baker. One week prior to the trial date, Able told Attorney that he wanted to plea bargain and that he was prepared to turn state's evidence and testify that Baker had loaned Carter the gun Carter used in the robbery. Able also said that he and Baker had shared in the proceeds of the robbery with Carter.

It is proper for Attorney to:

A. request court approval to withdraw as lawyer for both Able and Baker.

B. continue to represent Baker and, with Able's consent and court approval, withdraw as Able's lawyer.

C. continue to represent Able and, with Baker's consent and court approval, withdraw as Baker's lawyer.

D. continue to represent Able and Baker, but not call Able as a witness.

Question 50.

While presiding over the trial of a highly publicized antitrust case, ABCO v. DEFO, Judge received in the mail a lengthy letter from Attorney, a local lawyer. The letter discussed the law applicable to ABCO v. DEFO. Judge knew that Attorney did not represent either party. Judge read the letter and, without mentioning its receipt to the lawyers in the pending case, filed the letter in his general file on antitrust litigation.

Later, after reading the trial briefs in ABCO v. DEFO, Judge concluded that Attorney's letter better explained the law applicable to the case pending before him than either of the trial briefs. Judge followed Attorney's reasoning in formulating his decision.

Was it <u>proper</u> for Judge to consider Attorney's letter?

A. Yes, because Judge did not initiate the communication with Attorney.

B. Yes, if Attorney did not represent any client whose interests could be affected by the outcome.

C. No, unless Judge, prior to rendering his decision, communicated its contents to all counsel and gave them an opportunity to respond.

D. No, because Attorney is of record as counsel in the case.

B. Answers to Practice Questions

Answer 1

A is the best response, because it correctly identifies the duties regarding recommendations and disclosure under circumstances like these.

As a preliminary matter, note that option A uses the conjunction "and"; this means that the first part of the answer, concerning Attorney's duties of disclosure, *and* the second part of the answer, concerning a recommendation, must *both* be correct in order for the answer as a whole to be correct. Let's look at each one separately.

First, the duty of disclosure. The two codes vary slightly in the level of duty in this area. Under the MC, regarding bar applicants, attorneys *should* report to authorities all unfavorable information they possess regarding the character (or other qualifications) of a bar applicant. EC 1–3. Under MR 8.1(b), attorneys must respond candidly to requests from bar admission authorities for any unprivileged information about a bar candidate. Combining the two rules, you find that under both codes, Attorney *should* disclose Stu's embezzlement of the student bar association funds in response to the request from the bar authorities. The first part of answer A correctly reflects this standard.

Second, the duty regarding recommendations. Option A states that Attorney *may* make a recommendation as Attorney sees fit. In order for this to be correct, there would have to be no code provisions stating that Attorney *shouldn't* recommend Stu, and no provisions stating that Attorney *should* do so. In fact, that's the case. There are no provisions stating that a lawyer has a duty to recommend anyone for admission to the bar. As to not recommending someone, the codes both forbid lawyers from promoting "unqualified" candidates for admission to the bar. MR 8.1, DR 1–101(B). An applicant may be "unqualified" due to a defect in character, education, or "any other relevant attribute." DR 1–101(B). As a result, barring facts that indicate that Stu is unqualified, Attorney would be free to recommend him for admission. In fact, the facts clearly indicate why Attorney would be free to recommend Stu. While Stu *did* embezzle the SBA funds, his motivation in doing so—an emergency illness—coupled with the fact that he repaid the funds, indicate that Stu does not suffer any defects in character that would require that Attorney *not* recommend him for admission. The second part of option A correctly reflects this standard.

Since Option A correctly reflects the standards for both disclosure and recommendations, it's the best response.

B is not the best response, for two reasons: it fails to recognize that Attorney has no duty to recommend Stu, and it also ignores the fact that Attorney should disclose Stu's embezzlement *even if* he believes Stu is "reformed."

B recognizes that there are two central issues here: One, Attorney's duty concerning recommending Stu, and two, Attorney's duty of disclosure regarding Stu's embezzlement. Let's look at the recommendation duty first. Contrary to what B states, lawyers have no affirmative duty to recommend anyone; instead, the codes tell lawyers when they *cannot* recommend someone. Specifically, the rule is that a lawyer must not recommend an "unqualified" candidate for admission to the bar. MR 8.1, DR 1–101(B) (an applicant being "unqualified" if he suffers a defect in character, education, or "any other relevant attribute," DR 1–101(B)). When a bar applicant is not "unqualified," it's totally within a lawyer's discretion as to whether to recommend the applicant. Option B states that Attorney *should* recommend Stu; since it imposes a duty where none exists, it misstates a lawyer's duty concerning recommendations.

B also misstates a lawyer's duty concerning disclosing a bar applicant's defects in character. The two codes vary slightly in the level of duty in this area. Under the MC, regarding bar applicants, attorneys *should* report to authorities all unfavorable information they possess regarding the character (or other qualifications) of a bar applicant. EC 1–3. Under MR 8.1(b), attorneys *must* respond candidly to requests from bar admission authorities for any unprivileged information about a bar candidate. Combining the two codes, you find that Attorney *should* disclose Stu's embezzlement of the student bar association funds in response to a request from the bar authorities for information about Stu's character. Option B states that Attorney shouldn't disclose Stu's embezzlement if he believes Stu is of good moral character. What the "good moral character" qualification actually determines is whether Attorney may properly recommend Stu *at all;* if Attorney believed Stu lacked good moral character, it would be improper for him to recommend Stu in the first place. This has no bearing on whether Attorney must disclose his embezzlement, as the rules on disclosure indicate.

If you chose this response, it may be because you responded emotionally to the reason for Stu's embezzlement—the emergency illness—and decided that Stu deserves to be a lawyer in spite of the misuse of funds, and beyond that, you perhaps thought that bygones should be bygones, and you shouldn't mention it to the authorities for fear they'll put too much emphasis on it. You may be right that Stu deserves another chance; however, the rule is that Attorney may or may not recommend Stu, but even if he doesn't, he should disclose the wrongdoing to the authorities. Since option B recognizes neither of these, it's not the best response.

Option C is not the best response, because it mistakenly implies that the information about Stu is protected due to privilege.

Option C focuses on the issue of *disclosure* raised by these facts; that is, whether Attorney must/may disclose Stu's embezzlement to the authorities. The rule is that a lawyer must respond to any lawful demand for *non–confidential* information in relation to applications for bar admissions. DR 1–103(B), MR 8.1(b). What option C does is to focus on the non–confidential limitation, and conclude that the information here is confidential and thus not subject to disclosure. However, this mischaracterizes the facts; the information is *not* confidential. Under the MC, information is only protected if it is gained during a lawyer–client relationship and its disclosure would be embarrassing or detrimental to the client (or the client requested it be held confidential), DR 4–101(A) and (B); under the MR, all information about a client "relating to the representation" is protected, MR 1.6. The key here is that *Stu is not Attorney's client, and thus there can be no issue of confidentiality.* If you chose this response, you overlooked this fact (in addition, option C somewhat misstates the scope of confidentiality, since it doesn't matter from whom a lawyer learns the information about his client, so long as it fits within the scope of confidentiality discussed above). Since option C improperly addresses confidentiality, it's not the best response.

Option D is not the best response, because whether or not Stu has asked Attorney for a recommendation has no bearing on Attorney's duty to disclose the embezzlement.

Option D implies that where a bar applicant has not asked for a recommendation, a lawyer's duty is to withhold information about misconduct from bar authorities. In fact, this muddles a lawyer's duty regarding recommendations and his duty regarding disclosure of wrongdoing by a bar candidate, and misstates the standard for both. As to recommendations, a lawyer may recommend any qualified candidate for bar admission; whether or not the candidate has asked for a recommendation is immaterial.

As to disclosure, regardless of whether a candidate has solicited a recommendation, under both codes taken together, a lawyer should disclose a bar applicant's defects in character in response to a request from the bar authorities. The two codes vary slightly in the level of duty in this area. Under the MC, regarding bar applicants, attorneys should report to authorities all unfavorable information they possess regarding the character (or other qualifications) of a bar applicant. EC 1–3. Under MR 8.1(b), attorneys must respond candidly to requests from bar admission authorities for any unprivileged information about a bar candidate. Remember that where one lawyer code uses "should" and the other uses "must," the "should" controls, such that Attorney *should* disclose Stu's embezzlement of the student bar association funds in response to the bar authorities' request. Since option D mistakenly states that Attorney's duty to disclose is contingent on whether Stu has asked for a recommendation, it's not the best response.

Answer 2

D is the best response, because it represents the only set of facts constituting grounds for *mandatory* withdrawal.

The grounds for mandatory withdrawal are virtually identical under the codes. Under both DR 2110(B) and MR 1.16(a), a lawyer must withdraw from representation if continuing the representation will result in a legal or ethical violation; or the lawyer's physical or mental condition "materially impairs" (MR) or makes it "unreasonably difficult" (MC) to continue effective representation; or the client discharges the lawyer; or it's obvious the client's purpose is harassment or materially injuring someone. It's the first possibility—legal or ethical violation—that applies here. Here, if Attorney continues the representation knowing that Seller's affidavit contains falsehoods, he'll be violating the rule under which a lawyer cannot knowingly mislead a court, either with misrepresentations of his own or quoting those of his client. DR 7–102, MR 3.3.

Note that the modifier used in option D is "unless." This means that in order for the answer to be correct, the reasoning must be the only way the result given *cannot* occur. Applied here, you'd have to ask yourself: "Is there any way Attorney would have to withdraw if Attorney *didn't* know Seller's affidavit would contain false statements?" In fact, the answer to this is yes. If Attorney only believed Seller had caused the horse's injuries, and his investigation didn't prove conclusively that Seller *did* cause the injuries ("...ordinarily caused by prolonged neglect..."), grounds for mandatory withdrawal would not exist. What option D does, in effect, is to add a fact. Attorney's knowledge that Seller's statements to the court are false—which provides grounds for mandatory withdrawal. This information would not otherwise exist under the facts as stated in the problem. As a result, it's the best response.

A is not the best response, because Attorney's belief that the motion would not succeed would not create grounds for mandatory withdrawal.

The grounds for mandatory withdrawal are virtually identical under the codes. Under both DR 2110(B) and MR 1.16(a), a lawyer must withdraw from representation if continuing the representation will result in a legal or ethical violation; or the lawyer's physical or mental condition "materially impairs" (MR) or makes it "unreasonably difficult" (MC) to continue effective representation; or the client discharges the lawyer; or it's obvious the client's purpose is harassment or materially injuring someone. Comparing these with the facts in this problem, it becomes clear that Attorney's belief that the motion will fail would not constitute grounds for mandatory withdrawal.

What's underlying option A is the concept of the autonomy of the lawyer; that is, the extent to which a client can make a lawyer do something the lawyer believes will fail. In fact, the rule is that a client has the right to make major decisions in the representation (e.g., concerning the objectives of representation, affecting the merits of the case, and substantially prejudicing client's rights), and the lawyer makes the "strategic" decisions; that is, how to bring the client's goals to fruition. MR 1.2, EC 7–7. Whether to file for summary judgment would be within the client's power to decide, and the attorney's belief that the action the client desires won't succeed, or even that it *shouldn't* succeed, wouldn't be grounds for mandatory withdrawal. Since option A doesn't recognize this, it's not the best response.

B is not the best response, because it provides grounds for permissive withdrawal, not *mandatory* withdrawal.

The grounds for mandatory withdrawal are virtually identical under the codes. Under both DR 2110(B) and MR 1.16(a), a lawyer must withdraw from representation if continuing the representation will result in a legal or ethical violation; or the lawyer's physical or mental condition "materially impairs" (MR) or makes it "unreasonably difficult" (MC) to continue effective representation; or the client discharges the lawyer; or it's obvious the client's purpose is harassment or materially injuring someone. A client's refusal to follow his attorney's advice doesn't fit under any one of these, so Attorney wouldn't be subject to discipline for failing to withdraw on these grounds.

If you chose this response, you confused the grounds for *mandatory* withdrawal with those for *permissive* withdrawal. Under both codes, a client's insistence that his lawyer engage in conduct contrary to the lawyer's judgment and advice, *even if it doesn't violate ethical rules,* is grounds for permissive withdrawal. DR 2–110(C), MR 1.16(b). However, permissive withdrawal is just what the name implies; the lawyer may withdraw if he chooses, but he's neither obligated to continue the representation nor obligated to withdraw. Since option B doesn't provide grounds for mandatory withdrawal, it's not the best response.

C is not the best response, because it states an erroneous rule; in fact, an attorney *need* not accept his client's version of facts.

Lawyers have an obligation to zealously pursue the goals of their clients. However this duty is circumscribed by the lawyer's duty to the court, to see that justice is done. If you think about it for a minute, you can see that the rule as stated in option C cannot be true, because there are many occasions in which a lawyer's duty is contrary to what his client wants: for instance, a lawyer has a general duty not to use his client's perjured testimony. When you see a blanket statement like the one in option C— "Attorney must accept Seller's version of the facts"—always take a moment to think of situations where the statement *may not* be true. If you can think of even one, then the statement is incorrect, and the answer can't be the best response.

If you chose this response, you may have been thinking of the lawyer's duty to verify facts as stated by his client, which is an issue of competence. As a general rule, a lawyer has no obligation to verify a client's statement of facts, unless the circumstances reasonably indicate such a need. Even if this rule were applicable to these facts, there are circumstances indicating that Attorney shouldn't accept Seller's version of the facts; namely, his own investigation indicates that Seller may not be telling the truth. Nonetheless, the central problem with option C is that it states an incorrect rule of ethics, and as a result it cannot be the best response.

Answer 3

A is the best response, because it correctly identifies that Attorney is subject to discipline for helping Baker, who is not a licensed attorney, practice law.

The general rule on unauthorized practice is that a lawyer can't "aid" a non–lawyer in activities constituting the practice of law. DR 3–101(A), MR 5.5(b). As a general matter, offering advice and appearing in court are considered the practice of law. Here, Attorney employs Baker, who is not a licensed attorney, to appear in court on behalf of clients. When you distill the facts to this level, you can see that it's clear that Attorney has violated the ethics rules pertaining to unauthorized practice. However, as with many MPRE questions, this question is made more difficult by all the window–dressing in the facts. You're told that Baker has studied law extensively, thus creating the impression that he probably will render competent service; that the matters Attorney relegates to Baker are relatively minor; and, perhaps most importantly, you're told that the corporate clients consented to Baker's representation. The key point to remember is that *none of this makes any difference at all!* While clients are considered capable of consenting to some things that are otherwise code violations—most conflicts of interest, for instance—unauthorized practice isn't one of them. That's why it's important on MPRE questions to get to the "nut"—the central issue addressed in the question—and work your way back up from there, considering if consent can validate conduct and the like, without being influenced by the facts of the question. Since option A correctly addresses and resolves the central issue, which is that Attorney is aiding Baker in the unauthorized practice of law, it's the best response.

B is not the best response, because it does not address the central issue in the problem, even though it states a correct rule of law.

A "power of attorney" is a written instrument by which one person authorizes another to perform acts on his behalf (e.g., selling a piece of property). However, the reason it doesn't apply here is that "power of attorney" is really a misnomer; it doesn't really give the power to be one's attorney, but rather the power to act as a client, and make the decisions a client would normally make. The problem here isn't who makes the client–based decisions in the attorney–client relationship (i.e., the goals of the representation), but rather the one who performs the attorney function—and that person must be a licensed attorney. Since B doesn't recognize this, it's not the best response.

C is not the best response, because it misstates the law—client consent *cannot* validate unauthorized practice.

The general rule on unauthorized practice is that a lawyer can't "aid" a non–lawyer in activities constituting the practice of law. DR 3–101(A), MR 5.5(b). As a general matter, offering advice and appearing in court are considered the practice of law. Here, Attorney employs Baker, who is not a licensed attorney, to appear in court on behalf of clients. This is unauthorized practice in its purest form; what makes option C a little trickier is that it throws in an "informed consent" condition. In fact, what may have misled you into choosing option C is that you may have thought that the unauthorized practice prohibition is designed to protect the client in the first place, and as a result the client should be able to waive the prohibition after full consultation. This isn't bad reasoning, but there are other interests at stake; namely, those of the justice system, in assuring that only those competent to practice law (read: licensed attorneys) actually do so. As a result, a client cannot consent to a non–attorney representing him. Since C doesn't recognize this, it's not the best response.

D is not the best response, because whether or not Baker competently represents clients has no bearing on whether Attorney is subject to discipline for aiding a non–lawyer in the unauthorized practice of law.

The general rule on unauthorized practice is that a lawyer can't "aid" a non–lawyer in activities constituting the practice of law. DR 3–101(A), MR 5.5(b). As a general matter, offering advice and appearing in court are considered the practice of law. Here, Attorney employs Baker, who is not a licensed attorney, to appear in court on behalf of clients. As a result, Attorney has violated the rule on unauthorized practice, plain and simple. What makes D sneakier is that it takes a look at the end result, namely: Did Baker render competent service? In fact, it doesn't matter. If Baker *did* in fact act incompetently on Attorney's clients' behalf, the clients may have an action against Attorney for malpractice; but this has nothing to do with unauthorized practice. Since D doesn't recognize this, it's not the best response.

Answer 4

B is the best response, because it correctly identifies the fact that Attorney will be subject to discipline for violating Mafco's confidences.

The lawyer's duty of confidentiality, as it relates to disclosure, varies somewhat between the two codes of ethics. Under the MC, DR 4–101(B), as a general rule a lawyer must not knowingly reveal his client's confidences or secrets. A confidence is any communication protected by the attorney/client privilege; a secret is anything the client requests be held confidential, or whose disclosure would be embarrassing or detrimental to the client. DR 4–10l(A). The MR is somewhat broader, preventing the lawyer from revealing "information relating to representation of a client without the client's express or implied authorization." MR 1.6. Under the MC, the information about the intended manufacturing plant would be considered a "secret," because Mafco's president asked Attorney to keep the information confidential. Under the MR, it would be protected because it relates to Mafco's representation. As a result, because Attorney disclosed Mafco's plans to Investor without Mafco's consent, Attorney is subject to discipline.

While this problem is pretty straightforward, there is one fact that may be considered tricky, and it's the fact that Mafco was no longer Attorney's client when he disclosed Mafco's information to Investor. However, this doesn't affect Attorney's duty to protect Mafco's confidences under these facts, since the duty of confidentiality remains in force indefinitely. In any case, since option B correctly recognizes the fact that Attorney violated his duty of confidentiality toward Mafco, it's the best response.

A is not the best response, because it misrepresents the facts in the problem, creates a conflict of interest issue where none exists, and does not state the correct rule on conflicts of interest as they relate to former clients. Apart from that, it's a pretty good answer.

Option A states that Attorney took on Investor as a client, knowing that his interests might be adverse to those of Attorney's former client, Mafco. This misinterprets the facts, in that you're told that Investor was already one of Attorney's clients, not that Attorney was agreeing to represent Investor at the time of the disclosure. Thus, even if option A stated the law correctly, its misstatement of the facts means it could not be the best response.

As to its misstatement of the law, option A implies that Attorney's taking on Investor knowing that Investor's financial interests might be adverse to those of Mafco would constitute an impermissible conflict of interest. This isn't true, in at least two respects. The rule on conflicts of interests as to former clients has two elements: loyalty and confidentiality. As to loyalty, the rule is that a lawyer cannot represent another client in the same or a substantially related matter as a former client when the potential new client's interests are materially adverse to those of the former client, MR 1.9(a). As to the duty of confidentiality, the new representation must not involve the possibility that confidential information from the old client might be used against him. Option A muddles these two, by using the "might be adverse" language to imply that there's a loyalty problem with representing Investor. In fact, this isn't the case, since the matters Attorney handled on behalf of each client—purchasing land to build a plant, and tax advice about purchasing a utility—are not the same or even substantially related, thus not creating any "loyalty" problems. Second, as to confidentiality, even if Attorney had agreed to represent Investor for the purpose of buying the utility, there's nothing inherent in the representation that suggests that Attorney might *have* to disclose Mafco's information to Investor; the disclosure is more along the lines of convincing Investor that the purchase is a good idea, due to the potential bonanza in store for Investor if Mafco goes ahead with its building plans. While the duty of confidentiality is a central issue in these facts, and it underlies conflict of interest problems (as the above analysis indicates), option A does an end run around the principal issue here, which is a pure disclosure–of–confidential–information problem. As a result, it's not the best response.

Option C is not the best response, because Attorney's potential for discipline does not hinge on whether or not he profited from Investor's acquisition.

What option C does is to confuse the rules on disclosure and use, which are the two principal aspects of the lawyer's duty of confidentiality. Let's look at how the two differ. Generally speaking, the duty of non–disclosure, as its name implies, prevents a lawyer from disclosing to anyone else confidences and secrets of a client. The rules on *use* of client information, on the other hand, address what a lawyer may not *do* with his client's confidences and secrets. The rules vary a bit between the codes. Under the MC, DR 4–101(B), a lawyer may not: 1. use a confidence or secret of his client to the client's disadvantage, and 2. use a confidence or secret of his client for his own advantage or that of a third person *without* client's consent after full disclosure. Under the MR, Rule 1.8(b), the lawyer *may* use his client's confidential information to his own advantage as long as doing so doesn't disadvantage the client. What option C implies is that Attorney won't be subject to discipline for *disclosing* Mafco's information as long as he doesn't profit from *use* of that information. As the rules above indicate, this isn't how it works; instead, Attorney will be subject to discipline based purely on the fact that he disclosed Mafco's secret information without Mafco's consent, and that's pretty much all there is to it.

Interestingly enough, even if the facts were as C implies they were—namely, Attorney used Mafco's information for his own and/or Investor's benefit— the MPRE couldn't ask such a question, because the result would be *different* under the two codes! Under the MC, use that is advantageous to the lawyer or a third person isn't permissible without client's consent; under the MR, it is permissible without client's consent. Since the result would be different under the two codes, this is not a testable point.

In any case, since option C misstates and misapplies the rule on adverse use to facts involving disclosure, it's not the best response.

D is not the best response, because who initiated the conversation in which the disclosure took place is irrelevant to Attorney's being subject to discipline.

The lawyer's duty of non–disclosure, which is part of the duty of confidentiality, varies somewhat between the two codes of ethics. Under the MC, DR 4101(B), as a general rule a lawyer must not knowingly reveal his client's confidences or secrets. A confidence is any communication protected by the attorney/client privilege; a secret is anything the client requests be held confidential, or whose disclosure would be embarrassing or detrimental to the client. DR 4–101(A). The MR is somewhat broader, preventing the lawyer from revealing "information relating to representation of a client" without the client's express or implied authorization. MR 1.6. Under the MC, the information about the intended manufacturing plant would be considered a "secret," because Mafco's president asked Attorney to keep the information confidential. Under the MR, it would be protected because it relates to Mafco's representation. As a result, because Attorney disclosed Mafco's plans to Investor without Mafco's consent, Attorney is subject to discipline.

Option D suggests that a threshold issue in determining whether disclosure is permissible is whether someone else initiated the conversation in which the disclosure was made. When you think about it in this light, you can see how silly this is, since the mere fact that Investor happened to bring up the utility purchase doesn't give Attorney carte blanche to spill his guts on his other clients' confidential information. In fact, under the facts as they appear, Attorney's disclosure about Mafco's plans wasn't even really part of the meat of the conversation; it seems as though Attorney threw in the comment as an "icing on–the–cake" feature of the purchase!

Since option D focuses on a fact which is irrelevant to Attorney's being subject to discipline, it's not the best response.

Answer 5

B is the correct response, because it correctly identifies that of the three alternatives, only alternative II is permissible conduct for Attorney.

AS TO ALTERNATIVE I:

Alternative I is not an attractive choice because "difficulty of prevailing" is not grounds for withdrawal.

Option A suggests that lack of access to an expert witness, making it difficult to prevail, is grounds for either mandatory or permissive withdrawal. In fact, that's not the case. The grounds for mandatory withdrawal, under both codes, are as follows: 1. continued representation will result in a legal or ethical violation; 2. physical or mental condition of lawyer "materially impairs" (MR) or makes it "unreasonably difficult" (MC) to continue effective representation; 3. the lawyer is discharged by the client; or 4. it's obvious the client's purpose is harassment or materially injuring someone. DR 2–110(B), MR 1.16(a).

As to permissive withdrawal, common grounds between the MC and the MR are as follows: 1. client insists on a claim/defense that's unwarranted; 2. client seeks to pursue an illegal course of conduct; 3. continued representation is likely to violate law or ethical rules; 4. client makes it unreasonably difficult for lawyer to execute his duties effectively; 5. client insists lawyer engage in conduct that's "imprudent" (contrary to lawyer's judgment and advice); 6. client refuses to pay fees or expenses; 7. lawyer's inability to work with co–counsel; 8. mental or physical problem makes effective representation difficult. DR 2110(C), MR 1.16(b).

As these lists indicate, the fact that the odds of winning have been made more difficult due to lack of an expert witness would not constitute grounds for either mandatory or permissive withdrawal. In the absence of such grounds, the only proper thing for a lawyer to do is continue the representation to its natural conclusion. Since alternative I doesn't recognize this, it can't be part of the correct response.

AS TO ALTERNATIVE II:

Alternative II is an attractive choice, because it represents a proper basis on which a lawyer may advance the costs of litigation to his client.

The codes differ somewhat in their approach to advances to clients. Under the MC, the lawyer may advance his client the costs of litigation, investigation, medical exams, and getting and presenting evidence, *as long as the client remains ultimately liable for the debt,* DR 5–103(B). Under the MR, the rule is the same *except* that the MR don't require that the client remain ultimately liable for the costs. MR 1.8(e)(1), (2). Thus, under both codes taken together, it would be proper for Attorney to lend Publisher the cost of obtaining Wit's testimony, as long as Publisher ultimately agrees to pay Attorney back. Since Alternative II recognizes this, it can be part of the correct response.

AS TO ALTERNATIVE III:

Alternative III is not an attractive choice, because it represents, under both codes, an impermissible means of paying witnesses. The rule is that a lawyer cannot offer to, agree to, or actually pay a witness contingent on either the content of his testimony or the outcome of the case. DR 7–109(C), MR 3.4(b)(While MR 3.4(b) doesn't expressly forbid such payments, it does forbid inducements prohibited by law, and most jurisdictions forbid contingent payments to witnesses).

You may be wondering: what *is* permissible payment for witnesses? For *non–expert* witnesses, the lawyer may agree to pay expenses reasonably incurred by the witness in attending or testifying, and reasonable compensation to the witness for his loss of time in attending or testifying; expert witnesses are entitled to these as well as a reasonable fee for professional services. DR 7–109(C). What all this boils down to is that it's impermissible *as a matter of theory* for expert witnesses to receive contingent fees. In practice what happens is that experts are paid a small fixed fee for actual testimony and a contingency–based consulting fee, ABA Inf. Op. 1375 (1976); however, for purposes of the MPRE, you're only concerned with what happens in theory, and since contingent fees to witnesses are impermissible, alternative III cannot be part of the correct response.

Answer 6

B is the best response, because it correctly identifies the fact that Alpha will be liable for failing to provide competent service to Passenger.

There are three general ways in which a lawyer may be incompetent: 1. he lacks sufficient knowledge and skill to handle the matter; 2. he fails to prepare adequately in carrying out the representation; or 3. he neglects his duties to the client (including a failure to communicate with the client, or procrastination). DR 6–101, MR 1.3. Here, Alpha fits #3; by failing to advance Passenger's interests for ten months, Alpha neglected her duties to Passenger.

Note that this question indicates the extent to which facts must be crystal clear in a case where the modifier "because" is used, and the issue being tested is one that requires line–drawing, as neglect does. Here, Alpha refused to talk to either the opposing counsel or Passenger for ten months, up until one week before the statute of limitations was due to run out. While conduct that is less heinous could be considered neglectful, these facts make it absolutely clear that neglect is involved, and if Alpha is to avoid discipline, it must be on some basis other than lack of neglect.

In any case, since option B recognizes that Alpha will be subject to discipline due to neglect, it's the best response.

A is not the best response, because Alpha's being occupied with other clients would not release her from discipline for neglect.

The central problem with option A is the modifier it uses: "unless." Read another way, option A says that if Alpha was completely occupied with other clients during the ten months she neglected Passenger's work, she'll avoid discipline. This isn't true, and it means that A can't be correct.

Instead, Alpha will be subject to discipline for incompetence. There are three general ways in which a lawyer may be incompetent: 1. he lacks sufficient knowledge and skill to handle the matter; 2. he fails to prepare adequately in carrying out the representation; or 3. he neglects his duties to the client (including a failure to communicate with the client, or procrastination). DR 6–101, MR 1.3. Here, Alpha fits #3; by failing to advance Passenger's interests for ten months, Alpha neglected her duties to Passenger. Contrary to what option A states, a lawyer's heavy workload cannot excuse him from his duty of competent representation. DR 6–101(A)(3), MR 1.3. Since A doesn't recognize this, it can't be the best response.

C is not the best response, because its reasoning doesn't negate Alpha's incompetence.

There are three general ways in which a lawyer may be incompetent: 1. he lacks sufficient knowledge and skill to handle the matter; 2. he fails to prepare adequately in carrying out the representation; or 3. he neglects his duties to the client (including a failure to communicate with the client, or procrastination). DR 6–101, MR 1.3. Here, Alpha fits #3; by failing to advance Passenger's interests for ten months, Alpha neglected her duties to Passenger.

Option C suggests that because of the end result—Passenger's suit was filed before the statute of limitations ran out—Alpha should avoid discipline. In fact, this isn't the rule; instead, where delays are involved, you should determine if the delay was *unreasonable*. If it was, the attorney is subject to discipline, the rationale being that "unreasonable delay can cause a client needless anxiety and undermine confidence in the lawyer's trustworthiness." Comment, MR 1.3. As this option shows, unless you're dealing with malpractice, it's important not to be swayed by end results! In any case, since option C incorrectly states that Passenger's claims being filed on time releases Alpha from discipline, it's not the best response.

D is not the best response, because returning the $1,000 to Passenger would not release Alpha from liability, contrary to what D states.

There are three general ways in which a lawyer may be incompetent: 1. he lacks sufficient knowledge and skill to handle the matter; 2. he fails to prepare adequately in carrying out the representation; or 3. he neglects his duties to the client (including a failure to communicate with the client, or procrastination). DR 6–101, MR 1.3. Here, Alpha fits #3; by failing to advance Passenger's interests for ten months, Alpha neglected her duties to Passenger. Note that the conduct mandating discipline is *complete* when the neglect takes place; it doesn't matter if the attorney subsequently apologizes, repents, returns the money, or whether the complaint is ultimately filed on time, as happened here. Of course, had Alpha *not* returned the $1,000, she would *also* be subject to discipline for charging a fee she didn't earn. DR 2–106(A), MR 1.5(a). The rule with advance fees is that the lawyer can only keep as much as he earns through actual performance of services. However, since D ignores the fact that Alpha will be subject to discipline for neglect even though she returned the $1,000 fee, it's not the best response.

Answer 7

C is the best response, because it correctly recognizes the propriety of Alpha's motion for default judgment.

As a general matter, a lawyer has the duty to zealously pursue his client's interests within the bounds of law and propriety. DR 7–101(A), EC 7–1, MR 1.3. In this problem, Plaintiff's goal is to prevail in his personal injury suit against Defendant, as cheaply as possible. If Alpha can accomplish this goal with a default judgment—which will serve Plaintiff's goals all the more by saving Plaintiff the costs of a trial—then Alpha should do so, as long as there are no ethical reasons why he shouldn't do so. Under these facts, there are no countervailing reasons why Alpha *shouldn't* file for default.

Here's an example of how this might happen. Say that Defendant didn't have a lawyer, and that when he was served with process, he called Alpha and explained that he was in the hospital, and that his answer would be delayed until he got out of the hospital and could find a lawyer. Say in addition that Alpha knew that if he sought a default judgment when the time for filing the answer had expired, the default would subsequently be set aside, assuming that Defendant would file such a motion. In that case it would be reasonable for Alpha *not* to file for a default judgment, since it would be his professional judgment that waiving the default would be in Plaintiff's best interests (in that the contrary would waste Plaintiff's money; there'd be no substantive benefit, since a subsequent motion to set aside the default would likely succeed).

As the facts stand, there's no reason for Alpha not to seek a default judgment. Since C recognizes this, it's the best response.

A is not the best response, because Alpha's knowing that Defendant was represented by counsel has no effect on the propriety of Alpha's seeking a default judgment.

When a lawyer finds out that the opposing party is represented by a lawyer, the principal effect this has is to prevent the lawyer from communicating with the opposing party, without that party's consent. Thus, under these facts, this would mean that if Alpha wanted to communicate with Defendant, he'd have to do so through Beta. But that's not the case here. Under these facts, Defendant was properly served with process. With no answer filed before the time for filing expired, Alpha is left with one duty: to zealously pursue Plaintiff's goals within the bounds of the law, which in these facts, translates into Alpha seeking a default judgment. By doing so, Alpha is ensuring that Plaintiff will prevail, and saves Plaintiff the costs of a trial. Since option A doesn't recognize this, it's not the best response.

B is not the best response, for two reasons: It states an ethical principle that exists under only one of the codes, and it misapplies the rule to these facts.

Under the MC, DR 7–106(C)(5), a lawyer must comply with known local customs of courtesy or practice of the bar of a particular tribunal, and if he doesn't plan to do so, he must give opposing counsel timely notice of his intent not to comply. The problem is that there isn't an issue of professional courtesy under these facts; what option B *hints* at is that perhaps Alpha should have contacted Beta to remind him of the deadline, and ensure that Defendant notified him about the claim. There's no indication here that there's a custom of courtesy requiring a phone call to the opposing counsel when the deadline on a reply is approaching. Instead, Alpha has an overriding duty to zealously advocate his own client's best interests, and since they are best served by seeking a default judgment, Alpha acted properly in doing so.

In addition, option B can't be the best response because the Model Rules don't recognize the "courtesy" rule; by the time the Model Rules were drafted, the ABA considered this rule "too vague to be a rule of conduct enforceable as law." Thus, even if the rule was correctly applied to these facts, since applying the two codes would result in different answers, B cannot be the best response.

D is not the best response, because the fact that Insco will pay any judgment does not determine the validity of Alpha's seeking a default judgment.

What option D implies is that since Insco hired Beta to defend Defendant, a default judgment is fair because Insco will be liable for the failure of the lawyer it chose to file an answer to Plaintiff's complaint. Even though this is true, it really doesn't matter. Liability insurance policies typically provide that the insurance company will provide a lawyer to defend any suits (on behalf of the company and the policyholder) filed against the policyholder. This doesn't change the obligations of the opposing attorney, in this case, Alpha. Alpha still has a duty to pursue Plaintiff's goals within the bounds of law and propriety. When the opposing party fails to file an answer to a complaint, barring circumstances that wo 'd create an overriding duty *not* to seek a default judgment, doing so would be necessary as part of the lawyer's duty to zealously pursue his client's interests. Since D doesn't recognize this, it's not the best response.

Answer 8

C is the best response, because it identifies that the director's misinformation exonerates Attorney from discipline.

The issue here is the extent to which a lawyer is disciplinable for erroneous statements about the integrity of a judge or judicial candidate. The rules differ somewhat between the two codes. Under the Model Rules, MR 8.2(a), a lawyer may not make such a statement if the lawyer recklessly disregards the truth or falsity of the statement, or knows it's false (note that this is the "malice" standard from defamation). Under the MC, such statements are only prohibited if they are made with *actual knowledge* of falsity. Thus, under both codes taken together, Attorney would only be subject to discipline if she *knew* the statement about Judge was false. Option C tells you that Attorney won't be subject to discipline *if* she reasonably relied on the director's information. In order for C to be true, with its "if" modifier, then the reasoning need only be *plausible* under the facts (that is, there can't be anything in the facts to suggest it *couldn't* be true); the reasoning must address a central issue; and the result and the reasoning must agree. Under these facts, the reasoning is plausible; you're told in the facts that Attorney had confidence in the director and believed him as to Judge's reprimand, which comports with C's reasoning that Attorney "reasonably relied" on the information. This resolves a central issue, because if Attorney reasonably believed the director, she didn't know the statement about Judge was false, and thus wouldn't be subject to discipline. As this also shows, the result and the reasoning disagree, since Attorney's reasonable belief would exonerate her. Since option C recognizes this, it's the best response.

A is not the best response, because the contents of the official records are irrelevant.

Attorney's culpability for her misstatement, under both codes taken together, depends on whether or not she knew the statement was false. The rules differ somewhat between the two codes. Under the Model Rules, MR 8.2(a), a lawyer may not make a statement about the qualifications or integrity of a judge, adjudicatory officer, or judicial or legal candidate if the lawyer recklessly disregards the truth or falsity of the statement, or knows it's false (note that this is the "malice" standard from defamation). Under the MC, such statements are only prohibited if they are made with *actual knowledge* of falsity. Thus, under both codes taken together, Attorney would only be subject to discipline if she *knew* the statement about Judge was false. As this rule shows, it doesn't really matter if the official records of the commission would show that the statement was false, unless it was proven somehow that Attorney had seen the official records. Since there's no indication under these facts that that's the case, A is not the best response.

B is not the best response, because the actual falsity of Attorney's statement doesn't determine if she's culpable, but her level of awareness as to the falsity does.

Option B suggests that the only fact that determines Attorney's culpability is that Judge wasn't reprimanded. In fact, this doesn't correctly reflect the applicable rule. Instead, Attorney's culpability for her misstatement, under both codes taken together, depends on whether or not she knew the statement was false. The rules differ somewhat between the two codes. Under the Model Rules, MR 8.2(a), a lawyer may not make a statement about the qualifications or integrity of a judge, adjudicatory officer, or judicial or legal candidate if the lawyer recklessly disregards the truth or falsity of the statement, or knows it's false (note that this is the "malice" standard from defamation). Under the MC, such statements are only prohibited if they are made with *actual knowledge* of falsity. Thus, under both codes taken together, Attorney would only be subject to discipline if she *knew* the statement about Judge was false. Since option B doesn't recognize that the mere falsity of the statement alone isn't enough, it's not the best response.

D is not the best response, because the fact that Judge was a candidate in a contested election doesn't insulate Attorney from culpability.

Option D suggests that because Judge is running for office, it's "open season" on him, and Attorney can say anything about him without regard for its truth or falsity. If D were true, then Attorney could say, "Don't vote for Judge, because he has six wives and killed and ate one of his children," knowing that this is an outrageous lie, without fear of discipline. You know instinctively that this can't be the case. As this indicates, the central problem with option D is that the result doesn't follow from the reasoning; the fact that Judge is involved in a contested election *does not* mean that Attorney won't be culpable for wrongly stating that he'd been reprimanded.

In fact, Attorney's culpability for her misstatement, under both codes taken together, depends on whether she knew the statement was false. The rules differ somewhat between the two codes. Under the Model Rules, MR 8.2(a), a lawyer may not make a statement about the qualifications or integrity of a judge, adjudicatory officer, or judicial or legal candidate if the lawyer recklessly disregards the truth or falsity of the statement, or knows it's false (note that this is the "malice" standard from defamation). Under the MC, such statements are only prohibited if they are made with *actual knowledge* of falsity. Thus, under both codes taken together, Attorney would only be subject to discipline if she *knew* the statement about Judge was false. Since it's possible for Attorney to be subject to discipline *even though* Judge is a candidate in a contested election, D cannot be the best response.

Answer 9

B is the best response, because it correctly identifies that Attorney will be subject to discipline for implying that judges grant him special favors due to his campaign donations.

Under both codes, lawyers must not imply that they have the power to influence a public entity on improper or irrelevant grounds. DR 9–101(C), MR 8.4(e). This rule applies whether or not the lawyer has such influence, and even if he does, whether or not he actually uses it. The rationale is that such behavior undermines public confidence in the legal system. Here, Attorney is implying that judges will act favorably toward his clients, even if they don't deserve it, on the basis of his campaign donations. This is exactly the kind of conduct that the rule is aimed at. Since option B recognizes this, it's the best response.

A is not the best response, because although it arrives at the right result, it does so for the wrong reason: even if Attorney's contributions were made without regard to merit, this would not subject him to discipline; furthermore, option A ignores the true source of discipline for Attorney.

Only the Model Code, not the Model Rules, has a provision dealing with judicial elections: EC 8–6. It provides that lawyers should help make sure that only qualified people are elected to judgeships, and, beyond that, to protest earnestly against the appointment or election of those unsuited to such positions. Thus, if Attorney did, in fact, make contributions to judicial campaigns regardless of the fitness of the candidate, he'd be violating EC 8–6; however, since EC 8–6 is only aspirational, not mandatory, violating it only means that Attorney's conduct is *improper;* it wouldn't subject him to discipline. Furthermore, since there is no comparable provision under the Model Rules, this answer couldn't be correct, since the answers under the two codes would differ, making it impossible for A to be the best response.

Instead, Attorney will be subject to discipline for implying that judges will ignore the merits of Attorney's clients' positions, and instead be prejudiced toward them because of Attorney's campaign contributions. This is disciplinable, since lawyers must not imply that they have the power to influence a public entity (including a judge) on improper or irrelevant grounds. DR 9–101(C), MR 8.4(e). Since A doesn't recognize this, and states a basis on which Attorney would not be subject to discipline, it's not the best response.

C is not the best response, because the truth or falsity of Attorney's statements does not determine whether Attorney's comment is disciplinable.

Note that option C uses the qualifier "if"; this means that, in order for C to be the best response, the reasoning must be plausible under the facts (that is, there must not be anything in the facts to suggest it *couldn't* be true); the reasoning must address a central issue; and the result and the reasoning must agree. As to the first element, the reasoning is plausible under the facts, since there's nothing to indicate that, in fact, Attorney *didn't* make his stated donations to judicial campaigns, and it may well be that judges are swayed in favor of Attorney because of this (although if they are, they'll be subject to discipline under the Code of Judicial Conduct). Where option C falls apart is with the second element: it doesn't address a central issue in the question. The central issue here is whether Attorney's suggesting that he's bought off all the local judges is disciplinable. It's not the truth of the matter that's at issue here, but rather the *creation of the impression that it's true in the mind of the prospective client.* The rule is that, in order to preserve public confidence in the integrity of the judiciary, lawyers must not imply that they have the power to influence a public entity on improper or irrelevant grounds. DR 9–lOl(C), MR 8.4(e). Thus, it doesn't matter whether or not Attorney actually made the donations he claims to have made, and, even if he did, whether he has any intention of using any influence he has as a result to influence judges in favor of his clients; it's the mere act of creating the implication of impropriety under circumstances like these that forms the disciplinable offense. What all this means is that the truth of Attorney's statement wouldn't insulate him from discipline; if he satisfies the "implication of power" rule, he's subject to discipline. Since C doesn't recognize this, it's not the best response.

D is not the best response, because whether or not the prospective client retains Attorney does not determine whether Attorney's conduct is disciplinable.

Option D suggests that because the potential client didn't rely on Attorney's statement and retain Attorney, Attorney isn't subject to discipline. This in turn implies a "causation" element which doesn't, in fact, exist for conduct like this. Instead, the only thing that matters is whether or not Attorney implied that he had the power to influence a public entity (here, local judges) on improper or irrelevant grounds. This is all that's required for Attorney's conduct to be disciplinable, under DR 9–101(C) and MR 8.4(e); it's irrelevant whether the client subsequently hires him or not.

Note that option D indicates the danger in concentrating on end results in determining whether a lawyer's conduct is ethical, unless the issue is malpractice (in which case there must be prejudice to the client in order for the attorney to be liable). Instead, once the lawyer has undertaken the conduct in question, the ethical violation—if there is one—is complete. Since D doesn't recognize this, it's not the best response.

Answer 10

B is the best response, because it offers additional facts which would make it proper for Attorney to advise Judge.

The key here is establishing that Attorney's advising Judge doesn't constitute a violation of the Code of Judicial Conduct. Under MR 8.4(f), a lawyer can't knowingly aid a judge in violating the law or the CJC (no parallel provision in MC). Thus, if a course of conduct would subject a judge to discipline under the CJC, a lawyer's helping the judge to violate the CJC would subject the lawyer to discipline, too. The rule applicable to these facts involves *ex parte* communications about a pending or impending proceeding. As a general rule, a judge cannot have *ex parte* communications regarding a pending or impending proceeding not authorized by law, except that he can seek the advice of disinterested legal experts, under Canon 3(A)(4), as long as the judge notifies all the parties who was consulted and the substance of the advice given, and all parties are given a reasonable opportunity to respond to the advice. What this boils down to is that unless Judge asks for Attorney's advice, offering it would be unethical.

Note that option B uses the modifier "if." Thus, in order to be the best response, the reasoning must be plausible on the facts, it must resolve a central issue, and the result and the reasoning must agree. Here, B is plausible on the facts, because there's nothing to suggest that Judge didn't request Attorney's advice. It also resolves a central issue. Under these facts, you're not told whether or not Judge asked for Attorney's advice. This resolves a central issue, because given a request from the Judge, Attorney's conduct comports with CJC Canon 3(A)(4). Finally, the result and the reasoning agree, since the Judge's request does in fact make Attorney's conduct proper. Since option B recognizes this, it's the best response.

A is not the best response, because it doesn't address the issue of the propriety of *Attorney's* advising judge.

If option A was a correct statement of legal ethics, then any time a judge was concerned with the presentation of law by lawyers in the case, any lawyer could deluge him with advice. In fact, this isn't true, because such contact would help the judge violate the Code of Judicial Conduct, and knowingly aiding a judge in such a violation *itself* violates MR 8.4(f).

Under Canon 3(A)(4) of the CJC (concerning *ex parte* communications with disinterested legal experts), a judge cannot have *ex parte* communications regarding a pending or impending proceeding not authorized by law, except that he can seek the advice of disinterested legal experts, under Canon 3(A)(4), as long as the judge notifies all the parties who was consulted and the substance of the advice given, and all parties are given a reasonable opportunity to respond to the advice. What this boils down to is that unless Judge asks for Attorney's advice, offering it would be unethical. Although his dissatisfaction with the way the case was presented may be the *genesis* of Judge's request, without the request itself and the other elements of *ex parte* contact being satisfied, Attorney's conduct would be improper. In addition, the rule as stated in option A can't be a *real* rule, because it conditions the propriety of advice on a judge's being dissatisfied with the law as presented in court, and doesn't suggest how an attorney would know that the judge in a case was dissatisfied with the lawyers' presentations. Since option A doesn't recognize this, it's not the best response.

C is not the best response, because if Judge requests Attorney's advice, then his participation is proper.

Option C suggests that unless a lawyer is hired by a party, he cannot have any connection with a proceeding. This isn't necessarily true. The kind of participation outlined in these facts—offering disinterested legal advice—*can* be proper, as long as certain guidelines are met.

The central issue here is whether or not Attorney's offering advice constitutes an ethical violation. Under MR 8.4(f), a lawyer may not knowingly aid a judge in violating the CJC. Under CJC Canon 3(A)(4), a judge cannot have *ex parte* communications regarding a pending or impending proceeding not authorized by law, except that he can seek the advice of disinterested legal experts as long as he notifies all the parties who was consulted and the substance of the advice given, and all parties are given a reasonable opportunity to respond to the advice. What this boils down to is, given a request from Judge, Attorney's participation in the case is proper.

What may have misled you about option C is that *in some* circumstances it would be correct. Naturally, a lawyer cannot advise someone else's client; nor can he communicate with jurors about the merits of a case, even if he has nothing at all to do with the case. Those kinds of participation are improper; however, since the advice here *could* be proper under these facts (you're not given enough facts to know for sure—namely, you're not told if Judge requested Attorney's advice), and option C doesn't recognize this, it's not the best response.

D is not the best response, because the propriety of Attorney's advice doesn't depend on his notifying the parties of his intent.

The central issue here is whether or not Attorney's offering advice constitutes an ethical violation. Under MR 8.4(f), a lawyer may not knowingly aid a judge in violating the CJC. Under CJC Canon 3(A)(4), a judge cannot have *ex parte* communications regarding a pending or impending proceeding not authorized by law, except that he can seek the advice of disinterested legal experts as long as he notifies all the parties who was consulted and the substance of the advice given, and all parties are given a reasonable opportunity to respond to the advice. Note that this doesn't require that *Attorney* notify the parties of his intent to advise Judge, but rather Judge must notify them. Also, contrary to what option D states, *Judge* needn't notify the parties *before* he seeks the advice, as long as he gives them sufficient notice to respond to the advice. Thus, if you chose this response, you were thinking of Judge's duties on seeking disinterested legal advice, and overlooked the fact that prior notice isn't necessary.

Note that option D uses the modifier "unless." Thus, in order for it to be correct, the reasoning would have to be the only way the result could not occur. Under these facts, this would mean that the only way Attorney's conduct could be proper is if he gave prior notice to the parties of his intent to advise Judge. This isn't true; instead, the propriety of the conduct turns on whether or not Judge *asked* for advice. Otherwise, Attorney would be helping Judge conduct improper *ex parte* communications, and this would constitute an ethical breach. Since option D conditions the propriety of Attorney's conduct on erroneous requirements, it's not the best response.

Answer 11

D is the best response, because it identifies additional facts necessary to make Judge's contact with Attorney proper.

As a general rule, a judge cannot have *ex parte* communications regarding a pending or impending proceeding not authorized by law, except he can seek the advice of disinterested legal experts. Canon 3(A)(4). The exception is what's at work here. In order for the "disinterested legal expert" exception to insulate Judge from discipline for contacting Attorney, she would have to fulfill two additional requirements:

1. She'd have to notify all the parties who was consulted, and the substance of the advice given, and

2. She'd have to give all the parties a reasonable opportunity to respond to the advice.

Note, as a preliminary matter, that option D uses the modifier "unless." This means that in order for D to be the best response, the reasoning must be the only way the result *cannot* occur. If you apply the rules from Canon 3(A)(4) to the facts, you can see that this is true. If Judge doesn't inform the parties of Attorney's identity and the substance of his advice, and ask for their responses, she wouldn't be satisfying the requirements of 3(A)(4), her conduct wouldn't fit the "disinterested legal expert" exception, and she'd be subject to discipline as a result.

While they don't play a big role in this question, there are a couple things you should keep in mind about the disinterested legal expert exception. First, the judge doesn't have to seek the parties *consent* before consulting a legal expert; he need only *notify* them of the contact. Second, notice to the parties needn't come *before* the judge consults the expert; he may tell the parties afterward. Finally, the CJC recommends that a judge request *amicus curiae* briefs when he seeks disinterested legal advice, but it doesn't require it (and if the procedures above are followed, legal experts need not be asked to file *amicus curiae* briefs).

In any case, since option D correctly applies the rule on judge's contact with disinterested legal experts to these facts, it's the best response.

A is not the best response, because it doesn't provide a sufficient basis on which to determine whether or not Judge's conduct is proper.

Note that "because" is the modifier in option A. This means that, in order for it to be the best response, the following three elements must be satisfied: The reasoning must address and resolve a central issue; the facts in the question must completely satisfy the reasoning; and the result must be consistent with the reasoning. The problem with option A is in the first element—it doesn't address and resolve a central issue. Even though Attorney has no interest in the case, Judge's contact with him will still subject him to discipline *unless* he fits the "disinterested expert" exception to the bar on judge's communications concerning pending or impending proceedings. The rule is that a judge cannot have *ex parte* communications regarding a pending or impending proceeding not authorized by law, except that he *can* seek the advice of disinterested legal experts. Canon 3(A)(4). In order for the "disinterested legal expert" exception to insulate a judge from discipline for contacting an attorney as a disinterested expert, he would have to fulfill two additional requirements:

1. He'd have to notify all the parties who was consulted, and the substance of the advice given, and

2. He'd have to give all the parties a reasonable opportunity to respond to the advice.

As this shows, unless Judge's contact with Attorney satisfies these elements, she'll be subject to discipline, *even though* Attorney is, as option A correctly indicates, disinterested in the case. Since option A doesn't state a strong enough ground on which to insulate Judge from discipline, it's not the best response.

B is not the best response, because although it is correct, it is not as specific as another correct response, D, and it doesn't recognize the additional elements necessary to make Judge's contact with Attorney proper. Judges have a general duty of promoting justice, and this goal is mentioned in virtually every Canon in the Code of Judicial Conduct. However, this alone is not enough to justify a judge's behavior under some circumstances.

Note that option B uses the modifier "if." This means that, in order for B to be the best response, the reasoning must be plausible under the facts (that is, there can't be anything in the facts to suggest it couldn't be true); the reasoning must address a central issue; and the result and the reasoning must agree. Here, the reasoning is plausible under the facts; Judge could easily believe that seeking Attorney's advice serves the interests of justice. The problem is with the second element—the reasoning doesn't address a central issue. *Even if* contacting Attorney serves justice, it is impermissible *unless* the elements of CJC 3(A)(4), concerning disinterested legal experts, are satisfied. In order for the "disinterested legal expert" exception to insulate a judge from discipline for contacting an attorney as a disinterested expert, he would have to fulfill two additional requirements:

1. He'd have to notify all the parties who was consulted, and the substance of the advice given, and

2. He'd have to give all the parties a reasonable opportunity to respond to the advice.

Thus, even if contacting Attorney serves justice, if these additional elements aren't met, Judge will be subject to discipline. Since B doesn't recognize this, it's not the best response.

C is not the best response, because written consent of the parties is not necessary before a judge contacts a disinterested legal expert.

If you picked option C, you were on the right track in the sense that, in order for a judge to properly contact a disinterested legal expert about pending proceedings, he must *notify* the parties. However, C falls down in erroneously stating that this notice must take place *before* the judge seeks the outside advice, and that it must be *in writing*. Instead, under CJC 3(A)(4) these two elements must be met:

1. The judge would have to notify all the parties as to who was consulted, and the substance of the advice given, and

2. He'd have to give all the parties a reasonable opportunity to respond to the advice.

Although option C recognizes that notice to the parties is necessary, since it misstates the elements of proper advice from a disinterested legal expert, it's not the best response.

Answer 12

B is the best response, not so much because it addresses a central issue in the problem, but rather because it's the only one that makes a valid argument, addressing the "call" of the question, which can be supported by these facts.

This is an unusual question in that it plays a game of "hide the ball." It *seems* as though there ought to be an issue concerning conflict of interest, since you could justifiably say that Attorney's professional judgment in the case will be swayed by the fact that his prospective employers are present. However, the specific *question* doesn't address this conflict of interest, but rather asks only about Attorney's quoted statement. Thus, all you can look at is whether that statement, *standing alone,* is proper. The rule is that a lawyer cannot allude to any matter that he doesn't reasonably believe will be supported by admissible evidence. DR 7–106(C)(1); MR 3.4(e). Note that option B uses the modifier "if"; this means that, in order for B to be correct, the reasoning need only be *plausible* under the facts (that is, there can't be anything in the facts to suggest it *couldn't* be true); the reasoning must address a central issue; and the result and the reasoning must agree. Here, the reasoning is plausible under the facts, because there's nothing in the facts that indicates that Giant may not have failed to install safety devices in callous disregard for the safety of its employees. The second element, the "central issue" requirement, is troublesome, but as noted earlier, it addresses a more central issue than any of the other possible responses. Finally, the result and the reasoning agree, since if Attorney believes the statement is supportable by evidence, it's proper for him to say it. Since B recognizes this, it's the best response.

A is not the best response, because although it focuses on the correct issue, it doesn't identify the reason that Attorney's statement is proper.

Option A uses "because" as a modifier. To help see why A can't be the correct response, let's combine the reasoning of option A with the specific call of the question, and key facts from the question, into a statement: *Because opening statements are not evidence in a proceeding, it's proper for Attorney to call Giant callous, willful, and ignorant of the safety of its employees, in his opening statement.* Can you see why A can't be the best response? What it's saying is that, as long as a lawyer isn't offering evidence in a proceeding, he's free to level whatever charges he wants against Giant. For instance, you could change Attorney's statement to, "Giant failed to install safety devices because it's run by a bunch of greedy, scum–sucking pigs with foul and loathsome diseases who cheat on their spouses." You can see that the fact that the statement is in an opening statement doesn't make it proper!

Instead, the nature of Attorney's statement suggests that the potential problem with it is that the accusation may not be supportable with evidence. In fact, the rule that applies to lawyer statements is that a lawyer may not refer to inadmissible evidence, whether it's because he does not in good faith believe it's relevant, or because he doesn't reasonably believe it will be supported by admissible evidence. DR 7-106(C)(1), (2), MR 3.4(e). Here, what would make Attorney's statement proper, then, is his reasonable belief that it will be supported by admissible evidence. Since A overlooks this, and does not identify a reason why Attorney's statement might be proper, it's not the best response.

C is not the best response, because the fact that Attorney's prospective employers were present does not make the statement improper.

C is a tricky distractor, because it focuses on what your gut tells you *ought* to be the central issue here; namely, the fact that Attorney's professional judgment is likely to be swayed by the fact that he knows his future employers are watching him perform, and thus his personal interests may adversely impact his professional duties. One significant fact lessens the impact of this argument, namely that the Union's interests are in line with the government's; both are interested in the welfare of the employees.

Another factor which makes option C deceptively attractive is the conflict of interest involved in Attorney's having applied for a job with the Union. Under the MR, Rule 1.ll(c)(2)(MC has no provision), a government lawyer may not negotiate for private employment with any private party while the lawyer is participating personally and substantially in a matter involving that party. The rule is designed to prevent a government lawyer from having divided loyalties and prevent the appearance of impropriety. Here, the Union is not a party in the matter, and only one of the codes, the MR, prevents such conduct anyway, so *even though* there is the appearance of impropriety, Attorney's conduct would not be forbidden by the Rule. Furthermore, this wouldn't address the propriety of Attorney's making the statement at the hearing, but rather the propriety of his applying for a job with the Union in the first place, which isn't addressed in the question.

Instead, Attorney's statement will be considered proper if he believes that evidence will support the statement, DR 7–106(C)(1), MR 3.4(e); otherwise, it will be prohibited as a frivolous argument. Since option C overlooks this, and focuses on an issue that is not, in fact, essential to solving the problem, it's not the best response.

D is not the best response, because it mischaracterizes the facts—they do not, in fact, exceed the bounds of justifiable advocacy.

A lawyer has a duty to zealously pursue the goals of his client. However, this duty is bounded by law and propriety. What option D suggests is that Attorney's statement violates these boundaries. In theory, there are several ways Attorney could do this; for instance, if his statement would be considered degrading, undignified or discourteous, it would violate MR 3.5(c) and DR 7–106(C)(6); if Attorney didn't believe that evidence would support the statement, it would violate DR 7–106(C)(1) and MR 3.4(e); if it could be considered harassing or embarrassing, it would violate DR 7–106(C)(2), DR 7–102(A)(1), and MR 4.4.

In fact Attorney's statement doesn't violate any of these rules, and instead is proper, as long as he believes there will be evidence to support the statement. While Attorney's statement uses strong words, it is certainly no stronger than any you might find in the definition of various crimes and torts, and is normal, persuasive language. Since option D doesn't recognize this, it's not the best response.

Answer 13

Option D is the best response, because it correctly recognizes that all three statements would be permissible forms of advertising, under both codes.

AS TO ALTERNATIVE I:
Alternative I is permissible as valid qualification information.

The two codes differ greatly on their approach to permissible advertising. Under the MR, Rule 7.1, the only advertising that is *prohibited,* is that which is false and misleading. Under the MC, on the other hand, attorneys are told expressly what they may advertise; anything not included is prohibited. Generally speaking, under the MC, a lawyer may advertise virtually everything about fees (although there are format restrictions), and the information about the lawyer himself is limited to "resume" information (e.g., degrees, awards, bar memberships and posts held, professional licenses, and the like). Because the MC is stricter than the MR, if information would be permissible under the MC, it would also be permissible under the MR. As to the information in alternative I, DR 2–101(B) expressly permits information about schools, graduation dates, degrees, and scholastic distinctions. Since that's all that's included in alternative I, it's permissible.

AS TO ALTERNATIVE II:

Alternative II is permissible as valid service information.

The two codes differ greatly on their approach to permissible advertising. Under the MR, Rule 7.1, the only advertising that is *prohibited* is that which is false and misleading. Under the MC, on the other hand, attorneys are told expressly what they may advertise; anything not included is prohibited. In fact, almost everything about services offered is permissible under the MC, including name, address, phone number of firm, office hours and answering service hours, prepaid or group legal services in which the lawyer participates, credit cards accepted, limitations on areas of practice, and foreign languages spoken. DR 2–101(B). Because the MC is stricter than the MR, if information would be permissible under the MC, it would also be permissible under the MR. As to the information in alternative II, DR 2–101(B) expressly permits information about office and answering service hours. As a result, alternative II is permissible.

AS TO ALTERNATIVE III:

Alternative III is permissible as valid service information.

The two codes differ greatly on their approach to permissible advertising. Under the MR, Rule 7.1, the only advertising that is *prohibited* is that which is false and misleading. Under the MC, on the other hand, attorneys are told expressly what they may advertise; anything not included is prohibited. In fact, almost everything about services offered is permissible under the MC, including name, address, phone number of firm, office hours and answering service hours, prepaid or group legal services in which the lawyer participates, credit cards accepted, limitations on areas of practice, and foreign languages spoken. DR 2–101(B). Because the MC is stricter than the MR, if information would be permissible under the MC, it would also be permissible under the MR. As to the information in alternative II,

DR 2–101(B) expressly permits information about languages spoken. As a result, alternative II is permissible.

Answer 14

B is the best response, because it recognizes that the main problem with Attorney's agreement is that he's aiding Trustco in the unauthorized practice of law. In fact, under these facts, *aiding* is a pretty tame word; Attorney is violating almost every aspect of the prohibition against unauthorized practice.

Under DR 3–101(A) and MR 5.5(b), a lawyer isn't allowed to aid a non–lawyer in activities constituting the practice of law. As a general rule, offering advice, drafting documents and appearing in court are considered the "practice of law." Here, you're told that non–lawyer officers of Trustco would advise customers as to the details of trusts and wills. By taking part in this arrangement, then, Attorney is encouraging Trustco in the unauthorized practice of law.

Attorney is also violating the prohibition against splitting fees with non–lawyers. As a general rule, this is prohibited (although there are exceptions to this, including, for instance, a law firm's paying a deceased partner's estate a reasonable amount for a reasonable period of time after his death). DR 3–102(A) and MR 5.4(a). By accepting free rent in return for drafting wills and trusts, Attorney is, in effect, splitting fees with Trustco, and is subject to discipline for this.

Finally, Attorney's delegation of duties to Trustco would also constitute unauthorized practice. Delegation of lawyering duties to non–lawyers is only permissible if the supervising lawyer maintains a direct relationship with the client, supervises the delegated work, and has complete professional responsibility for the work product. EC 3–6. Here, Attorney has no contact with the clients whatsoever; thus, even if you could characterize Attorney as delegating work to non–lawyers, his conduct would not comport with the rules on unauthorized practice.

As this shows, no matter how you slice it, Attorney is in the soup for his agreement with Trustco. Since B recognizes this, it's the best response.

A is not the best response, because the prohibition against agreements restricting a lawyer's right to practice wouldn't apply to these facts.

Option A is correct to the extent that it recognizes that there is a rule under which a lawyer may not restrict his right to practice. Specifically, under MR5.6 and DR 2–108, there are two aspects to this prohibition: First, a lawyer can't make a partnership or employment agreement that restricts his right to practice *after the relationship terminates* (unless the agreement concerns retirement benefits); and second, a lawyer can't be part of an agreement in which a restriction on the lawyer's right to practice is part of a settlement between private parties.

Option A implies that the first part of this rule should apply to the facts here. In fact, it doesn't, because restrictions on practice *while an employment relationship continues* are valid; after all, a law firm can validly prohibit its members from maintaining their own practice while they work for the firm. Thus, the "restriction on practice" rule wouldn't subject Attorney to discipline under these facts.

Instead, what option A ignores is the central issue here, which is that Attorney is assisting Trustco in the unauthorized practice of law, which violates DR 3–101(A) and MR 5.5(b). Those rules provide that a lawyer isn't allowed to aid a non–lawyer in activities constituting the practice of law. As a general rule, offering advice and appearing in court are considered the "practice of law." Here, you're told that non–lawyer officers of Trustco would advise customers as to the details of trusts and wills. By taking part in this arrangement, then, Attorney is encouraging Trustco in the unauthorized practice of law. Since option A overlooks this, and misapplies the "restriction on practice" rule to these facts, it's not the best response.

C is not the best response, because it misstates the ethical rules: a lawyer is not subject to discipline for failing to charge a client. If anything, the ethical rules are designed to prevent lawyers from *overcharging* their clients; they are permitted, and in the case of indigents requiring legal services, they are encouraged to offer their services free of charge.

Note that option C uses the modifier "because." In order for C to be correct, if the call of the question and the reasoning in option C are combined, option C's reasoning should explain the call of the question. In combining the two, you come up with this statement: "Attorney is not subject to discipline for entering into the agreement with Trustco, because he isn't charging the customer for his services." When you look at it in this way, you can see that what C is saying is that the fact that Attorney isn't charging for his services exonerates him from discipline he would otherwise face. Your knowledge of the ethical rules in general tells you that simply not charging for services doesn't insulate a lawyer from discipline. For instance, if a lawyer takes on a client and then completely botches the case through incompetence, he won't avoid discipline by failing to charge for his services.

Instead, what option C ignores is the central issue here, which is that Attorney is assisting Trustco in the unauthorized practice of law, which violates DR 3101(A) and MR 5.5(b). Those rules provide that a lawyer isn't allowed to aid a non–lawyer in activities constituting the practice of law. As a general rule, offering advice and appearing in court are considered the "practice of law." Here, you're told that non-lawyer officers of Trustco would advise customers as to the details of trusts and wills. By taking part in this arrangement, then, Attorney is encouraging Trustco in the unauthorized practice of law. Since option C overlooks this, and mistakenly implies that not charging for services insulates Attorney from discipline, it's not the best response.

Option D is not the best response, because it mischaracterizes the facts, and ignores the central reason Attorney will be subject to discipline: he's aiding Trustco in the unauthorized practice of law.

Option D states that Attorney isn't giving advice to Trustco's customers. In fact, if "giving advice" is taken to mean "practicing law" on behalf of the clients, then Attorney *is* advising them. The practice of law, as a general matter, includes advising clients, drafting documents, and appearing in court. If you overlooked this, you were probably misled by the facts in the problem which state that Attorney would never meet with the customer, nor charge the customer for his services in preparing documents on the customer's behalf.

As to the "central issue" problem with option D, it overlooks the central question posed, which is whether or not entering into the arrangement with Trustco subjects Attorney to discipline. This doesn't turn on whether or not Attorney actually advises Trustco's customers at all, but rather, whether or not the agreement means that Attorney is assisting Trustco in the unauthorized practice of law, which violates DR 3-101(A) and MR 5.5(b). Those rules provide that a lawyer isn't allowed to aid a non–lawyer in activities constituting the practice of law. As a general rule, offering advice and appearing in court are considered the "practice of law." Here, you're told that non-lawyer officers of Trustco would advise customers as to the details of trusts and wills. By taking part in this arrangement, then, Attorney is encouraging Trustco in the unauthorized practice of law. Since option D overlooks this, and mischaracterizes the facts, it's not the best response.

Answer 15

C is the best response, because it recognizes that since Attorney previously represented both Husband and Wife in the dispute, he can't thereafter represent either one if there is a subsequent problem with the settlement.

As option C correctly implies, the central problem here is a conflict of interest. While it's appropriate for a lawyer to mediate a dispute between current or former clients, the following conditions must be met:

1. The lawyer must consult with each client concerning the implications of common representation (e.g., advantages, risks, and effect on attorney–client privilege between commonly represented clients [i.e., there is no privilege]);

2. The lawyer must obtain each client's consent;

3. The lawyer must reasonably believe the clients can resolve their dispute in their best interests (if they are antagonistic toward each other or seem headed for contentious litigation, mediation isn't appropriate);

4. The lawyer must reasonably believe there will be no improper effect on his responsibilities to each client (e.g. he must believe his impartiality will not be threatened); and

5. The lawyer must inform both clients that he cannot represent either one in the dispute (that is, the lawyer can't take sides).

(MR 2.2; EC 5–20 basically agrees.)

The problem here is with #5 — having represented both Husband and Wife in mediating their dispute, Attorney can't subsequently take sides and represent one against the other. This is exactly what's represented in the reasoning to Option C.

Note that while option C focuses on the mediation aspect of these facts, there's another equally good reason why Attorney couldn't represent Wife against Husband: conflict of interest. Under these facts, Attorney is apparently still representing Husband; as part of his duty of loyalty to Husband, he couldn't act as an advocate in a case *against* Husband. Nonetheless, since C offers a sound argument for why Attorney couldn't properly represent Wife against Husband, it's the best response.

A is not the best response, because it refers to attorney/client privilege in multiple representation situations, *not* the propriety of Attorney's representing Wife, and it arrives at the wrong result.

When a lawyer has current or former clients who disagree, he may mediate the dispute between them, if the following conditions are met:

1. The lawyer must consult with each client concerning the implications of common representation (e.g., advantages, risks, and effect on attorney-client privilege between commonly represented clients [i.e., there is no privilege]);

2. The lawyer must obtain each client's consent;

3. The lawyer must reasonably believe the clients can resolve their dispute in their best interests (if they are antagonistic toward each other or seem headed for contentious litigation, mediation isn't appropriate);

4. The lawyer must reasonably believe there will be no improper effect on his responsibilities to each client (e.g., he must believe his impartiality will not be threatened); and

5. The lawyer must inform both clients that he cannot represent either one in the dispute (that is, the lawyer can't take sides.)

(MR 2.2; EC 5-20 basically agrees.)

What option A implies is #1 above, under which there is no attorney-client privilege as to information the attorney receives in the presence of the other client. However, this has nothing to do with the propriety of Attorney's representing Wife against Husband; this instead is determined by #5, under which a lawyer cannot represent either client against the other in the dispute. That's the case here. Attorney can't represent Wife against Husband because he previously mediated the dispute (in addition, his representing Wife against Husband would violate his duty of loyalty to Husband, constituting an impermissible conflict of interest). Since option A doesn't recognize this, it's not the best response.

B is not the best response, because it misapplies the rules of confidentiality to this fact pattern.

What option B implies is that what's involved here is a matter of disclosing Husband's confidential information, and that Husband's defrauding Wife and Attorney provides a basis for such disclosure. In fact, there are several instances under which an Attorney may disclose his client's confidential information for his own benefit, including:

1. Adverse claim from client (e.g., malpractice, convicted former client challenges result of criminal trial on grounds of ineffective assistance of counsel);

2. Protect reputation against attack from any source, even if no lawsuit has been filed against the lawyer;

3. Fee dispute with client (e.g., to establish claim itself by proving what services were performed, or to collect fee by attaching former client's property).

DR 4-101(C)(4), MR 1.6(b)(2)

In fact, had Husband defrauded Attorney, this would provide a basis for disclosing Husband's confidential information, to the extent necessary to protect Attorney's reputation, under #1, above. The problem with this is that it doesn't address the question, which is whether or not it would be proper for Attorney to represent Wife against Husband. This involves issues of loyalty, not just confidentiality, and Attorney's duty of loyalty, as Husband's attorney, means that he could not represent anyone in a case against Husband. Specifically, under these facts, Attorney can't represent Wife against Husband because he previously mediated a dispute between the two, and, having done so, he can't "take sides" in the dispute. The thing that makes B tricky is the fact that it addresses one of the theories underlying conflict of interest, namely, confidentiality, as well as the theory that's actually at issue here–loyalty. Nonetheless, since option B doesn't recognize that the problem is loyalty and not confidentiality, it's not the best response.

D is not the best response, because Husband's being represented by independent counsel would not make the representation proper.

Note that option D uses the modifier "unless." As a result, in order for D to be correct, the reasoning must be the only way the result cannot occur; if you can think of even one other way the result might come about, D cannot be correct. With this in mind, in order for D to be correct, the following statement would have to be true: "Attorney is free to represent Wife as long as Husband now has his own lawyer." In fact, this isn't true, because even if Husband has his own lawyer, Attorney can't represent Wife against him, due to his duty of loyalty to Husband (unless he gets Husband's informed consent to do so, and there's no indication of this under these facts). What D suggests is that the concern under facts like these is that the "left-out" client isn't represented by counsel. Instead, the problem is that the "left-out" client here, Husband will have his lawyer appearing against him, which violates Attorney's duty of loyalty to Husband. Specifically, under these facts, Attorney can't represent Wife against Husband because he previously mediated a dispute between the two, and, having done so, he can't "take sides" in the dispute. Since D doesn't recognize this, it's not the best response.

Answer 16

A is the best response, because it recognizes that I, II, and III are all *not* objectionable under either code.

AS TO ALTERNATIVE I:

Alternative I is expressly permissible trial publicity, under MR 3.6(c) and DR 7-107.

Both the Model Code and the Model Rules place significant restrictions on permissible trial publicity. The Model Code prohibits statements by lawyers if there's a "reasonable likelihood" of prejudicial impact on the proceedings. The Model Rules are more liberal, prohibiting only extrajudicial statements that the lawyer should realize have a "substantial likelihood" of materially prejudicing the proceeding. Both codes give lists of statements which lawyers involved in investigating or litigating a civil or criminal matter may make. These include:

1. The general nature of a claim or defense;

2. Information in a public record (e.g., indictment, criminal complaint);

3. The existence, general scope, and nature (offense, claim, or defense) of an investigation (as well as the identity of those involved, including officers and agencies, except where local law prohibits this);

4. The scheduling and result of any step in litigation;

5. A request to the public for help in obtaining evidence, or information about it;

6. A warning of danger concerning the behavior of anyone involved if it's reasonable to believe there's a likelihood of substantial harm to anyone or to the public interest; and

7. In a criminal case, the accused's identity, residence, occupation, and family status;

8. In a criminal case, if accused hasn't been apprehended, information necessary to aid in apprehension;

9. Fact, time, and place of arrest.

As #9 indicates, the place of arrest is expressly permissible trial publicity. Since Alternative I reflects this, it's correct.

AS TO ALTERNATIVE II:
Alternative II is expressly permissible trial publicity, under MR 3.6(c) and DR 7-107.

Both the Model Code and the Model Rules place significant restrictions on permissible trial publicity. The Model Code prohibits statements by lawyers if there's a "reasonable likelihood" of prejudicial impact on the proceedings. The Mode Rules are more liberal, prohibiting only extrajudicial statements that the lawyer should realize have a "substantial likelihood" of materially prejudicing the proceeding. Both codes give lists of statements which lawyers involved in investigating or litigating a civil or criminal matter may make. These include:

1. The general nature of a claim or defense;

2. Information in a public record (e.g., indictment, criminal complaint);

3. The existence, general scope, and nature (offense, claim, or defense) of an investigation (as well as the identity of those involved, including officers and agencies, except where local law prohibits this);

4. The scheduling and result of any step in litigation;

5. A request to the public for help in obtaining evidence, or information about it;

6. A warning of danger concerning the behavior of anyone involved if it's reasonable to believe there's a likelihood of substantial harm to anyone or to the public interest; and

7. In a criminal case, the accused's identity, residence, occupation, and family status;

8. In a criminal case, if accused hasn't been apprehended, information necessary to aid in apprehension;

9. Fact, time, and place of arrest.

As #2 indicates, information publicly available, like the contents of an indictment, is permissible trial publicity. Since Alternative II reflects this, it's correct.

AS TO ALTERNATIVE III:

Under #1, a lawyer may publicly state the nature of a defense, which is all Attorney, under these facts, is doing. What makes Alternative III a *little* tricky is that while a not guilty plea may be announced *a guilty plea is considered unduly prejucicial, and thus may not be publicly disclosed by a lawyer associated with the proceedings!* What makes the difference here is the fact that the plea is *not* guilty. Since Alternative III picks up on this distinction and recognizes that this makes the statement permissible, it's correct.

Answer 17.

D is correct, because it reflects the fact that none of the conduct listed would violate either the Model Code or the Model Rules.

AS TO ALTERNATIVE I:

Alternative I is correct because it reflects the fact that Alpha may properly solicit contributions to Beta's campaign, regardless of whether he may appear before Beta when he becomes a judge.

There are several rules, in both codes, which contribute to alternative A's being proper, considering that, for conduct to be proper, it must not be discouraged or prohibited by either code. Most importantly, EC 8-6 encourages lawyers to aid in the selection of qualified judges (the MR have no parallel provision). Under these facts, Alpha believes that Beta is better qualified than Delta, so it would be proper for Alpha to encourage Beta's candidacy. In addition, MR 8.4(f) states that a lawyer can't knowingly aid a judge in violating the law or the Code of Judicial Conduct (no parallel provision in MC). This means that if the CJC prohibited a judicial candidate from establishing a campaign committee to solicit endorsements from lawyers who may appear before the candidate when he becomes a judge, then it would be improper for Alpha to solicit such endorsements, as well. In fact, the CJC expressly permits a judicial candidate to set up a campaign committee and have others solicit endorsements on his behalf. CJC 7(B)(2). Thus, it would be proper for Alpha to solicit such endorsements for Beta.

If you didn't think Alternative I was proper, it's probably because you were thrown by the "...are likely to appear before Beta if Beta becomes a judge" language. There is language like this in the Code of Judicial Conduct, but it doesn't refer to judicial campaign activities, but rather to judges financial activities, under Canon 5. That Canon requires that a judge regulate his financial activities so as to minimize the risk of conflict with his official duties. Specifically, this requires that a judge refrain from financial and business dealings that tend to (a) reflect adversely on his impartiality; (b) interfere with proper performance of his judicial duties;(c) exploit his judicial position; or (d) involve him in frequent transactions with lawyers or persons likely to come before the court on which he serves. As you can see, the language of (d) is what may have made you think Alternative I isn't proper. Beyond that, it's quite foreseeable that a lawyer might endorse Beta to curry favor with him and because he thinks he'll win, regardless of whether the lawyer thinks Beta will make a fine, upstanding judge. This disregard for his ability might have struck you as creating the appearance of impropriety. What all this shows is the nit-picking kind of an exam the MPRE really is, and just how detailed your knowledge of the codes has to be. In any case, soliciting public endorsements is something perfectly proper under both the lawyer codes and the CJC. Since Alternative I recognizes this, it's correct.

AS TO ALTERNATIVE II:

Alternative II is correct because it realizes that Alpha may properly solicit contributions for Beta's campaign from other lawyers.

In order for such conduct to be proper, it would have to be OK under either code. In fact, that's the case, although you take a roundabout circuit to arrive at that result. First, EC 8-6 encourages lawyers to aid in the selection of qualified judges (the MR have no parallel provision). Under these facts, Alpha believes that Beta is better qualified than Delta, so it would be proper for Alpha to encourage Beta's candidacy. In addition, MR 8.4(f) states that a lawyer can't knowingly aid a judge in violating the law or the Code of Judicial Conduct (no parallel provision in MC). This means that if the CJC prohibited a judicial candidate from establishing a campaign committee to solicit endorsements from lawyers who may appear before the candidate when he becomes a judge, then it would be improper for Alpha to solicit such endorsements, as well. In fact, the CJC expressly permits a judicial candidate to set up a campaign committee and have others solicit contributions on his behalf. CJC 7(B)(2). Thus, it would be proper for Alpha to solicit such contributions for Beta. (Note that there aren't restrictions on such solicitation, and as a result, there's no reason why Alpha *couldn't* seek contributions from lawyers likely to appear before Judge Beta, or anyone else, for that matter.)

Again, if you didn't think Alternative I was proper, it's probably because you were thrown by the "...are likely to appear before Beta if Beta becomes a judge" language. There is language like this in the Code of Judicial Conduct, but it doesn't refer to judicial campaign activities, but rather to a judge's financial activities, under Canon 5. That canon requires that a judge regulate his financial activities so as to minimize the risk of conflict with his official duties. Specifically, this requires that a judge refrain from financial and business dealings that tend to (a) reflect adversely on his impartiality; (b) interfere with proper performance of his judicial duties; (c) exploit his judicial position; or *(d) involve him in frequent transactions with lawyers or persons likely to come before the court on which he serves.* As you can see, the language of (d) is what may have made you think Alternative II isn't proper, since money is involved and thus it could be construed as "financial activity." Beyond that, it's quite foreseeable that a lawyer might contribute to Beta's campaign to curry favor with him and because he thinks he'll win, regardless of whether the lawyer thinks Beta will make a fine, upstanding judge, and this might have struck you as creating the appearance of impropriety. What all this shows is the nit-picking kind of an exam the MPRE really is, and just how detailed your knowledge of the codes has to be. In any case, soliciting contributions is something perfectly proper under both the lawyer codes and the CJC. Since Alternative II recognizes this, it's correct.

AS TO ALTERNATIVE III:

Alternative III is correct, since Alpha may properly indicate, in public, that he opposes Delta.

In order for a course of conduct to be proper, there must be nothing in either code discouraging or prohibiting the conduct. Alternative III is interesting in this respect, because the problem doesn't tell you that Delta is unfit or unqualified to be a judge, but simply that Alpha believes Beta is *better* qualified than Delta. The reason this makes Alternative III more interesting is that there simply *isn't* anything in the codes about opposing the candidacy of people who aren't unfit or unqualified for judicial office, which means it *must* be proper!

Even though there's nothing directly on point in either code, let's look at the provisions that are closest to these facts. EC 8-6, which is the only provision in either code addressing directly the issue of lawyers supporting/ opposing candidates for judicial office, says that, as a *positive* duty, lawyers should support for judgeships only those candidates who are qualified; as a *negative* duty, lawyers should vigorously protest the election of those who are unfit or unqualified. Inherent in the concept of supporting those who are qualified is the idea that it's all right for lawyers to publicly oppose their opponents. Of course, in doing so, Alpha couldn't violate the ethical rules, for instance, by spreading malicious lies about Delta. However there isn't anything indicated here other than mere public opposition, and so you'd have to assume that in doing so Alpha wouldn't step on any other ethical rules. Since Alternative III recognizes that public opposition is permissible under both codes, it's correct.

Answer 18

A is the best response, because it recognizes that Attorney's ad doesn't violate either the Model Code or the Model Rules.

The two codes differ dramatically in their approach to attorney advertising. Under the MC, DR 2–101, attorneys are told expressly what they may advertise; anything not included is prohibited. Under the far more liberal MR approach, Rule 7.1, anything relevant that's not "false or misleading" may be advertised. As a result, for advertising to pass muster under both codes, it must appear in the MC, and it must not be false or misleading. First, let's look at the Model Code. There are three aspects of the ad to examine: The fact that a professional actor makes the pitch; the telephone number; and the fee information.

A pitch by a professional actor is not prohibited under the Model Code. Instead, the MC addresses only *what's said;* it doesn't particularly matter who conveys the information. The phone number is expressly permitted by DR 2–101(B)(1). The fee information is a little more troublesome, in the sense that Attorney really isn't advertising a fee, but rather is making a general statement about her fee being less than what might be expected. The statement is more suitably analyzed under the general rule about advertising provided in DR 2–101(A), which provides that a lawyer must not make a public statement containing a false, fraudulent, misleading, deceptive, self-laudatory or unfair statement or claim. When you look at what's actually being said in the statement, you can see that it really *can't* violate the rule, because it's too vague, something like puffery. Thus, the ad is permissible under the Model Code.

The Model Rules, as stated earlier, only prohibit "false and misleading" ads, under Rule 7.1. Because the ad satisfies the Model Code, it *has* to satisfy the Model Rules, since the Rules are more liberal than the Code.

These are the most important elements of the ad. However, note the "administrative" information that you're told in the last paragraph; namely, that Attorney approved the prerecorded ad, is keeping a copy of it, and is keeping a record of when it was made. This is required under the Model Code under DR 2–101(D). The Model Rules only require that a copy of the ad be kept for two years after it was last disseminated, along with a record of when and where it was used. MR 7.2. Here again, Attorney satisfies these requirements.

Since option A recognizes that the ad is permissible under both codes, it's the best response.

B is not the best response, because Attorney's statement about fees is permissible *whether or not* her fees are lower than those generally charged locally.

B is very tricky because of all the elements of Attorney's ad, the fee statement is the most suspect. Both codes prevent ads that are "false and misleading," and although Attorney's statement is too vague to violate either code's rules on advertising, it's not hard to see how it *might* be misleading. However, *even if it were, the reasoning in B wouldn't be correct!* That's because B is unnecessarily restrictive. Note that it uses the modifier "unless"; this means that in order for B to be true, the only way the statement could be proper is if Attorney's fees were lower than those generally charged in the area where she practices. The problem with this is it doesn't really reflect what Attorney said in her ad. She said that her fees might be "lower than you think"; this doesn't necessarily mean she's saying she charges less than other attorneys in the area for the same service, because what "you think" doesn't depend on what those other attorneys charge. For instance, if Attorney charges $100/hour, and "you think" her fees would be $150/hour, then her fees are lower than you think, *regardless* of what local attorneys charge. Since option B doesn't pick up on this, although it's a tempting choice, it's not the best response.

C isn't the best response, because using a professional actor doesn't make the ad improper.

Option C suggests that the only person who may appear in a lawyer's ad is the lawyer himself. In fact, neither code has this restriction. Instead, as long as the ad fits the list of permissible advertising contents under the MC, DR 2–101, and it's not "false and misleading" under the MR, Rule 7.1, it will be permissible. Neither code is concerned with *who says* what in the ad, but rather the *content* of the ad itself. If you chose this response, you may have been thinking of the requirement under the Model Code that information in an ad must be presented in a dignified manner. However, under these facts, you're not told enough to determine whether or not the actor used is dignified; if Attorney used Bozo the Clown, who squirted a flower at the camera as he performed Attorney's ad, you could say he'd be venturing somewhat south of dignified. However, the mere use of a professional actor, without additional facts, wouldn't pose "dignity" problems.

In fact, the content of Attorney's ad doesn't violate either code, and since it also meets the administrative requirements (e.g., maintaining copies of the ad) of DR 2–101(D) and MR 7.2, it's proper. Since option C doesn't recognize this, it's not the best response.

D is not the best response, because whether or not Attorney charges for an initial consultation does not determine if the ad is proper.

In order for an ad to be permissible under the MR, Rule 7.1, it must not be "false or misleading." Under the MC, DR 2–101, it must fit within a long list of permissible advertising information. In fact, under DR 2–101(B)(20), lawyers are permitted to advertise fees for an initial consultation. However, this doesn't mean that they must do so; instead, when a class of information appears in the Model Code under DR 2101(B), it means that information may be advertised. Thus, the absence of any mention of a fee for an initial consultation doesn't make Attorney's ad improper.

Note that the modifier option D uses is "if." This means that, in order for D to be correct, the reasoning would have to be plausible under the facts (that is, there couldn't be anything in the facts to suggest it couldn't be true); the reasoning would have to address a central issue; and the result and the reasoning would have to agree. The problem here is with the second element—the reasoning doesn't address a central issue, because, as stated earlier, whether or not Attorney actually charges a fee for an initial consultation doesn't determine whether the ad is proper. In fact, the content of the ad doesn't violate either code, and since it also meets the administrative requirements (e.g., maintaining copies of the ad) of DR 2–101(D) and MR 7.2, it's proper. Since option D doesn't recognize this, it's not the best response.

Answer 19

D is the best response, because it recognizes that of the three alternatives, only alternative I will subject Prosecutor to discipline.

AS TO ALTERNATIVE I:

Alternative I is not correct, because sending a staff member to consult with Deft would be not only improper but disciplinable, since it was done without Attorney's consent.

As a general rule, a lawyer has the duty not to exercise improper influence over proceedings. One type of conduct which this prohibits is communication with an opposing party, without that party's attorney's consent. DR 7–104(A)(1), MR 4.2. That's really all there is to it; however, there are a couple of "red herrings" in the facts here which might have thrown you. First, you have the fact that Prosecutor himself didn't communicate with Deft, he had a *non–lawyer staffmember* do so. This doesn't change the result, because the rule applies whether the lawyer himself communicates with a represented opposing party, or he has someone else do so; in fact, as a rule of thumb, anything a lawyer is prohibited from doing is also disciplinable if he has someone else, lawyer or not, do it in his place.

Second, and more troublesome, is Prosecutor's sneaking suspicion that Attorney isn't acting in Deft's best interests in turning down the plea bargain, because Prosecutor believes that Attorney is looking for headlines at Deft's expense. The problem is that *this doesn't change the fact that Prosecutor can't communicate with Deft!* Prosecutor's duty remains the same: namely, he cannot communicate with Deft without Attorney's consent.

If you slipped up on this, it may be because this strikes you as totally unfair to Deft. Well, you're right. It is. However, the issue of whether or not Attorney's behavior is ethical is a separate question—in fact, it's the next question on the exam. The fact remains that Prosecutor's duty is not to communicate with Deft without Attorney's consent, and since Prosecutor had a staff member do just this, he's subject to discipline, and since disciplinable conduct is inherently improper, Alternative I, which doesn't recognize this, is not correct.

AS TO ALTERNATIVE II:

Alternative II is correct because it incorporates Prosecutor's duty to seek justice.

The duties of prosecutors differ from those of lawyers most significantly in terms of zealous representation; namely, prosecutors have a duty to seek justice, not convictions. This has a number of interesting ramifications; for instance, the prosecutor must generally disclose to the defense all information tending to negate guilt or mitigate the offense; the prosecutor must take reasonable steps to see that the defendant has a chance to get counsel and knows how this is done; the prosecutor has a duty to act on the basis that the defendant is presumed innocent and reaps the benefit of reasonable doubt; and the duty that applies here, namely that prosecutors may only conduct prosecutions where, objectively speaking, probable cause exists. DR 7–103(A), MR 3.8(a).

In terms of Alternative II, this means that, *whatever* crime Prosecutor seeks to pursue, it's permissible as long as it's supported by probable cause. In these facts, Prosecutor would be willing to plea bargain Deft down to joy–riding, so he clearly believes that there's probable cause to believe Deft committed the crime. As a result, it would be proper for Prosecutor to file a motion to dismiss, and then prosecute Deft on the joyriding charge. Since Alternative II recognizes this, it's correct.

AS TO ALTERNATIVE III:

Alternative III is correct because it recognizes that Prosecutor is not violating his duty to seek justice if he goes ahead and prosecutes Deft on the auto theft charge.

The duties of prosecutors differ from those of lawyers most significantly in terms of zealous representation; namely, prosecutors have a duty to seek justice, not convictions. This has a number of interesting ramifications; for instance, the prosecutor must generally disclose to defense all information tending to negate guilt or mitigate the offense; the prosecutor must take reasonable steps to see that the defendant has a chance to get counsel and knows how this is done; the prosecutor has a duty to act on the basis that the defendant is presumed innocent and reaps the benefit of reasonable doubt; and the duty that applies here, namely that prosecutors may only conduct prosecutions where, objectively speaking, probable cause exists. DR 7–103(A), MR 3.8(a).

The wrinkle in these facts is that Prosecutor would be willing to accept a plea bargain for joy–riding, the lesser offense, and so your gut reaction might be that he's not seeking justice if he attempts to convict Deft of the greater offense, auto theft. The facts are tricky because you're expressly told that Prosecutor believes it's in the interest of justice to let Deft plead guilty to joy–riding, and those words—*interest of justice*—are exactly what Prosecutor has a duty to seek. However, there's another phrase that's equally important, and it's this one: *"Prosecutor reasonably believes that Deft committed the offense."* What this means is that the auto theft charge is supported by probable cause, and that makes it proper for Prosecutor to pursue the charge. Put another way, the "interest of justice" here isn't mutually exclusive with the prosecutor's belief about the crime committed; although letting Deft plea–bargain is in the interest of justice, this doesn't mean that pursuing the auto theft charge *isn't,* as long as it's supported by probable cause. What this indicates more than anything else is the importance of reading carefully. In any case, since Alternative III recognizes that it would be proper for Prosecutor to vigorously pursue the auto theft charge, it's correct.

Answer 20

C is the best response, because it recognizes that Prosecutor must know that Attorney actually put her own interests before Deft's in order for Prosecutor to properly contact the authorities.

The general rule is that a lawyer has a duty to report to the appropriate authorities any unprivileged information he has as to another lawyer's misconduct. What this means is that you have to determine two things from these facts; first, whether Attorney's conduct constitutes an ethical violation, and second, whether Prosecutor knows about it.

Before we look at this in detail, note that option C uses the modifier "unless." What this means is that in order for it to be correct, the reasoning must be the only way the result cannot occur. Under these facts this is made a bit more interesting in that there are *two* elements to the reasoning: Attorney's misconduct and Prosecutor's knowledge. In order for Option C to be the best response, if both of these elements exist, Prosecutor should report Attorney to the disciplinary authorities, and if either or both of them don't, Prosecutor has no such duty. Let's analyze the facts.

Attorney violated the conflict of interest rules under these facts if she let her personal interest in garnering publicity affect her judgment in representing Deft. MR 1.7, DR 5–105(A), (B), EC 5–2. Note that this isn't clear from these facts; all you know is that, objectively speaking, it doesn't seem as though Attorney is acting in Deft's best interests, and you know she has a motive for not doing so—her political ambitions. However, because option C uses the modifier "unless," it's not necessary that Attorney's misconduct be obvious from the facts; it need only be plausible, and because of what you're given, it's perfectly plausible that Attorney did in fact let her own interests overwhelm her duties to Deft.

Having addressed Attorney's ethical violation, let's look at how this affects Prosecutor. If Prosecutor knows about Attorney's misconduct, he has a duty to report it. DR 1–103(A) (the MR 8.3(a) limits the "reportable" acts to those which raise a substantial question as to a lawyer's honesty, trustworthiness, or fitness as a lawyer in other respects; but this isn't all that much of a limitation, since almost every ethics rule violation could be construed to fit these categories). Both of the codes require that a lawyer *know* of the violation before the duty to report it kicks in. Here again, note that the facts don't *tell* you that Prosecutor knows why Attorney didn't recommend the plea bargain to Deft; but because option C uses the modifier "unless," this need only be plausible under the facts, and there's nothing to indicate that Prosecutor *couldn't* know about it.

Taken together, the misconduct and the knowledge tell you that Prosecutor has a duty to report Attorney. If either one of them is missing, no duty exists. Since option C conditions Prosecutor's duty to report on both of these elements, it's the best response.

Option A isn't the best response, because the end result of Attorney's behavior does not determine Prosecutor's duty to report her to the authorities.

As a general rule, a lawyer's duty to report another lawyer's misconduct depends on whether the lawyer has unprivileged knowledge of the other lawyer's ethical violation. DR 1–103(A), MR 8.3(a). The problem with option A is that it doesn't address either Attorney's ethical violation—which is not at all clear from the facts as given—nor whether Prosecutor knows about it. Instead, it does something which you have to be very careful to watch out for: it predicates discipline on the end results of the conduct. It's important to remember that the only time *end results* matter, in legal ethics, is in malpractice, where there must be detriment to the client in order for the attorney to be liable. Other than that, if a lawyer breaks the rules, *it doesn't matter what the results of his violation are!*

Let's look at option A in detail. Since "because" is the modifier, the following statement would have to be true: "Prosecutor should report Attorney to the disciplinary authorities because she refused to plea bargain, and Deft suffered a detriment as a result." Let's put it another way, which would also have to be true: "If Deft suffered detriment from Attorney's refusal to plea bargain, Prosecutor should report Attorney to the authorities." In order for A to be correct, the "If" clause here would have to provide the reason why the second clause, "Prosecutor should report Attorney," should occur. In fact, this isn't the case. As stated earlier, a lawyer has a duty to report others' ethical violations to the disciplinary authorities. The problem with the statement is that the fact that Attorney didn't plea bargain doesn't necessarily mean that she violated the ethics rules. For instance, if Attorney believed, due to her professional experience, that it was in Deft's best interests to go to trial and not accept the plea bargain, then Attorney would have been perfectly correct in refusing to plea bargain. If you look at the facts closely, you can see that you're never told that Attorney let her own interests in publicity adversely affect Deft's representation; you're only told that Prosecutor *suspects* that might be the case. What this shows is what option A overlooks: Attorney's *motivation* for refusing to plea bargain. If Deft's best interests are the motivating facts, then the statement above isn't true. Furthermore, option A overlooks the fact that Prosecutor would have to have *knowledge* of Attorney's motivation in order for the duty to report her to the authorities kicks in. Since option A overlooks all of this, it's not the best response.

B is not the best response, because the *result* of Attorney's conduct doesn't determine whether or not Prosecutor should report her to the disciplinary authorities.

As a general rule, a lawyer's duty to report another lawyer's misconduct depends on whether the lawyer has unprivileged knowledge of the other lawyer's ethical violation. DR 1–103(A), MR 8.3(a). The problem with option A is that it doesn't address either Attorney's ethical violation—which is not at all clear from the facts as given—nor whether Prosecutor knows about it. Instead, it does something which you have to be very careful to watch out for: it predicates discipline on *end results*. It's important to remember that the only time end results matter, in legal ethics, is in malpractice, where there must be detriment to the client in order for the attorney to be liable. Other than that, if a lawyer breaks the rules, *it doesn't matter what the results of his violation are!* If you were thrown by this, it's probably because you figured that whether or not Prosecutor has to report Attorney depends on whether Attorney was using Deft to get publicity, and the fact that she got publicity means that Prosecutor was correct in his belief that Attorney wasn't acting with Deft's best interests in mind—and that since this is an improper conflict of interest, Prosecutor should report Attorney.

The central problem with this is that it doesn't provide any evidence that Attorney actually violated the ethics rules, which in turn would create the basis for Prosecutor's duty to report her to the authorities. To see why, let's put a reasonable interpretation on Attorney's actions. Say that Attorney didn't plea bargain because she felt, based on her professional judgment, that it was in Deft's best interests to go to trial. If that was the case—and there's nothing in these facts to say it *couldn't* be—then Attorney was perfectly proper in what she did, and *regardless* of whether she got widespread publicity as a result of the trial, she wouldn't have violated the ethics rules, and there'd be no basis on which Prosecutor would be duty–bound to report her to the authorities. What this tells you is that Attorney's receiving widespread publicity doesn't provide a reason for Prosecutor to report her, and, since "if" is the modifier, in order for option B to be the best response, the reasoning would have to address a central issue. Since it doesn't do so, B isn't the best response.

D is not the best response, because even if Attorney zealously and competently represented Deft, she could still have violated the ethics rules, and if Prosecutor knew about this violation, Prosecutor would have a duty to report it to the disciplinary authorities.

As a general rule, a lawyer's duty to report another lawyer's misconduct depends on whether the lawyer has unprivileged knowledge of the other lawyer's ethical violation. DR 1–103(A), MR 8.3(a). Thus, there are two elements that must be satisfied in order to create the duty to report: 1. there must be an ethical violation by one lawyer, and 2. knowledge of that violation by a second lawyer. What makes option D tricky is that it *seems* to eliminate the basis on which Attorney could have violated the ethics rules, which would mean that Prosecutor would have no duty to report Attorney. Stated another way, what option D is actually saying is, "There are only two ways Attorney could have violated the ethics rules: either she violated her duty of zealous representation, or she violated her duty of competent representation. Assuming she didn't do either of these, she couldn't have violated the ethics rules, and thus there's no reason for Prosecutor to have to report her." The problem is that option D *doesn't eliminate* one very plausible basis on which Attorney could have violated the rules: *conflict of interest.* Attorney violated the conflict of interest rules under these facts if she let her personal interest in garnering publicity affect her judgment in representing Deft. MR 1.7, DR 5–105(A), (B), EC 5–2. Thus, even if Attorney *did* competently and zealously represent Deft, she could *still* have violated the ethics rules by letting her personal interest in garnering publicity affect her representation of Deft, and if she did so, *and* Prosecutor knew about this, Prosecutor would have a duty to report her. Note that what this tells you is the importance of remembering that one course of conduct can violate *several different ethics rules.* What it also means is that option D is very sneaky, and it's perfectly understandable if you chose it. Nonetheless, since option D overlooks the conflict of interest angle, it's not the best response.

Answer 21

A is the best response, because it correctly recognizes that asking Driver a question that Attorney knows will result in a false answer subjects Attorney to discipline.

Under both codes, a lawyer may not knowingly present false evidence. MR 3.3(a)(4), DR 7–102(A)(4). This can come about, as these facts indicate, not just by offering pieces of evidence that are false, but in asking questions to which the Attorney knows the answer will be false. DR 7–102, MR 3.3. Under these facts, you're told pretty explicitly that Driver is going to perjure himself if Attorney asks him his name. First, you have a motive, in that if Driver tells his real name, he will face an increased penalty for drunk driving since it will be obvious that it will be his second offense, and not his first; second, you're told that Driver asked Attorney not to disclose his real name; and finally, and most importantly, Driver told Attorney that he'd lie about his name if called as a witness. What this means is that Attorney simply cannot ask Driver his name, since he knows Driver's going to lie.

What's most interesting about this question is not the rule itself, which is pretty straightforward, but rather the number of issues the facts raise that could have been the focus of the question. Perhaps the most glaring one is the issue of disclosure—namely, whether, since he knew that his client would perjure himself and that he had to call him as a witness, Attorney's duty of candor would require that he divulge Driver's threatened fraud to the court. Of course, there's a very good reason why this couldn't be the focus of the question—the result would be different under the two codes.

Under the Model Rules, Attorney would probably have to disclose the information to the court, and under the Model Code, because the information is a client secret, he *couldn't* do so. In fact, the very fact that there are so many different issues that could have been raised by these facts is what makes it a little tricky; all of the distractors focus on rules that apply to issues that could have been raised, but weren't. In any case, since option A correctly identifies that Attorney will be subject to discipline for asking Driver his name knowing that Driver will respond with a lie, it's the best response.

B is not the best response, because even if Driver did commit a felony in giving an assumed name when he obtained his license, this fact won't subject Attorney to discipline for asking his name at trial.

Note that the modifier option B uses is "if." This means that, in order for it to be correct, the reasoning need only be plausible under the facts (that is, there can't be anything in the facts to suggest it couldn't be true); the reasoning must address a central issue; and the result and the reasoning must agree. Here, as to the first element, it's entirely possible that Driver committed a felony by giving a false name when he applied for a driver's license. It's the second element that's the problem, because even if this was a felony, it doesn't address Attorney's culpability for asking Driver his name at trial. What the reasoning in option B is referring to is Attorney's duty of *disclosure.* As part of the duty of candor, lawyers must disclose information on a fraud occurring during representation. DR 7–102(B)(1), MR 3.3(a)(2). There are a couple of reasons why this doesn't apply here: First, what's at issue here is Attorney's disciplinability for *asking Driver his name;* it isn't a question about whether Attorney would be subject to discipline for failing to disclose Driver's true identity. Second, even if it were a disclosure question, Attorney wouldn't be liable for nondisclosure because the fraud was completed before the representation began; if a fraud is complete before the lawyer begins to represent the client, the lawyer has no duty to disclose the fraud.

Instead, the rule that applies here is that lawyers may not knowingly present false evidence. MR 3.3(a)(4), DR 7–102(A)(4), and they must not ask questions that they know will result in false answers. DR 7–102, MR 3.3. Here, Attorney asked Driver his name, knowing that Driver was going to perjure himself, and this subjects Attorney to discipline. Since B doesn't recognize this, it's not the best response.

C is not the best response, because its reasoning refers to whether Attorney should/must disclose Driver's identity, and that's not what's at issue here. What's at issue here is whether or not Attorney can ask Driver, as a witness, a question that Attorney knows Driver will answer with a lie.

The phrase, "...obtained during the course of representation" is the language of confidentiality. As a general rule, lawyers have a duty neither to disclose nor use their clients' confidences and secrets. As to disclosure, as a general rule, lawyers must not knowingly reveal their clients' confidences or secrets gained in the professional relationship. The rules differ slightly between the two codes. Under the MC, a confidence is any communication protected by the attorney–client privilege; a secret is anything his client requests be held confidential, or whose disclosure would be embarrassing or detrimental to the client. DR 4–101(A). The MR is more general, preventing the lawyer from revealing information relating to the representation of a client, without the client's express or implied authorization. MR 1.6. *If the question here asked whether Attorney could disclose Driver's true identity, these rules would be applicable, and Driver's identity would be protected.* However, that's not what you're asked—instead, you're asked whether Attorney is subject to discipline for asking Driver his name while Driver is testifying as a witness. Since Attorney isn't disclosing anything, the rules on disclosure aren't applicable! This is *very* sneaky because many of the facts in the question lead you down the garden path to believe that the question will address confidentiality. You're told that Attorney learned Driver's big secret during the representation, and that Driver asked Attorney to keep the information confidential. However, the question doesn't address this at all; all that matters is that Attorney knows that if he asks Driver his name when Driver testifies, Driver is going to lie. The rule that applies is that a lawyer must not ask a witness questions that he knows will result in false answers, DR 7–102 and MR 3.3, and that a lawyer may not knowingly present false evidence. MR 3.3(a)(4), DR 7–102(A)(4). That's really all there is to it. Since C focuses on an issue that isn't presented by this question, it's not the best response.

D is not the best response, because it ignores the central issue, which is whether or not Attorney will be subject to discipline for asking Driver his name.

Note that option D uses the modifier "unless." This means that, in order for it to be correct, the reasoning must be the only way the result *cannot* occur. Also, "No, unless..." is the flip side of "Yes, if...," and if the answer is true in one of these forms, it will be in the other form, too. Here, by "switching" option D, you come up with the following statement: "Yes, if Driver's true name is an issue in the proceeding." This means that if Attorney asks Driver his name, and the name is an issue in the proceeding, Attorney will be subject to discipline, under option D. When it's put this way, you can see that it doesn't make logical sense; if Driver's name is considered an issue in the proceeding, then Attorney should ask about it, and according to option D, doing so will subject him to discipline. Clearly there can't be a rule that requires this, and in fact, there isn't. Instead, the rule is that a lawyer must not ask questions of witnesses that he knows will result in false answers. DR 7–102, MR 3.3, and a lawyer may not knowingly present false evidence. MR 3.3(a)(4), DR 7 102(A)(4). Since option D doesn't recognize this, it's not the best response.

Answer 22

A is the best response, because it correctly recognizes that only alternative III represents disciplinable behavior.

AS TO ALTERNATIVE I:

Alternative I is correct, since it recognizes that a lawyer may properly agree to pay a witness's expenses reasonably incurred by a witness in attending or testifying at trial.

The codes differ in their approach to permissible witness fees, in that the Model Code is specific, and the Model Rules are not (although the most important thing to remember under both is that contingent fees to witnesses are prohibited). Under the Model Code, DR 7–109(C), a lawyer cannot offer to, agree to, or actually pay a witness fees which are contingent on either the content of the witness's testimony or the outcome of the case. However, a lawyer may agree to pay a witness: 1. expenses reasonably incurred by a witness in attending or testifying; 2. reasonable compensation to a witness for his loss of time in attending or testifying; and 3. a reasonable fee for the professional services of an expert witness. The Model Rules, Rule 3.4(b), only prohibit payments to witnesses that are prohibited by law. In this instance, since the Model Code is specific and the Model Rules aren't, you'd have to follow the Model Code to arrive at the correct answer. As #1 in the list indicates, it's proper to agree to pay a witness for expenses incurred in attending the trial or testifying, and Wit's travel expenses would fit this description. Since alternative I recognizes that it's proper for Attorney to reimburse Wit for these expenses, it's correct.

AS TO ALTERNATIVE II:

Alternative II is correct, since it recognizes that Attorney may properly reimburse Wit for wages lost while he attends trial.

The codes differ in their approach to permissible witness fees, in that the Model Code is specific, and the Model Rules are not (although the most important thing to remember under both is that contingent fees to witnesses are prohibited). Under the Model Code, DR 7–109(C), a lawyer cannot offer to, agree to, or actually pay a witness fees which are contingent on either the content of the witness's testimony or the outcome of the case. However, a lawyer may agree to pay a witness: 1. expenses reasonably incurred by a witness in attending or testifying; 2. reasonable compensation to a witness for his loss of time in attending or testifying; and 3. a reasonable fee for the professional services of an expert witness. The Model Rules, Rule 3.4(b), only prohibit payments to witnesses that are prohibited by law. In this instance, since the Model Code is specific and the Model Rules aren't, you'd have to follow the Model Code to arrive at the correct answer. As #2 indicates, it's perfectly proper to pay a witness his "opportunity cost"—that is, what he would have made had he not had to attend the trial. Since alternative II recognizes this, it's correct.

AS TO ALTERNATIVE III:

Alternative III isn't correct, because it contains the one thing that is definitely a bogeyman in witness fees—namely, a contingent payment.

The codes differ in their approach to permissible witness fees, in that the Model Code is specific, and the Model Rules are not (although the most important thing to remember under both is that contingent fees to witnesses are prohibited). Under the Model Code, DR 7–109(C), a lawyer cannot offer to, agree to, or actually pay a witness fees which are contingent on either the content of the witness's testimony or the outcome of the case. However, a lawyer may agree to pay a witness: 1. expenses reasonably incurred by a witness in attending or testifying; 2. reasonable compensation to a witness for his loss of time in attending or testifying; and 3. a reasonable fee for the professional services of an expert witness. The Model Rules, Rule 3.4(b), only prohibit payments to witnesses that are prohibited by law (although most jurisdictions forbid contingent payments). In this instance, since the Model Code is specific and the Model Rules aren't, you'd have to follow the Model Code to arrive at the correct answer. As the rule above illustrates, a lawyer can't pay a witness depending either on what he says, or what the client recovers. As a result, agreeing to feed Wit

5% of the ultimate booty would subject Attorney to discipline. Since alternative III doesn't recognize this, it's not correct.

Answer 23

A is the best response, because it correctly identifies that the gift is permissible, and the reason why: it's given to Judge as part of a public testimonial to her.

As a general rule, neither a judge, nor anyone in her family who lives with her, may accept any gift, bequest, favor, or loan from anyone. CJC 5(C)(4). However, there are several important exceptions to this rule; in fact, for most purposes, it's probably only important to remember that the gifts and favors that are prohibited are those that suggest an improper influence on the judge. Nonetheless, CJC 5(C)(4) offers a list of gifts which a judge may accept:

1. a gift incident to a public testimonial to the judge;

2. books supplied by a publisher on a complimentary basis for official use;

3. invitations to judge and spouse to attend bar-related functions devoted to improving the law, legal system, or administration of justice;

4. ordinary social hospitality;

5. gift, bequest, favor, or loan from a relative;

6. wedding or engagement gifts;

7. loans from lending institutions in the regular course of business on the same terms offered to non–judges;

8. scholarships or fellowships awarded on the same basis as to anyone else;

9. any other gift, bequest, favor, or loan, as long as the donor is not a party or anyone whose interests have come or are likely to come before the judge, so long as, if the value exceeds $100, the judge reports it as if it were compensation.

As #1 indicates, a judge may accept a gift incident to a public testimonial. That's exactly what's going on in these facts. Perhaps the only thing that's even slightly tricky about this question is the fact that the portrait is worth $4,000 and it comes in part from lawyers who practice in City's courts, and presumably before Judge. That brings up something that's very important to remember in relation to gifts to judges; namely, even if the gift is permissible under Canon 5, it must *still* not create an appearance of impropriety, or it will violate Canon 2 of the CJC. There's no real suggestion of impropriety in these facts; you don't see any lawyers schmoozing with Judge, or commenting that now Judge will "know who her friends are." Instead, you're told that she's served for many years as a director of the organization, that the organization is never involved in litigation, and that she isn't paid for her work on the charity's behalf. As a result, there's no real reason why Judge shouldn't accept the portrait, and since option A recognizes this, it's the best response.

Option B is not the best response, because whether Judge is compensated for her services to the organization or not is irrelevant in determining if she may properly accept the portrait.

Note that option B uses the modifier "because." If B were true, then you could take its reasoning, make it into an "if" clause, combine it with the call of the question, and that statement would be true, as well. When you do this, you wind up with this statement: "If Judge did not receive compensation for her services to the charitable organization, then it would be proper for her to accept a $4,000 portrait as a gift." You can see that Judge's not accepting pay for her work doesn't create the reason why the gift is acceptable. Instead, judges may only accept gifts that do not create a conflict with their judicial duties, and which don't create the appearance of impropriety. Here, even if Judge didn't accept pay for her services to the organization, it's still possible that accepting the gift would be improper. Let's look at how this might be true. Say that some of the lawyers were representing tobacco companies in cases that were upcoming in Judge's court, and they made it plain to Judge that they expected to see a "return" on their gift to her. If this were true, their gift would suggest that they were trying to improperly influence Judge, and she couldn't properly accept the gift. CJC 5(C)(4).

Instead, the reason Judge may accept the gift is that it's incident to a public testimonial to her. This is expressly permitted under CJC 5(C)(4). In addition, even if a gift meets the requirements of Canon 5, it must not create an appearance of impropriety under Canon 2. The gift here doesn't; it's clearly given in recognition of Judge's efforts on behalf of the charitable organization, and not as a nefarious attempt to improperly influence Judge. As a result, it's proper for Judge to accept the portrait, and since option B doesn't recognize the reason why, it's not the best response.

C is not the best response, because the fact that the gift cost over $1,000 in and of itself doesn't determine the propriety of accepting it.

As a general rule, neither a judge, nor anyone in her family who lives with her, may accept any gift, bequest, favor, or loan from anyone. CJC 5(C)(4). However, there are several important exceptions to this rule; in fact, for most purposes, it's probably only important to remember that the gifts and favors that are prohibited are those that suggest an improper influence on the judge. Furthermore, even if a gift is appropriate under Canon 5, it must still not create an appearance of impropriety under Canon 2.

Canon 5(C)(4) offers a list of exceptions to the "no gifts" rule, and one of those is a gift incident to a public testimonial to a judge. That's what's going on here, and that's why the gift is proper. However, C isn't a terrible answer, in the sense that the sheer expense of a gift can create the appearance of impropriety, or otherwise suggest that the donors are trying to improperly influence the judge. It's just that under these facts, this idea doesn't hold a lot of water; you're told that Judge has served the charity for many years, and there's no real indication that the gift is anything other than an honest "thank you" for her efforts on the charity's behalf. Another tip–off that C can't be the best response is the dollar amount; it isn't as though a gift worth $1,000 is all right, and a gift of $1,001 isn't. If you chose this response, it may be because you were thinking about the reporting requirements of Canon 6. A judge is required to report gifts whose value exceeds $100, as if the gift were compensation, if the donor is someone whose interests haven't and aren't likely to come before the judge. As you can see, the gift here is incident to a public testimonial, so it doesn't fit this rule, and even if it did, the amount is $100, not $1,000. Since option C doesn't cite the applicable rule and arrives at the wrong result, it's not the best response.

D is not the best response, because the mere fact that the donating lawyers practice in City's courts isn't enough to make the gift improper.

As a general rule, neither a judge, nor anyone in her family who lives with her, may accept any gift, bequest, favor, or loan from anyone: CJC 5(C)(4). However, there are several important exceptions to this rule; in fact, for most purposes, it's probably only important to remember that the gifts and favors that are prohibited are those that suggest an improper influence on the judge. Furthermore, even if a gift is appropriate under Canon 5, it must still not create an appearance of impropriety under Canon 2. With these rules in mind, it's easy to see why you might have chosen option D; the fact that lawyers who gave the portrait may well, and probably have, come before Judge does create a hint that they may expect a *quid pro quo* for their gift. However, if you picked up on this, you picked up on a detail way too subtle to be the basis of an MPRE question. Under these facts, you're hit over the head with just how honest this gift is; you're told that Judge has striven diligently on the charity's behalf for many years, that the organization hasn't been involved in litigation, and that the gift is incident to a public testimonial to Judge, which is expressly permitted by the list of permissible gifts under CJC 5(C)(4); that the lawyers donating for the portrait appear in City's courts is the only hint of impropriety, and it's just not enough to support such a conclusion on a multiple–choice exam like the MPRE. For the gift to be improper, you'd need facts like statements by the donating lawyers that the Judge "ought to know on which side her bread is buttered" or that they had some controversial litigation coming up in her court shortly. You aren't given anything like this, and the fact that you're given several facts the other way—suggesting that the gift is entirely proper—means there's no question but that the gift is proper. Since D doesn't recognize this, it's not the best response.

Answer 24

A is the best response, because it correctly reflects the rule on limitations on practice as they must appear on a law firm's letterhead.

 The rule is that while the same law firm name can be used in different jurisdictions, the letterhead must indicate any jurisdictions in which the firm has an office but in which partners and/or associates can't practice. DR 2–102(D), MR 7.5(b). Alpha, Beta, and Delta's stationery meets this requirement, since the limitations on each lawyer's practice are clearly stated. Perhaps the only possibly tricky thing about this question is that Alpha and Beta can't practice in the same state together, but there's no rule that requires that lawyers in the same firm all be admitted to practice in at least one common state. Since option A correctly recognizes that the limitations on practice stated for each member of the firm make the letterhead permissible, it's the best response.

Option B is not the best response, because it states a requirement that does not, in fact, exist.

The rule is that while the same law firm name can be used in different jurisdictions, the letterhead must indicate any jurisdictions in which the firm has an office but in which partners and/or associates can't practice. DR 2–

102(D), MR 7.5(b). As this rule shows, there is no requirement that all members of the firm be admitted to practice in at least one common state. When you think about it, that wouldn't be a very workable rule if it *did* exist. In any case, since option B places a non-existing requirement on letterheads, it's not the best response.

C is not the best response, because it misstates the rule on permissible letterheads.

Under DR 2–102(D) and MR 7.5(b), the same firm name can be used in all jurisdictions; in fact, the real limitation is that it must reflect any jurisdictions in which the firm has an office but in which partners and/or associates aren't admitted to practice. If you think about it in practical terms, you can see how impossible it would be for huge law firms to change their names from state to state. In any case, since option C places a restriction on letterheads that doesn't exist, it's not the best response.

D is not the best response, because the letterhead is permissible whether or not Delta actively practices in both First and Second.

Note that option D uses the modifier "unless." In order for D to be correct, then, the reasoning must be the only way the result cannot occur; if you can think of even one other way the result might come about, D can't be correct. In fact, Delta's flitting from First to Second for his practice has no impact on the propriety of the letterhead. Instead, regardless of whether Delta actively practices in First and Second, the letterhead will be permissible as long as it lists any jurisdictions in which the first has an office but in which partners and/or associates aren't admitted to practice. DR 2-102(D), MR 7.5(b). In fact, even if Delta *did* actively practice in both First and Second, if the limitations on practice weren't listed on the letterhead, the members would be subject to discipline. Since option D doesn't recognize this, it's not the best response.

Answer 25

C is the best response, because it correctly recognizes that the likelihood Attorney will be called as a witness makes it improper for Attorney to act as an advocate in the case.

As a general rule, a lawyer cannot accept or continue employment where it's obvious he may be called as a witness on a client's behalf during the proceedings, with the following three exceptions: 1. the testimony relates to an uncontested issue; 2. the testimony relates to the nature and value of legal services rendered in the case; or 3. disqualification of the lawyer would work a substantial hardship on the client. MR 3.7, DR 5–102(A), (B), 5–101(B) . The reason for this rule is that the interests of witness and advocate are inconsistent; as an advocate, the lawyer's duty is to argue his client's case. As a witness, on the other hand, the lawyer must objectively state facts. This puts him in a position of arguing his own credibility; furthermore, his advocacy makes him easily impeachable (due to his interest) and thus a less effective witness. EC 5–9.

Under these facts, it couldn't be made any more clear that Attorney is going to be called as a witness—Son is challenging the will on grounds of testamentary capacity, and attorney prepared the will and is the only surviving witness to its execution. As a result, the above–stated rule against lawyers' testifying in cases they're trying would come into play. Since the facts fit none of the exceptions, Attorney cannot properly represent Executor in the case. Since C recognizes this, it's the best response.

A is not the best response, because the result and the reasoning don't agree.

The problem here is the potential of a lawyer's having to appear as a witness in a case he's trying. As a general rule, a lawyer cannot accept or continue employment where it's obvious he may be called as a witness on a client's behalf during the proceedings, with the following three exceptions: 1. the testimony relates to an uncontested issue; 2. the testimony relates to the nature and value of legal services rendered in the case; or 3. disqualification of the lawyer would work a substantial hardship on the client. MR 3.7, DR 5–102(A), (B), 5–101(B). Here, Attorney will almost certainly be called as a witness. The central issue in the case is testamentary capacity; Attorney not only prepared the will, but is the sole surviving witness to its execution. What option A does is to focus on the fact which makes it most likely that A will be called as a witness, but offering this as a reason why Attorney *may* represent Executor. In fact, just the opposite is true; the fact that Attorney will appear as a witness means he *may not* represent Executor. If you chose this response, it could be that you misread the call of the question, expecting it to ask if Attorney was subject to discipline, not whether the representation was proper—because if that *was* the question, A would be the best response, since it identifies the central reason why Attorney will be called as a witness, and thus the main reason why he can't act as an advocate in the case. However, since A arrives at the wrong result, it's not the best response.

B is not the best response, because it ignores the central issue; namely, the propriety of serving as both advocate *and* witness in the same case.

B's reasoning—that Attorney's testimony will support the will's validity—implies that his conduct is proper because he's satisfying his duty of loyalty to Testator. Loyalty only comes into question when there's a conflict of interest issue. The problem is that the issue here doesn't involve conflict of interest at all; the only hint of truth in B is that the only way Attorney could testify is on behalf of the validity of the will, because he prepared it; he couldn't, for instance, attack its validity. Instead, the question here asks you whether or not Attorney could properly represent Executor in the will's probate; and the issue this throws up is whether or not Attorney can act as an advocate in a case where he will almost certainly be called as a witness. The facts tell you that Son is challenging the will on grounds of testamentary capacity. Attorney prepared the will and is the sole surviving witness to its execution, so he's the most obvious witness in the case. The rule is that a lawyer cannot accept or continue employment where it's obvious he may be called as a witness on a client's behalf during the proceedings, with the following three exceptions: 1. the testimony relates to an uncontested issue; 2. the testimony relates to the nature and value of legal services rendered in the case; or 3. disqualification of the lawyer would work a substantial hardship on the client. MR 3.7, DR 5–102(A), (B), 5–101(B). Since the facts here fit none of the exceptions, it will not be proper for Attorney to represent Executor in the will challenge. Since B doesn't recognize this, and instead focuses on loyalty, which is not an issue in the problem, it's not the best response.

D is not the best response, because it implies a duty of loyalty to Son that doesn't exist.

What option D is implicitly focusing on is the duty of loyalty to former clients (like Testator). The rule is that a lawyer cannot represent another client in the same or a substantially related matter as a former client when that client's interests are materially adverse to the former client's interests. MR 1.9(a). What this means given these facts is that Attorney could not take on representation challenging the validity of the will, or opposing Testator's interests in any way. If you look at what's going on here, Attorney is fulfilling his duty of loyalty to Testator if he represents Executor, because Executor's position is that the will is valid as it stands; it's *Son* who's challenging its validity, and thus, ironically enough, it's *Son's* position that would violate Attorney's duty of loyalty to Testator, *regardless* of whether he's Testator's heir at law or not.

In fact, what option D overlooks entirely is the central problem here, which is not a matter of whom Attorney is representing in the case, but the fact that he intends to act as both advocate *and* witness in the same case. He is certain to be called as a witness because he both wrote the will and is the only surviving witness to its execution. The rule is that a lawyer cannot accept or continue employment where it's obvious he may be called as a witness on a client's behalf during the proceedings, with the following three exceptions: 1. the testimony relates to an uncontested issue; 2. the testimony relates to the nature and value of legal services rendered in the case; or 3. disqualification of the lawyer would work a substantial hardship on the client. MR 3.7, DR 5–102(A), (B), 5–101(B). Since the facts here fit none of the exceptions, it will not be proper for Attorney to represent Executor in the will challenge. Because option D overlooks this issue and focuses instead on the issue of conflict of interest, it's not the best response.

Answer 26

D is the best response, because it recognizes that only by fully explaining everything in the file can Attorney avoid discipline for attempting to limit his liability for malpractice.

The issue here is whether Attorney's conducting and taping the final interview could be construed as an attempt to limit his malpractice liability to his client. If so, the interview would violate both codes. Under the MR, a lawyer may only prospectively limit his liability for malpractice if the client consents after being advised by separate counsel, and applicable law allows it. MR 1.8(h). Under the MC, a lawyer may not prospectively attempt to limit his liability to his client for his personal malpractice. DR 6–102. The key here is that Attorney isn't trying to limit his liability; rather, he's trying to preserve evidence in case his client does sue him for malpractice. While the taped interview may discourage Attorney's clients from suing him, it's not a limitation on his liability. Only if Attorney didn't discuss the whole client file with the client could this be seen as an impermissible attempt to limit his liability by hiding from the client things about the representation that might create liability.

In addition, note that only by discussing the entire file in good faith could Attorney avoid discipline for an impermissible conflict of interest. The rule is that a lawyer can't let personal interests affect his judgment in representing clients. MR 1.7, DR 5–105(A),(B),EC 5–2. If Attorney does not completely and thoroughly discuss the client file with the client in the taped interview, he'll be letting his personal interest in avoiding malpractice liability outweigh the best interests of his client.

Regardless of whether you analyze the question in terms of limiting malpractice liability or conflict of interest, it's clear that Attorney must fully explain everything in the file, in good faith, in order to avoid discipline. Since option D recognizes this, it's the best response.

A is not the best response, because it misstates the ethics rules.

Option A conditions Attorney's discipline on whether he's preserving evidence for a possible malpractice claim. In fact, neither code prevents a lawyer from doing this. If you chose this response, it's probably because you were thinking of all the other things related to malpractice that a lawyer can't do. For instance, take lawyers' attempts to prospectively limit liability to clients for malpractice. Both codes frown on this, and the Model Code forbids it entirely, DR 6-102. (Under MR 1.8(h), a lawyer may only prospectively limit his liability for malpractice if the client consents after being advised by separate counsel, and applicable law allows it.) Or consider lawyers' negotiating settlements of clients' malpractice claims against them. This too is discouraged, and is only possible if the lawyer first advises the client, in writing, to obtain the advice of separate counsel concerning the settlement. MR 1.8(h)(no parallel provision in MC).

Instead of looking at what the codes expressly say about malpractice— since they don't expressly prohibit preserving evidence for malpractice claims—look at what might be unsavory about Attorney's taped–interview practice. For instance, if Attorney was letting his personal interests (in avoiding malpractice) affect his judgment on behalf of his clients, this would be a disciplinable conflict of interest. MR 1.7, DR 5–105(A), (B), EC 5–2. Furthermore, if Attorney left out certain elements of the representation in the interview, this could be viewed as an impermissible attempt to limit malpractice liability by hiding from the client things about the representation that might create liability. However, since option A ignores these and instead focuses on something that *isn't* disciplinable, and it mistakenly states that it *is* disciplinable, it's not the best response.

B is not the best response, because these facts don't clearly indicate that Attorney *is* acting adversely to client.

Note that option B uses the modifier "because." As a result, for B to be correct, the reasoning must address and resolve a central issue; the facts in the question must completely satisfy the reasoning; and the result must be consistent with the reasoning. Option B falls down on the second element. Option B says that Attorney was acting adversely to the client, and the facts don't show this; if anything, the taped interview, although it admittedly helps Attorney insulate himself from malpractice, may actually give the client an opportunity to voice any misgivings he has, and clear up any questions about his case or the legal system itself, and in this respect the taped interview program would be laudatory. Instead, in order for B to be correct, the facts would have to indicate that Attorney was doing something impermissible in the interview (for instance, playing hide–the–ball with elements of the representation that were handled somewhat south of skillfully). Alternatively, B could have made Attorney's disciplinability conditional on his doing something impermissible in the interview (e.g., "Yes, if Attorney misrepresents elements of the representation that could form the basis for malpractice liability").

This problem aside, if Attorney had acted adversely to the client in some way, he'd be subject to discipline for conflict of interest, by letting his personal interest (in avoiding malpractice) affect his judgment in representing clients. MR 1.7, DR 5–105(A), (B), EC 5–2. Even though B recognizes that acting adversely to a client would subject Attorney to discipline, because it mischaracterizes the facts, it's not the best response.

C is not the best response, because the timing of the interview would not determine whether or not it would subject Attorney to discipline.

What option C implies is that Attorney's duties, as reflected in his conducting the taped interview, are different during the representation and after the representation, and that a duty of some sort is lifted once the representation terminates. Looking at the two duties most applicable to these facts—limiting malpractice liability and conflict of interest—the timing of the taped interview makes no difference. Let's look at malpractice first. Both codes frown on lawyers' attempts to prospectively limit liability to clients for malpractice, and the Model Code forbids it entirely, DR 6–102. (Under MR 1.8(h), a lawyer may only prospectively limit his liability for malpractice if the client consents after being advised by separate counsel, and applicable law allows it.) Thus, if there were something about Attorney's interviews that constituted a prospective limitation on malpractice liability, it wouldn't matter whether the representation had concluded or not. As to conflict of interest, a lawyer is not allowed to let his personal interests affect his judgment in representing clients. MR 1.7, DR 5–105(A),(B), EC 5–2. Since this relates to representation but doesn't put a time limit on when the conduct must take place, it too isn't impacted by whether or not the representation has ended. Since option C focuses on something that doesn't determine the disciplinability of Attorney's conduct, it's not the best response.

Answer 27

C is the best response, because it correctly applies the rule on a lawyer's decision–making authority in the area of reasonable requests from opposing counsel.

Lawyers have the right to agree to reasonable requests of opposing counsel that do not prejudice the rights of the client (e.g., court procedures, continuances, waiver of procedural formalities, and the like), under DR 7–101(A)(1) and MR 1.3, Comment—*regardless of what their clients want.* Applying this rule to the facts, you can see that agreeing to Beta's request for a five–day extension is Alpha's decision alone, unless doing so would prejudice Plaintiff's rights. Under these facts, it's not clear whether or not the extension would prejudice Plaintiff's rights or not, but since option C conditions Alpha's disciplinability on the existence of prejudice, it doesn't matter, since it's *plausible* that the extension wouldn't harm Plaintiff.

What makes this question a little tricky is that the rule on reasonable requests seems to disagree with the lawyer's duty to zealously advocate his client's interests within the bounds of the law, the feeling being that if Plaintiff wants Alpha to stick it to Defendant, then, by gum, Alpha ought to have to do so. If it helps to remember the rule, you should think of response to reasonable requests as an exception to the duty of zealous advocacy.

In addition, keep in mind that Alpha could have refused to agree to the extension, and he'd be acting perfectly properly in that case as well. The point is that it's Alpha's decision as to whether to grant the extension, and if Alpha agrees to it, Plaintiff's rights must not be prejudiced by the decision. Since option C recognizes that the propriety of the decision rests on whether Plaintiff's rights are prejudiced by the extension, and that if they aren't, it's entirely Alpha's decision whether to grant the extension, it's the best response.

A is not the best response, because it overlooks the fact that the decision involved here isn't Plaintiff's to make.

The only way that Alpha could be subject to discipline for failing to follow her client's orders was if the client had the power to make a decision, and Alpha disobeyed that decision. That's not the case here. In fact, lawyers have the right to agree to reasonable requests of opposing counsel that do not prejudice the rights of the client (e.g., court procedures, continuances, waiver of procedural formalities, and the like), under DR 7–101(A)(1) and MR 1.3, Comment—*regardless of what their clients want.* As this rule indicates, the only way that Plaintiff could have the power to make a decision on the continuance would be if granting the continuance would prejudice Plaintiff's rights. There's no indication in these facts that the extension would do so, and thus the answer choice would have to create prejudice in order to give the decision–making authority to Plaintiff.

If you chose this response, it's probably because you figured making Beta stick to strict deadlines is legal, and that, as part of her duty of zealous advocacy, Alpha has a duty to pursue Plaintiff's goals within the bounds of the law. That's not bad thinking, and it would prevail if there weren't a more specific rule stating otherwise. Nevertheless, since option A mischaracterizes the decision as being Plaintiff's to make and not Alpha's, it's not the best response.

B is not the best response, because it mischaracterizes the decision on granting the extension as being Plaintiff's, and not Alpha's.

Option B suggests that the only way Alpha could escape discipline would be to have Plaintiff agree to grant the extension. What this does is to say that the decision on the extension belongs to Plaintiff. In fact, it doesn't; the rule is that lawyers have the right to agree to reasonable requests of opposing counsel that do not prejudice the rights of the client (e.g., court procedures, continuances, waiver of procedural formalities, and the like), under DR 7–101(A)(1) and MR 1.3, Comment—*regardless of what their clients want.* Thus, unless granting the extension would prejudice Plaintiff's rights—and there's no suggestion under these facts that it would—Alpha is free to grant the extension without Plaintiff's consent. This is a bit sneaky in the sense that there are many types of otherwise–improper conduct that can be made permissible with client consent, the most obvious being most conflicts of interest. However, it's not the case here. Since B overlooks the fact that, without facts indicating the extension would prejudice Plaintiff's rights, Alpha has the right to grant the extension, it's not the best response.

D is not the best response, because Beta's fault doesn't determine whether or not Alpha was proper in granting the extension.

Note that option D uses the modifier "because." This means that, if you make an "if...then" statement out of its reasoning and the call of the question, that statement must be true in order for D to be the best response. Combining the two, you wind up with this statement: "If Beta was not at fault in causing the delay, Alpha won't be subject to discipline for granting the extension." What this does is make the propriety of Alpha's decision contingent upon whether or not Beta was responsible for the delay. When you see it this way, it makes it more obvious that this can't be true. Regardless of who was responsible for the delay, Alpha properly granted the extension *unless* doing so prejudiced Plaintiff's rights, in which case Plaintiff should have been asked to make the decision. That's because the rule is that lawyers have the right to agree to reasonable requests of opposing counsel that do not prejudice the rights of the client (e.g., court procedures, continuances, waiver of procedural formalities, and the like), under DR 7–lOl(A)(l) and MR 1.3, Comment—*regardless of what their clients want.* The fault or lack of it in creating the need for the request is irrelevant. Since option D doesn't recognize this, it's not the best response.

Answer 28

C is the best response, because it identifies the fact that Alpha's reasonable belief in the truth of his statements insulates him from discipline.

Under these facts, Alpha is making statements about the qualifications and integrity of a judge, Beta. The rules on such statements vary slightly between the two codes. Under MR 8.2(a), a lawyer may not make a statement concerning the qualifications or integrity of a judge, adjudicatory officer, or judicial or legal candidate if the lawyer recklessly disregards the truth or falsity of the statement or knows that it's false (note that this is the "malice" standard from defamation). The MC only prohibits statements made with *actual knowledge* of falsity. DR 8–102(A). Taken together, this means that in order for Alpha to be subject to discipline, he'd have to have known that his statements about Beta were false. What clues you in to the fact that Alpha didn't violate this rule is that you're told Alpha "reasonably believed" Beta undertook illegal and unethical campaign practices. This

0

means that Alpha cannot be subject to discipline for his statements, making C the best response.

A is not the best response, because it misstates the standard by which you determine if Alpha's statements subject him to discipline.

The reasoning in A refers to EC 8–6, which requires that when a lawyer criticizes a judge, he must be sure his statement is true, use respectful language, and avoid petty criticisms, since doing otherwise "tend[s] to lessen public confidence in our legal system." The problem with option A is that it takes this language out of context, changes it from a rationale into a rule, and raises it to the level of a disciplinable offense. What EC 8–6 is saying is that if a lawyer's criticisms are false, disrespectful and petty, *then* they will tend to lessen respect in the legal system, and that's to be discouraged. It's not the "lessening confidence" aspect *itself* that makes the statements disciplinable.

Instead, the only way Alpha could be subject to discipline for his statements, under both codes taken together, is if he knew they were false. (The rules on such statements vary slightly between the two codes. Under MR 8.2(a), a lawyer may not make a statement concerning the qualifications or integrity of a judge, adjudicatory officer, or judicial or legal candidate if the lawyer recklessly disregards the truth or falsity of the statement or knows that it's false (note that this is the "malice" standard from defamation). The MC only prohibits statements made with *actual knowledge* of falsity. DR 8–102(A). You know Alpha doesn't meet the "knowingly false" standard, since the facts tell you that Alpha "reasonably believed" his statements were true. Thus, regardless of whether or not Alpha's statement might lessen confidence in the legal system, since his statements beat the "knowingly false" standard, he won't be subject to discipline. Since A doesn't recognize this, it's not the best response.

B is not the best response, because it places a requirement on Alpha's comments that doesn't, in fact, exist. What B suggests is that in order for criticisms of judges to be permissible, they must be directed at the judges' defects in legal knowledge. In fact, this isn't the case. The rules on such statements vary slightly between the two codes. Under MR 8.2(a), a lawyer may not make a statement concerning the qualifications or integrity of a judge, adjudicatory officer, or judicial or legal candidate if the lawyer recklessly disregards the truth or falsity of the statement or knows that it's false (note that this is the "malice" standard from defamation). The MC only prohibits statements made with *actual knowledge* of falsity, DR 8–102(A). Taken together, this means that in order for Alpha to be subject to discipline, he'd have to have known that his statements about Beta were false. Since the facts tell you that Alpha reasonably believed his comments were true, he won't be subject to discipline for them.

If you chose this response, you may have been thinking about the language of EC 8–6, which requires that lawyers' criticisms of judges have as their motivation a desire to improve the legal system. While comments directed at judges' legal knowledge (or lack thereof) certainly meet this standard, ensuring that judges who are elected to their positions are ethical and law-abiding in their election practices serves the same goal—and that was the source of Alpha's statements. In any case, even if EC 8–6 did apply, it's only aspirational, not mandatory, so that even if Alpha's comments weren't aimed at improving the legal system, he wouldn't be subject to discipline; his statements would merely be improper.

In any case, since B incorrectly states that Alpha's disciplinability depends on whether his comments were directed at Beta's legal knowledge, it's not the best response.

D is not the best response, because Beta's access to the press does not determine whether or not Alpha's comments subject him to discipline.

What option D suggests is that if Beta has the ability to engage in a mud-slinging contest with Alpha in the local press, then Alpha's free to say anything he wants about Beta. In fact, that's not the case; Alpha has "defamation-like" restrictions on the types of comments he can make about Beta, or any judge. The rules on such statements vary slightly between the two codes. Under MR 8.2(a), a lawyer may not make a statement concerning the qualifications or integrity of a judge, adjudicatory officer, or judicial or legal candidate if the lawyer recklessly disregards the truth or falsity of the statement or knows that it's false (note that this is the "malice" standard from defamation). The MC only prohibits statements made with *actual knowledge* of falsity. DR 8–102(A). Taken together, this means that in order for Alpha to be subject to discipline, he'd have to have known that his statements about Beta were false. Since the facts tell you that Alpha reasonably believed his comments were true, he won't be subject to discipline for them.

As these rules indicate, the attacked judge's access to the press doesn't make an otherwise disciplinable comment proper. Since D doesn't recognize this, it's not the best response.

Answer 29

C is the best response, since it recognizes that the contribution will be proper as long as it's donated to Judge's campaign committee.

There are a couple of rules which make the conduct described in C proper (and therefore nondisciplinable). First, MR 8.4(f) states that a lawyer can't knowingly aid a judge in violating the law or the Code of Judicial Conduct (no parallel provision in the MC). Thus, if Attorney violated any of the campaign contribution rules in the CJC, he'd be subject to discipline. However, the CJC expressly permits a judicial candidate to set up a campaign committee to solicit contributions from everyone, including lawyers. CJC 7(B)(2). As a result, it's perfectly proper for Attorney to make his contribution to Judge's campaign committee.

If you didn't choose this response, there may have been a couple things that bothered you: First, the size of Attorney's contribution, and second, the fact that he and Judge are business partners. As to the size of the contribution, you may have thought that such a large contribution smacks of impropriety, and thus might violate Canon 2 of the CJC, which requires that a judge avoid even the appearance of impropriety in all his activities. However, without additional facts suggesting that Attorney expected something in return for his donation or any other facts suggesting that the generous contribution may affect Judge's professional judgment, the mere size of the donation in this case wouldn't violate Canon 2. Second, the fact that Judge and Attorney are business partners may create a problem under Canon 5 of the CJC, which requires that judges regulate their financial activities so as to minimize the risk of conflict with their official duties. However, this doesn't address the propriety of the campaign contribution, and *that's* the call of the question here.

Note, incidentally, that option C uses the modifier "if." This means that in order for it to be correct, the reasoning must be plausible under the facts; the reasoning must address a central issue; and the result and the reasoning must agree. Here, there's nothing to suggest that Attorney *didn't* make the contribution to Judge's campaign committee. This resolves a central issue, because if the donation were made directly to Judge, it would violate the CJC and subject Attorney to discipline; and finally, assuming the contribution was made to the campaign committee, it would, as C states, insulate

Attorney from discipline. Since option C addresses and correctly resolves the central issue under these facts, it's the best response.

A is not the best response, because whether or not Attorney represents clients before Judge's court or not, *this doesn't resolve the propriety of the campaign contribution.*

What A suggests is that Attorney's representing clients in cases that may come before Judge precludes him from making a contribution to Judge's re–election campaign. It's easy to see why you might choose this response, because such a contribution smacks of a bribe. However, by the same token, lawyers are supposed to promote the campaigns of those they believe will make qualified judges. EC 8–6. The lawyers most likely to know this, on a professional basis, are those who argue cases before the judge. The way this conflict is resolved is that attorneys may make campaign contributions to the campaign committees of judges, regardless of whether they appear before them in court or not. CJC 7(B)(2). Of course, if there were additional facts suggesting that the contribution would affect Judge's conduct or judgment on the bench, then the contribution would violate Canon 2 of the CJC; but there aren't any facts here suggesting that the contribution smacks of a bribe, so this isn't an issue here. (Note that if Attorney's conduct would help Judge violate the CJC, Attorney would be subject to discipline under MR 8.4(f).)

Option A is tricky because an obvious issue in these facts, and one you were probably thinking about if you chose this response, is the impact of Judge's owning real estate with Attorney. This suggests that there may be a problem under Canon 5 of the CJC, which requires that a judge regulate his financial activities so as to minimize the risk of conflict with his official duties. Among other things, this requires that a judge refrain from financial and business dealings that tend to involve him in frequent transactions with lawyers or persons likely to come before the court on which he serves. Thus, the language in option A fits a rule that could very well determine if it's proper for Judge to co–own property with Attorney. However, that's not the question here; the question here only deals with the propriety of Attorney's campaign contribution. Since option A doesn't recognize this, it's not the best response.

B is not the best response, because the propriety of Attorney's contribution doesn't depend on discussing it with Judge beforehand.

In order to see why B can't be correct, let's combine its reasoning with the call of the question into an "If...then" statement. If the resulting statement is correct, then B would be correct. Combining the two, you get "If Judge and Attorney don't discuss the matter of a campaign contribution before it's made, then Attorney will be subject to discipline for contributing $10,000 to Judge's campaign." In fact, no rule in either the ethical codes or the CJC require notice before a donation is made. What is required, instead, under CJC 7(B)(2), is that any such donations be made to the judge's campaign committee, not to the judge personally. In addition, Canon 2 requires that a judge must avoid even the appearance of impropriety, which a very large donation, or one given under circumstances indicating a bribe, might create. As long as these conditions are met, it simply doesn't matter whether the judge is notified about the donation before it's made. Since option B doesn't recognize this, it's not the best response.

D is not the best response, because the long–standing relationship between Attorney and Judge doesn't provide a basis on which the contribution is proper.

Under MR 8.4(f), a lawyer is not allowed to aid a judge in violating the Code of Judicial Conduct. Thus, Attorney's contribution to Judge's campaign cannot violate the CJC. The rule on campaign contributions is found in CJC 7(B)(2), and it is that any such donations must be made to the judge's campaign committee, not to the judge personally. Beyond that, Canon 2 requires that a judge must avoid even the appearance of impropriety (which a large donation or one given under circumstances indicating a bribe might create). As long as Attorney's donation, then, is made to Judge's campaign committee, Attorney won't be subject to discipline.

What option D refers to, in an oblique kind of way, is the basis on which lawyers should support candidates for judicial office. Under EC 8–6, lawyers are encouraged to aid in selecting only qualified people for judicial positions. What Attorney's and Judge's long–standing personal and business relationship would provide is experience from which Attorney could determine if Judge is qualified for the bench. The problem with applying this to these facts is that it's far too general; it simply doesn't provide a specific reason for which Attorney's contribution might not be disciplinable (beyond that, since it's only an ethical consideration, failing to follow it would merely be improper; it wouldn't subject Attorney to discipline).

In any case, since option D does not provide a basis on which Attorney can avoid discipline, even though it arrives at the correct result, it's not the best response.

Answer 30

D is the best response, because it recognizes that none of the activities mentioned violates either the rules on advertising or solicitation.

AS TO ALTERNATIVE I:

Alternative I will not subject Alpha to discipline, because it doesn't constitute solicitation, and all its elements are on the list of permissible advertising in the Model Code.

There are two principle issues involved in alternative I: the means of dissemination, which creates a possible solicitation issue, and the content of the flyer itself.

The fact that Alpha is placing the ads in the artists' booths gives rise to a solicitation issue. Solicitation is initiating contact with a potential client for the purpose of being retained for compensation, and, due to the possibility of overreaching, it is *generally* impermissible (although there are significant exceptions, for instance, accepting employment arising from public speaking engagements). The key here is that Alpha isn't engaging in any personal contact with the artists; merely leaving copies of the flyer lying around. Thus there isn't the possibility of overreaching, and the prohibitions against solicitation don't apply.

With the solicitation issue out of the way, let's look at the flyer as advertising. (Note that advertising and solicitation differ in terms of their *audience*—the audience for advertising is general, and for solicitation, it's personal.) The codes differ substantially in their approach to advertising. Under the MR, Rule 7.1, the only advertising that is prohibited is that which is false and misleading. Under the MC, on the other hand, attorneys are told expressly what they may advertise; anything not included is prohibited. Generally speaking, under the MC, a lawyer may advertise virtually everything about fees (although there are format restrictions), and the information about the lawyer himself is limited to "résumé" information (e.g., degrees, awards, bar memberships and posts held, professional licenses, and the like). Because the MC is stricter than the MR, if the information would be permissible under the MC, it would also be permissible under the MR. As to the information in Alpha's flyer, DR 2–101(B) expressly permits information about office address and phone, education and degrees, and limitations on practice. Thus, all the information in Alpha's flyer is permissible. Since alternative I recognizes that the restrictions on dissemination and content are satisfied in these facts, it's correct.

AS TO ALTERNATIVE II:

Alternative II's conduct does not subject Alpha to discipline, since a retainer agreement is a permissible form of advertisement.

The codes differ substantially in their approach to advertising. Under the MR, Rule 7.1, the only advertising that is prohibited is that which is false and misleading. Under the MC, on the other hand, attorneys are told expressly what they may advertise; anything not included is prohibited. Generally speaking, under the MC, a lawyer may advertise virtually everything about fees (although there are format restrictions), and the information about the lawyer himself is limited to "résumé" information (e.g., degrees, awards, bar memberships and posts held, professional licenses, and the like). Because the MC is stricter than the MR, if the information would be permissible under the MC, it would also be permissible under the MR.

The permissibility of including the retainer agreement in the flyer would hinge on whether it complies with the "fee information" restrictions of DR 2–101 (in which all the elements of permissible lawyer advertising are mentioned). While almost any kind of fee information may be included in a lawyer's ad, the thrust of the Model Code restrictions is on disclosure; specifically, it seems as though what the Code authors were concerned about was that lawyers might withhold fee information from their ads, which would make the ads misleading (e.g., stating a fixed fee that in fact only applies to a small percentage of cases). If anything, by including his retainer agreement in his advertising piece, Alpha is fully disclosing his fee arrangement, and in doing so completely satisfies any disclosure requirements of DR 2–101.

While including a retainer agreement in an ad may strike you as kind of crass, it's not impermissible under either code, which means that Alpha won't be subject to discipline for his conduct.

AS TO ALTERNATIVE III:

Alternative III will not subject Alpha to discipline, because the conduct it describes doesn't violate the rules on solicitation.

The key here is that Alpha isn't engaging in any personal contact with the artists; he's simply leaving his van parked at the fair entrance. Thus, as long as Alpha doesn't personally approach any fairgoers, there isn't the possibility of overreaching, and the prohibitions against solicitation don't apply. Since the conduct described doesn't violate the rules on solicitation, Alpha won't be subject to discipline for it.

Answer 31

D is the best response, because it cites a condition which would make Attorney's conduct proper.

The rule is that a lawyer may advise his client to disobey a court order *only* when he has a good–faith belief that no valid obligation exists. DR 7–106(A), EC 7–25, MR 3.4(c). Otherwise, violating such an order will subject the attorney to discipline.

The facts here tell you that Attorney reasonably believes Witness shouldn't answer questions. You're also told that Attorney advised Witness not to answer on grounds that Witness had a constitutional right not to do so. When you compare these facts to the rule, you can see that the only "missing link" is whether or not Attorney had a good–faith belief that Witness's constitutional rights did in fact mean that he need not answer the questions. Simply advising Witness to use his constitutional rights as a shield doesn't necessarily mean that Attorney has a good–faith belief that this is why Witness shouldn't have to answer the questions. Thus, in order to be the best response, D would have to resolve this ambiguity—and it does.

Note that option D uses the modifier "if." Thus, in order to be the best response, the reasoning would have to be plausible under the facts (that is, there can't be anything in the facts to suggest it *couldn't* be true); the reasoning would have to address a central issue; and the result and the reasoning would have to agree. The reasoning is plausible because there's nothing in the facts to suggest that Attorney *lacks* a good–faith belief in the "constitutional rights" argument. Even more importantly, this resolves a central issue by giving Attorney ethical grounds on which to challenge the court order. Finally, as D recognizes, given a good–faith belief that Witness need not answer the questions, Attorney will not be subject to discipline for advising Witness not to answer. As a result, D is the best response.

A is not the best response, because it's not supported by the facts, and even if it was, it doesn't necessarily mean Attorney would be subject to discipline.

Option A uses the modifier "because." This means that A can only be correct if the reasoning addresses and resolves a central issue, the facts in the question completely satisfy the reasoning, and the result is consistent with the reasoning. Option A runs into problems with both of the first two elements. For one thing, the facts don't tell you unequivocally that Attorney's advice is not legally sound. If, in fact, Witness's constitutional rights would protect him from answering the questions, then Attorney's advice is legally sound. You aren't told how valid the argument *is,* but there simply isn't enough in the facts to conclude that it isn't legally sound.

Even if the facts did indicate conclusively that the argument isn't legally sound—namely, that Witness's constitutional rights *don't* give him a basis for refusing to answer the questions—this doesn't necessarily mean that Attorney is subject to discipline. The rule is that a lawyer may advise his client to disobey a court order *only* when he has a good–faith belief that no valid obligation exists. DR 7–106(A), EC 7–25, MR 3.4(c). Note that the actual existence or non–existence of the obligation to comply doesn't matter—*it's whether or not the Attorney has a good faith belief that it doesn't exist.* Thus, even if the argument was not legally sound, if Attorney had a good–faith belief that the argument was sound, he wouldn't be subject to discipline, and *that's* the heart of the question; by not resolving this, option A is avoiding the central issue in the question. As a result, it's not the best response.

B is not the best response, because it mischaracterizes Attorney's advice.

Option B is a *very* attractive distractor, because a casual glance at the facts shows you that Attorney is advising Witness to disobey a court order, which, as the facts tell you, is a crime. Under both the codes, an attorney may not counsel his client in conduct that the attorney knows is illegal or fraudulent. DR 7–102(A)(7), MR 1.2(d). The key fact that makes this inapplicable here is that, if Attorney has a good–faith belief that Witness has no obligation to answer the questions, he may properly advise Witness not to answer. DR 7 106(A), EC 7–25, MR 3.4(c). These two rules aren't contradictory, because if Attorney has a good–faith belief that Witness has no obligation to answer the questions, he isn't advising Witness to do anything illegal! Obviously the linchpin to this argument is the existence of the good–faith belief that Witness' constitutional rights give him a basis for refusing to answer the questions. While the facts don't unequivocally tell you this, they broadly hint at it, by telling you that Attorney reasonably believes it's not in Witness' best interest to answer, and his advice is to back up this argument on constitutional grounds. In order for B to be correct, the facts would have to unequivocally tell you just the opposite—that Attorney was advising Witness to commit a crime. Since B mischaracterizes the facts, it can't be the best response.

C is not the best response, because it's reasoning would not insulate Attorney from discipline.

What option C tells you is that if Attorney counseled Witness to commit an offense other than one involving moral turpitude, he won't be subject to discipline. In fact, this isn't true. Regardless of whether the client's proposed crime involves moral turpitude, the rule is that a lawyer may not counsel his client in conduct that the attorney knows is illegal or fraudulent. DR 7–102(A)(7), MR 1.2(d). Thus, under these facts, if Attorney counseled Witness to commit a crime, he'd be subject to discipline regardless of whether the crime involved moral turpitude or not. (Incidentally, contrary to what C states, there's really no way Witness' offense *could* constitute moral turpitude, since it's fairly obvious from these facts that all he did was refuse to answer questions at the hearing. Without some rather bizarre additional facts, there's no way moral turpitude could come into the picture at all.)

If you chose this response, you were thinking of lawyers disciplined for *their own* misconduct. Specifically, you must have been thinking of DR 1–102(A)(3), which prohibits lawyers from engaging in moral turpitude crimes, since that's the only provision in either code which mentions moral turpitude. (The Model Rules have no such provision, prohibiting only conduct involving dishonesty, fraud, deceit, misrepresentation, or any other conduct reflecting adversely on the attorney's fitness to practice law. MR 8.4. This conduct is also prohibited under DR 1–102.) As you can see, the conduct here isn't Attorney's, but Witness', and thus Attorney's disciplinability will turn on the propriety of his advising Witness to violate a court order and refuse to answer questions. The rule on this is as follows: If Attorney has a good–faith belief that Witness has no obligation to answer the questions, he may properly advise Witness not to answer. DR 7–106(A), EC 7–25, MR 3.4(c). Thus, a correct response to the question would have to address whether or not Attorney had a good–faith belief that Witness' constitutional rights should insulate him from answering the questions, since that's the only ambiguous issue in these facts. Since C doesn't recognize this, it's not the best response.

Answer 32

D is the best response, because it provides a basis on which Attorney can properly disclose the fact that Client left her with the box.

The central issue here is determining whether there are grounds on which Attorney could properly violate his duty of confidentiality toward Client.

Note as a preliminary matter that Client's information is subject to the duty of confidentiality. The coverage differs somewhat between the two codes. Under the MC, a lawyer must not knowingly reveal a confidence or secret of his client gained in the professional relationship. A confidence is any communication protected by the attorney/client testimonial privilege; a secret is anything that the client requests be confidential, or whose disclosure would be embarrassing or detrimental to the client. DR 4–1Ol(A). Under the MR, the lawyer must not reveal "information relating to representation of a client" without the client's express or implied authorization. MR 1.6. Under these facts, the information about Client's box would qualify under both codes. Under the MC, it's a secret, because Client asked Attorney not to disclose it, and under the MR it's protectable because it relates to the representation.

Since the information is protected as confidential under both codes, in order for Attorney to escape discipline for disclosing it, there must be an *exception* to the duty of confidentiality that applies to these facts. Under both codes, DR 4–1Ol(C)(4) and MR 1.6(b)(2), a lawyer may disclose confidential information to the extent reasonably necessary to establish a defense to a criminal charge or civil claim against the lawyer based on conduct involving the client (note, in fact, that such disclosure is permissible *whenever* the lawyer's reputation is attacked, whether or not a lawsuit or criminal charge is launched against him). Here, Attorney is being charged with receiving stolen property. His defense must include the fact that he got the jewelry box from Client, in order to exonerate himself. As a result, Attorney's self–interest allows him to disclose the information, *to the extent necessary,* even though it is confidential.

Incidentally, note that the modifier in option D is "if." This means that the reasoning must be plausible under the facts, it must resolve a central issue, and the result and reasoning must agree. Here, it's extremely likely that Attorney will have to disclose where he got the box in order to defend himself. This resolves a central issue by providing Attorney with an exception to the confidentiality rules. Finally, as D states, this means that Attorney won't be subject to discipline for disclosing the source of the box. As a result, D is the best response.

A is not the best response, because it doesn't take into account a likely reason why Attorney should be able to disclose the information and avoid discipline.

What option A does correctly is to establish that Client's information is covered by the duty of confidentiality, under both codes. Specifically, A establishes that the information is protectable as a "secret" under the Model Code, since secrets include anything that the client requests be confidential, or whose disclosure would be embarrassing or detrimental to the client. DR 4–101(A). By stating that Client instructed Attorney not to tell anyone about the jewelry box, the information fits this description. (Note that the Model Rules would also protect the information, since Rule 1.6 protects all "information relating to representation of a client".)

If you chose this response, you overlooked the fact that Attorney will be able to disclose the information because it fits an *exception* to the rules against disclosure—namely, Attorney's defense. Under both codes, DR 4–101(C)(4) and MR 1.6(b)(2), a lawyer may disclose confidential information to the extent reasonably necessary to establish a defense to a criminal charge or civil claim against the lawyer based on conduct involving the client (note, in fact, that such disclosure is permissible *whenever* the lawyer's reputation is attacked, whether or not a lawsuit or criminal charge is launched against him). It's hard to imagine Attorney's being able to conduct his defense to the "receiving stolen goods" charges *without* disclosing that he got the box from Client.

Note that option A uses the modifier "because." This would have to mean that the fact that Client told Attorney not to rat about the box *necessarily* means that Attorney would be subject to discipline for disclosing the information. The existence of the defense exception means Attorney isn't necessarily subject to discipline, and since option A doesn't realize this, it's not the best response.

B is not the best response, because it doesn't recognize a likely reason why Attorney will avoid discipline, and it states as conditional a fact that is certain from the facts—namely, that disclosing the information will be detrimental to Client.

What option B does correctly is to establish that Client's information is covered by the duty of confidentiality, under both codes. Specifically, B establishes that the information is protectable as a "secret" under the Model Code, since secrets include anything that the client requests be confidential, or whose disclosure would be embarrassing or detrimental to the client. DR 4–l0l(A). By conditioning Attorney's discipline on whether the disclosure is detrimental to Client's interests, B suggests that the information is subject to the duty of disclosure. (Note that the Model Rules would also protect the information, since Rule 1.6 protects all "information relating to representation of a client.")

There are a couple of problems with this characterization. Most importantly, it ignores the fact that even if the information is protected, Attorney will nonetheless be able to disclose it to the extent necessary for his defense. Under both codes, DR 4–101(C)(4) and MR 1.6(b)(2), a lawyer may disclose confidential information to the extent reasonably necessary to establish a defense to a criminal charge or civil claim against the lawyer based on conduct involving the client (note, in fact, that such disclosure is permissible *whenever* the lawyer's reputation is attacked, whether or not a lawsuit or criminal charge is launched against him). Thus, even if disclosure would be detrimental to Client's interests, disclosing it wouldn't necessarily subject Attorney to discipline, contrary to what option B states.

The other problem with option B, which is minor by comparison, is that by using the modifier "if," it suggests that there's a question as to whether or not the disclosure would be detrimental to client's interests. If you look at the facts you can see that there's no way the disclosure *couldn't* be detrimental to Client; he dumped a "hot" antique jewel box on his lawyer. Thus, "if" isn't an appropriate modifier—"because" would have been.

In any case, the main problem with option B is that it ignores the "defense" exception to the duty of confidentiality, making B not the best response.

Option C is not the best response, because whether or not the jewelry box is involved in the dispute between Partner and Client is irrelevant to whether Attorney may properly disclose the fact that Client gave him the jewelry box.

What option C suggests is that the information from Client is not subject to the duty of confidentiality, and so Attorney is free to disclose where he got the jewelry box. The problem with this is that the information is protected by the duty of confidentiality. Under the MC, a lawyer must not knowingly reveal a confidence or secret of his client gained in the professional relationship. A confidence is any communication protected by the attorney/client testimonial privilege; a secret is anything that the client requests be confidential, or whose disclosure would be embarrassing or detrimental to the client. DR 4–lOl(A). Under the MR, the lawyer must not reveal "information relating to representation of a client" without the client's express or implied authorization. MR 1.6. Contrary to what C states, the information would be protected under both codes. Under the Model Code, it would be protected as a "secret," since Attorney learned it during the relationship, and Client asked him to keep it under his hat. Under the Model Rules, the information would "relate to the representation," because Client gave it to Attorney to keep it out of the property dispute with Partner (in fact, this "relate to the representation" scope cuts a very broad swath under the Model Rules). As a result, the information is confidential, and therefore in order to avoid discipline for disclosing it, it would have to fit an exception to the confidentiality rules. Although C overlooks it, the information fits the "defense" exception to confidentiality. Under both codes, DR 4–lOl(C)(4) and MR 1.6(b)(2), a lawyer may disclose confidential information to the extent reasonably necessary to establish a defense to a criminal charge or civil claim against the lawyer based on conduct involving the client (note, in fact, that such disclosure is permissible *whenever* the lawyer's reputation is attacked, whether or not a lawsuit or criminal charge is launched against him). This is the real reason Attorney will avoid discipline. Thus, even though option C arrives at the correct result, because its reasoning misses the mark, it's not the best response.

Answer 33

C is the best response, because it correctly characterizes Alpha's proposed representation as an impermissible conflict of interest.

As a general rule, a lawyer may not take on or continue representing a client if either doing so will be directly adverse to another client, or the representation may be materially limited by the lawyer's duties to someone else. MR 1.7, DR 5–105(A), (B). Option C focuses on a particularly sneaky facet of this rule, as it relates to current clients; namely, a lawyer may not represent one client against another, current client *even in a totally unrelated case.* That's what's going on here. Even though you're only representing Builder on the contract issue, you can't take *any* position against him, even on something totally unrelated to the contract problem—including the zoning case. As you can see, the rule on this is pretty straightforward, and perhaps the only thing that makes it tricky is that it's counterintuitive.

Incidentally, keep in mind that this only applies to *current* clients, not former ones. The lawyer's duty of loyalty to former clients only means he cannot represent another client in the same or a substantially related matter as a former client when that client's interests are materially adverse to the former client's interests. MR 1.9(a). Thus, under these facts, if Builder had been a former client, representing Neighbor would be perfectly proper. However, since he's a current client, Alpha can't represent anyone against him on any matter, and since C recognizes this, it's the best response.

A is not the best response, because Alpha can't represent anyone against Builder *regardless* of how unrelated the two matters are.

As a general rule, a lawyer may not take on or continue representing a client if either doing so will be directly adverse to another client, or the representation may be materially limited by the lawyer's duties to someone else. MR 1.7, DR 5–105(A), (B). As it applies to *current* clients (like Builder), this prohibits a lawyer from representing a client (Neighbor) against a current client *even in a totally unrelated case.* Thus, even if—as is the case here—the two matters are totally unrelated, the new representation will still be prohibited.

If you chose this response, you may have been relying on your intuition, which would tell you that Alpha could probably represent both Builder and Neighbor adequately. That's what makes A a good distractor; it seems as though it ought to be correct, but in fact it doesn't represent the actual rule. Alternatively, you may have been thinking of the duty of loyalty to former clients, not current ones, under which a lawyer cannot represent another client in the same or a substantially related matter as a former client when that client's interests are materially adverse to the former client's interests. MR 1.9(a). If Builder had in fact been a former client of Alpha, this would be correct, but the first line of the facts tell you he's a *current* client. Finally, you may have chosen A because the wording in the reasoning seemed familiar. If so, you're probably remembering the language from the rules on joinder of claims in Civil Procedure; as the rule above indicates, the ethics rules refer to the same or a substantially related matter, *not* common issues of law or fact.

In any case, since A doesn't recognize that the representation is prohibited even thought the positions are unrelated, it's not the best response.

B is not the best response, because its reasoning doesn't determine the propriety of Alpha's dual representation, and it arrives at the wrong result.

If you chose this response, you were probably thinking of the rule on representing clients with conflicting legal positions. As a general rule, a lawyer may take on a new client whose legal position would be directly opposite to that of an existing client. However, a lawyer may not assert a position on one client's behalf if success would be detrimental to another client. That's what option B is getting at; what it's suggesting is that since one case is judicial and the other administrative, your arguments on behalf of one can't be detrimental to the other. However, it's not the legal argument that you make for either Builder or Neighbor that's at issue here, since the breach of contract action and the zoning action couldn't have any adverse effect on each other, but rather the impact representing Neighbor would have on your duty of loyalty. As a general rule, a lawyer may not take on or continue representing a client if doing so either will be directly adverse to another client, or the representation may be materially limited by the lawyer's duties to someone else. MR 1.7, DR 5–105(A), (B). As it applies to *current* clients (like Builder), this prohibits a lawyer from representing a client (Neighbor) against a current client *even in a totally unrelated case.* Thus, even if—as is the case here—the two matters are totally unrelated and appear in different kinds of proceedings, the new representation will still be prohibited. Since B doesn't recognize this, it's not the best response.

Option D is not the best response, because whether or not the cases are appealable to the same court does not determine whether there's an impermissible conflict of interest in these facts.

If you chose this response, you were probably thinking of the rule on representing clients with conflicting legal positions. As a general rule, a lawyer may take on a new client whose legal position would be directly opposite that of an existing client. However, a lawyer may not assert a position on one client's behalf if success would be detrimental to another client. If the two cases here were appealable to the same court, and the legal position Alpha had to take in favor of one would adversely impact the legal position of the other, he'd have an impermissible conflict of interest. However, this isn't applicable here; it's not the legal positions that are at issue, but rather Alpha's duty of loyalty to Builder, his current client. Beyond *that*, the legal positions Alpha would have to take on each client's behalf

aren't contradictory, since the positions have no relationship whatsoever—
one is a breach of contract case, and the other concerns zoning.

As to the duty of loyalty, the general rule is that a lawyer may not take on
or continue representing a client if doing so either will be directly adverse
to another client, or the representation may be materially limited by the
lawyer's duties to someone else. MR 1.7, DR 5–105(A), (B). As it applies
to *current* clients (like Builder), this prohibits a lawyer from representing
a client (Neighbor) against a current client *even in a totally unrelated case.*
Thus, regardless of whether the cases are appealable to the same court, the
fact that representing Neighbor would require Alpha to oppose Builder
makes representing Neighbor impermissible. Since option D doesn't recognize this, it's not the best response.

Answer 34

A is the best response, because it recognizes that Attorney's failure to interview Wit constitutes incompetence.

A lawyer has a duty to provide competent service. There are three general
ways an attorney can be incompetent: he can lack sufficient knowledge
and skill to handle the matter; he can fail to prepare adequately in carrying
out the representation; and he can neglect his duties to the client (including
a failure to communicate with the client, or procrastination). DR 5–101,
MR 1.1, 1.3. The problem in these facts is with the second element: preparation. A lawyer preparing for a trial must, among other things, undertake
any necessary legal research, prepare whatever motions or requests for instructions are necessary, review any relevant documents, and investigate
relevant factual issues, which would include interviewing witnesses. Here,
Attorney failed to interview the only witness, a failure which is compound-
ed by the fact that Wit's testimony would have helped Plaintiff. As a result,
Attorney didn't prepare adequately, and he'll be subject to discipline for
incompetence. DR 6–101(A)(2), MR 1.1.

Perhaps the only fact that makes this question tricky is that Attorney believed Plaintiff's testimony alone would be persuasive, and that Wit's testimony wouldn't be necessary. In many areas of legal ethics, the lawyer's
beliefs can save him from discipline; however, competence isn't one of
them. It must be a reasonable professional judgment that motivates the
lawyer to make a decision on what preparation must be done; an *unreasonable* belief won't make proper otherwise incompetent work.

Incidentally, you may have noticed that Attorney will also be liable to Plaintiff for malpractice based on negligence. The rule is that the lawyer must exercise the skill, prudence, diligence, and knowledge possessed by general practitioners of ordinary skill, experience, and capacity who perform similar services in the same (or a similar community). If a failure to live up to this standard results in damages to a client (or an intended beneficiary of the lawyer's services), the lawyer is subject to liability for malpractice based on negligence. Here, Attorney's negligent failure to interview Wit made Plaintiff lose the case, and thus Attorney will be liable for malpractice.

In any case, since option A correctly recognizes that Attorney's representation was incompetent, it's the best response.

B is not the best response, because Wit's availability for subpoena does not change the incompetent nature of Attorney's trial preparation.

A lawyer has a duty to provide competent service. There are three general ways an attorney can be incompetent: he can lack sufficient knowledge and skill to handle the matter; he can fail to prepare adequately in carrying out the representation; and he can neglect his duties to the client (including a failure to communicate with the client, or procrastination). DR 6–101, MR 1.1,1.3. The problem in these facts is with the second element: preparation. A lawyer preparing for a trial must, among other things, undertake any necessary legal research, prepare whatever motions or requests for instructions are necessary, review any relevant documents, and investigate relevant factual issues, which would include interviewing witnesses. Thus, the problem with Attorney's preparation under these facts is that he chose *not to investigate* Wit at all, and *this* is what makes Attorney's work incompetent; whether or not Wit can be subpoenaed has no impact on this at all. Since option B mistakenly conditions Attorney's discipline on Wit's being subject to subpoena, it's not the best response.

C is not the best response, because the mere fact that the highway patrol records disclose the *existence* of a witness is enough to subject Attorney to discipline for failing to interview Wit.

A lawyer has a duty to provide competent service. There are three general ways an attorney can be incompetent: he can lack sufficient knowledge and skill to handle the matter; he can fail to prepare adequately in carrying out the representation; and he can neglect his duties to the client (including a failure to communicate with the client, or procrastination). DR 6–101,

MR 1.1, 1.3. In preparing for trial, a lawyer must, among other things, investigate relevant factual issues, which would include interviewing witnesses. Under these facts, Attorney learns from the highway patrol records that there is *only one* disinterested witness, Wit. Regardless of what Wit would say, Attorney's duty of competence to Plaintiff would demand that Attorney interview Wit, and if his testimony is favorable, call him as a witness, and if it isn't, come up with some means of attacking it. Thus, the fact that Attorney doesn't know the substance of Wit's testimony from the highway patrol records doesn't remove his duty to interview him. Since option C doesn't recognize this, it's not the best response.

D is not the best response, because it mischaracterizes the facts, and, beyond that, Attorney's belief alone would not be sufficient to exonerate him from discipline.

First, let's look at how D misstates the facts. By using the modifier "if," D tells you that Attorney's belief that Plaintiff's testimony would suffice must be *plausible* under the facts. While this normally means that there can't be anything indicating it can't be true, the converse is also required; that is, the facts *can't* indicate that the reasoning is *unequivocal*. Instead, it must be simply *plausible*. The problem is that there's absolutely no question that Attorney believes that Plaintiff's testimony would suffice, because the facts tell you expressly that "Attorney believed that Plaintiff's testimony would be persuasive." Because this appears plainly in the facts, it can't be considered conditional.

Even if D did correctly characterize the facts, it couldn't be the best response, because Attorney's belief would not be sufficient to insulate him from discipline. It's understandable if you chose this response, because in many areas of legal ethics, the lawyer's beliefs can save him from discipline; however, competence isn't one of them. It must be a reasonable professional judgment that motivates the lawyer to make a decision on what preparation must be done; an *unreasonable* belief won't make proper otherwise incompetent work. Under these facts, it's unreasonable for Attorney not to interview Wit, especially in light of the fact that he's the only witness to the accident. Without Wit, it's a coin–toss as to whether the jury will believe Plaintiff or Defendant, and that makes it unreasonable for Attorney to rely on Plaintiff's testimony alone. Since option D doesn't recognize that Attorney's conduct was incompetent regardless of his faith in Plaintiff's testimony, it's not the best response.

Answer 35

C is the best response, because it correctly recognizes that it's the client's decision whether or not to accept settlement offers.

The rule is that the client has the right to make major decisions about the representation. EC 7–7, 7–8, MR 1.2(a). This includes the right to accept or reject offers of settlement by the other party. What this means is that the attorney has a duty to tell the client about settlement offers, and abide by the client's decision on them. A failure to do so is improper under the Model Code, and disciplinable under the Model Rules. (The attorney makes decisions about strategy, that is, implementing his client's goals.)

The fact that throws a wrench into the works is the waiver in the retainer agreement. This is particularly tricky because, under the MR, at least, the client *can* authorize the lawyer to reject offers below a set amount without consulting the client. MR 1.4, Comment. However, this is really only a form of antecedent decision–making on the client's part, and doesn't change the fact that accepting or rejecting a settlement is part of the client's decision–making power. What makes the agreement here different is that Attorney is forcing Client to give up his decision–making authority *all together*. What also makes this deceptive is that there are many areas in legal ethics where a client's consent can make otherwise–improper conduct proper, conflict of interest being the most common area where a client can normally consent to an otherwise improper conflict. In any case, since option C correctly recognizes that Attorney's conduct improperly strips Client of his decision–making authority over settlements, it's the best response.

A is not the best response, because Client's consent can't validate Attorney's conduct under these facts.

The rule is that the client has the right to make major decisions about the representation. EC 7–7, 7–8, MR 1.2(a). This includes the right to accept or reject offers of settlement by the other party. What this means is that the attorney has a duty to tell the client about settlement offers, and abide by the client's decision on them. A failure to do so is improper under the Model Code, and disciplinable under the Model Rules. (The attorney makes decisions about strategy, that is, implementing his client's goals.)

What makes option A so tricky is that, to a certain extent, a client *may* properly cede his decision making authority, at least when it comes to settlement offers, to his attorney. Under the MR, at least, the client *can* authorize the lawyer to reject offers below a set amount without consulting the client. MR 1.4, Comment. However, this is really only a form of antecedent decision–making on the client's part, and doesn't make it possible for a client to waive his decision–making authority on settlements offers *in total,* which is what's going on here. What makes option A even trickier is that there *are* many areas in legal ethics where a client's consent can make otherwise–improper conduct proper. For instance, in most cases a client can OK an otherwise–impermissible conflict of interest. What all this adds up to is that it's entirely understandable why you chose option A, even though it's not the best response.

B is not the best response, because Attorney's skill at evaluating settlement offers does not make the decision hers and not Client's.

The rule is that the client has the right to make major decisions about the representation. EC 7–7, 7–8, MR 1.2(a). This includes the right to accept or reject offers of settlement by the other party. What this means is that the attorney has a duty to tell the client about settlement offers, and abide by the client's decision on them. A failure to do so is improper under the Model Code, and disciplinable under the Model Rules. (The attorney makes decisions about strategy, that is, implementing his client's goals.) Of course, Attorney's evaluation skills would come into play in Client's decision, in the sense that it's Attorney's duty to advise Client as to the benefits and detriments of any given settlement offer, and his opinion as to whether or not Client should accept it. Nonetheless, this doesn't change the fact that the ultimate decision as to whether to accept the offer is Client's, not Attorney's. Since option B doesn't recognize this, it's not the best response.

D is not the best response, because the method of payment doesn't determine who makes the decision on whether to accept settlement offers.

The rule is that the client has the right to make major decisions about the representation. EC 7–7, 7–8, MR 1.2(a). This includes the right to accept or reject offers of settlement by the other party. What this means is that the attorney has a duty to tell the client about settlement offers, and abide by the client's decision on them. A failure to do so is improper under the Model Code, and disciplinable under the Model Rules. (The attorney makes decisions about strategy, that is, implementing his client's goals.) Thus, regardless of whether Attorney is paid on a fixed, contingent or hourly basis, the right to accept settlement offers belongs to Client.

If you chose this response, you probably put a lot more thought into this question than most people, in that you might have been thinking about *why* the attorney oughtn't to be able to accept settlement offers. If an attorney is to be paid on a contingent fee, he'll be likely to put his own interest in hauling in a bundle of loot over the interests of his client, and hold out for a larger settlement, or force a trial, based on his own interests. On a fixed or hourly basis, the motivation to subvert his client's interests would be far less. While this is sound thinking, the rule remains that regardless of the fee basis, the attorney doesn't have the right to accept or reject settlement offers. Since D doesn't recognize this, it's not the best response.

Answer 36

B is the best response, because it identifies the central problem with the firm name: It includes Gamma's name.

As a general rule, the name of a law firm cannot be misleading. There are two separate issues in this particular problem: One, whether Beta's name may be included after his death, and two, whether Gamma's name may be included based on the arrangement between him and Alpha. Option B resolves the Beta issue correctly, because it doesn't mention Beta's inclusion in the name as being grounds for discipline. The rule is that when a lawyer dies or retires, the firm may go on using his name. DR 2-102(B), MR 7.5, Comment. The rationale for this is that it's important to be able to identify the law firm by the name it's been using, and this outweighs the danger of the name's being misleading. Thus, including Beta's name in the firm name is proper.

As option B recognizes, what makes Alpha disciplinable is the fact that he and Gamma are not, in fact, partners. The rule is that lawyers can't hold themselves out as partners if they aren't. Partners must have an agreement detailing their rights and responsibilities, and part of this must be to share each other's liabilities and responsibilities. DR 2–102(C), MR 7.5(d). Under these facts, you don't have a partnership; instead, you have an office–sharing arrangement. Since this makes Alpha subject to discipline, and B recognizes this, it's the best response.

A is not the best response, because it's not Beta's presence in the firm name that subjects Alpha to discipline, but *Gamma's.*

As a general rule, the name of a law firm cannot be misleading. If you chose this response, it could be because you were thinking of this rule, and figured that a firm name that includes a dead person would be misleading. It's not bad thinking, but the rule is that when a lawyer dies or retires, the firm may go on using his name. DR 2–102(B), MR 7.5, Comment. The rationale for this is that the importance of being able to identify the law firm by a name it's been using outweighs the danger of the name's being misleading. Thus, including Beta's name doesn't make the firm name impermissible. Instead, it's Gamma's name that raises problems, since he and Alpha aren't really partners; they just share offices. The rule is that it's impermissible for lawyers to hold themselves out as—i.e., call themselves— partners if they aren't, in fact, partners. DR 2–102(C), MR 7.5(d). *This* is what makes Alpha subject to discipline. Although option A comes to the right result, since it attributes Alpha's disciplinability to Beta's name and not Gamma's name in the firm name, it's not the best response.

C is not the best response, because it ignores the central issue—namely, that Gamma's name cannot appear in the firm name—and arrives at the wrong conclusion as a result.

Option C correctly identifies that Beta's name may properly appear in the firm name. The rule is that when a lawyer dies or retires, the firm may go on using his name. DR 2–102(B), MR 7.5, Comment. Thus, as long as Beta was a member of the firm when he died or retired, use of his name will be proper—and C correctly recognizes this. However, option C takes for granted that the use of Gamma's name is proper, and *that's* where the problem is. The rule is that lawyers who are not partners may not hold themselves out as partners. DR 2–102(C), MR 7.5(d). By using their names in the same law firm name, Alpha and Gamma are holding themselves out as partners. This makes the firm name impermissible, and since C overlooks this, it's not the best response.

D is not the best response, because what Gamma's doing doesn't provide a basis for including his name in the law firm name.

The rule is that lawyers who are not partners may not hold themselves out as partners. DR 2–102(C), MR 7.5(d). Partners must have an agreement detailing their rights and responsibilities, and part of this must be to share each others' liabilities and responsibilities. What you have here, instead, is an office–sharing arrangement. Neither code prohibits such arrangements, as long as, among other things, care is taken to ensure the confidentiality of each attorney's clients, and the attorneys don't claim to be partners. By putting themselves together under a common name, Alpha and Gamma are holding themselves out as partners. Since D mistakenly states that an of-fice–sharing arrangement is a valid basis on which to use a common firm name, it's not the best response.

Answer 37

B is the best response, because it correctly identifies that Attorney's role in the matter on behalf of the government prohibits her from representing Deftco.

The problem here is a conflict of interest, specifically as it relates to law-yers moving from government work to private practice. The rule is that a former government lawyer is prohibited from representing a private client in a matter in which he participated personally and substantially while working for the government, without consent from the appropriate govern-mental agency. MR 1.11(a); DR 9–101(B) is interpreted similarly. Here, you're told that Attorney was very involved with the Deftco case as a gov-ernment lawyer; thus, option B hits the nail on the head when it identifies this as the central reason Attorney can't represent Deftco after leaving the government.

What makes option B a little tricky is that Attorney is representing Deftco, not the landowners. Your gut feeling might be that since Attorney was act-ing adversely to Deftco when she worked for the government, and now she'll be working on Deftco's behalf against the landowners (as to whom Attorney has no confidential information), there's really no problem be-cause Attorney won't be using information *about* Deftco *against* Deftco. However, what this ignores is that part of the rationale for restricting former government lawyers is the concern that a private client could enjoy an unfair advantage due to access to confidential government information, obtainable only from a prior government lawyer; furthermore, there's the belief that a lawyer shouldn't be in a position where the anticipation of benefits to private clients might affect a lawyer's performance for the gov-ernment. As a result, the "personal and substantial" participation is enough to prohibit Attorney from representing Deftco, regardless of the position she took on the government's behalf. Since option B recognizes this, it's the best response.

A is not the best response, because Attorney will be subject to discipline for representing Deftco regardless of whether the prior judgment deter-mines Deftco's liability.

Note that because option A uses the modifier "unless," this must mean that the reasoning is the only way the result could not occur. As a result, in order for option A to be correct, the following statement would have to be true: "Attorney will not be subject to discipline for representing Deftco if the judgment in the prior case is determinative of Deftco's liability." This isn't true; the rule is that a former government lawyer is prohibited from representing a private client in a matter in which he participated personally and substantially while working for the government, without consent from the appropriate governmental agency. MR 1.ll(a); DR. 9–lOl(B) is interpreted similarly. Here, you're told that Attorney was very involved with the Deftco case as a government lawyer; thus, Attorney can't represent Deftco after leaving the government, *regardless* of whether the prior case determines Deftco's liability. Since A doesn't recognize this, it's not the best response.

C is not the best response, because Attorney's competence in the matter won't make the representation proper.

What option C does is to ignore the central issue here—namely, a conflict of interest due to Attorney's move from the government to the private sector. The rule is that a former government lawyer is prohibited from representing a private client in a matter in which he participated personally and substantially while working for the government, without consent from the appropriate governmental agency. MR 1.ll(a); DR 9–lOl(B) is interpreted similarly. Under these facts, it's made pretty plain that Attorney was heavily involved in a matter on behalf of the government, and so she cannot represent Deftco in the same matter after leaving the government.

If you chose this response, you were focusing on one of the competing policies that went into creating the restrictions on former government employers. Namely, a government lawyer shouldn't face restrictions in his future employment so stiff as to act as a deterrent against entering public service. MR 1.11, Comment. However, on the other side is the government's concern that the power or discretion vested in public authority might be used for the special benefit of a private client, and that a lawyer shouldn't be in a position where the anticipation of benefits to private clients might affect a lawyer's performance for the government. Thus, *some* restrictions on future employment of government attorneys is appropriate, and since C doesn't recognize this, it's not the best response.

D is not the best response, because Attorney cannot represent Deftco *regardless* of whether the information is public or not.

D implicitly recognizes that the central issue here is a conflict of interest, due to Attorney's move from government work to private practice. That's because one of the two duties underlying conflict of interest rules is confidentiality (the other is loyalty). However, if you chose this, you weren't thinking of confidentiality as it relates to conflict of interest—in that a lawyer can't take on a client if doing so would require that he disclose another client's confidences—but rather as it relates to disclosure of a client's secrets. As to *former* clients, an attorney's duty of confidentiality is lifted as to matters that are now "publicly" known. If you chose this response because of its "matter of public record" language, this is the rule you were thinking of. The problem is that this doesn't resolve the conflict of interest in this problem, which doesn't depend on confidential information. Instead, the rule is that a former government lawyer is prohibited from representing a private client in a matter in which he participated personally and substantially while working for the government, without consent from the appropriate governmental agency. MR 1.ll(a); DR 9–lOl(B) is interpreted similarly. Under these facts, it's made pretty plain that Attorney was heavily involved in a matter on behalf of the government, and so she cannot represent Deftco in the same matter after leaving the government.

Of course, part of the *rationale* for the restriction on former government lawyers is to prevent the improper use of confidences gained while the lawyer worked on behalf of the government. If that were the only concern, then the fact that all the information became public thereafter should remove the restriction. However, it's not the only concern; the other part of the rationale is the belief that a lawyer shouldn't be in a position where the anticipation of benefits to private clients might affect a lawyer's performance on behalf of the government. As a result, the mere fact that all Attorney's information on the matter has since become public does not make representing Deftco proper. Since option D doesn't recognize this, it's not the best response.

Answer 38

C is the best response, because it recognizes that the problem with the Alpha–Beta arrangement is the lack of consent from Plaintiff.

The central issue under these facts is two-pronged: whether or not the fee–splitting arrangement is proper, and whether the association with Beta is proper. In fact, the missing element from *both* of these, as option C indicates, is the lack of consent from Plaintiff.

As a threshold issue, associating with Beta was one of three appropriate courses of action for Alpha when he realized he was in over his head in representing Plaintiff. A lawyer has a duty to represent his clients competently. If, after undertaking a client, the lawyer realizes he's not competent to handle the matter, he has three choices: one, withdraw, DR 6–101(A), DR 2–110(B)(2), EC 6–3, MR 1.1 and 1.16(a)(1); two, undertake the work or study necessary to gain competence in the matter, EC 6–3, 6–4, MR 1.1, as long as this doesn't result in unreasonable expense or delay and the lawyer in fact becomes competent; or three, associate with a lawyer competent in the matter, *with the client's consent.* DR 6–101(A)(1), MR 1.1. The problem here is that Alpha didn't seek Plaintiff's consent before associating with Beta, and by disclosing Plaintiff's confidential information to Beta, Alpha violated his duty of confidentiality to Plaintiff.

As to the fee–splitting, the problem there, too, is the lack of consent from Plaintiff. The standards under the two codes differ slightly. Under the Model Code, the client must consent to the arrangement, the fee must be reasonable, and the division must reflect the services performed and responsibilities assumed by each lawyer. DR 2–107. The Model Rules don't require the last element; as long as the lawyers assume joint responsibility for the work, the fee is reasonable, and the client consents, it doesn't matter who actually did the work (although if the fee division isn't proportional to the work performed, the client's consent must be in writing). MR 1.5(e). Thus, *both* codes require client consent, which is lacking under these facts.

Since option C recognizes that the lack of consent invalidates both the association and fee–splitting aspects of the Alpha–Beta arrangement, it's the best response.

A is not the best response, because the fact that the fee to Plaintiff didn't increase doesn't make the arrangement proper.

Option A focuses on one of the elements necessary for a valid fee–splitting arrangement between lawyers; namely, the fee must be reasonable. DR 2-107, MR 1.5(e) (note that this means that even an increase may be permissible, as long as the fee would still be reasonable.) However, what option A ignores is that Plaintiff's *consent* is necessary both for the fee-splitting and for Alpha's associating with Beta in the first place. Let's look at each of these problems—the association and the fee–splitting—separately.

Under these facts, you learn that Alpha didn't think he could competently represent Plaintiff in every aspect of the representation. One of the courses of conduct proper under such circumstances is to associate with a lawyer competent in the matter, *with the client's consent.* DR 6–101(A)(1), MR 1.1 (the other proper courses are to withdraw, or study to become competent in the matter, at no unreasonable expense or delay to the client). What's missing here is Plaintiff's consent, and on this issue alone, Alpha's conduct was improper. Even if that *had* been proper, the fee–splitting arrangement would have submarined Alpha. The rules differ slightly between the codes, although consent is necessary for each of them. Under the MC, the client must consent to a fee–splitting arrangement, the fee must be reasonable, and the division must reflect the services performed and responsibilities assumed by each lawyer. DR 2–107. The MR don't require the last element; provided that the lawyers assume joint responsibility for the work, the fee is reasonable, and the client consents, it doesn't matter who actually did the work. MR 1.5(e). Thus, under *both* codes, what's missing in these facts is Plaintiff's consent. As a result, the fact that the fee itself is the same for both lawyers as it would have been for Alpha alone does not validate Alpha's conduct. Since option A doesn't recognize this, it's not the best response.

B is not the best response, because it ignores the fact that Plaintiff's lack of consent to the arrangement makes it improper.

Option B focuses on one of the elements necessary for a valid fee–splitting arrangement between lawyers, under the Model Code; namely, the fee must be divided in proportion to the services performed and the responsibilities assumed by each. DR 2–107 (this element is *not* required by the Model Rules, although if the fee division isn't proportional to the work performed by each lawyer, the client's consent to the arrangement must be in writing. MR 1.5(e)). However, what option B ignores is that Plaintiff's *consent* is necessary both for the fee–splitting and for Alpha's associating with Beta in the first place. Let's look at each of these problems—the association and the fee-splitting—separately.

Under these facts, you learn that Alpha didn't think he could competently represent Plaintiff in every aspect of the representation. One of the courses of conduct proper under such circumstances is to associate with a lawyer competent in the matter, *with the client's consent.* DR 6–101(A)(1), MR 1.1 (the other proper courses are to withdraw, or study to become competent in the matter, at no unreasonable expense or delay to the client).

What's missing here is Plaintiff's consent, and on this issue alone, Alpha's conduct was improper. Even if that *had* been proper, the fee–splitting arrangement would have submarined Alpha. The rules differ slightly between the codes, although consent is necessary for each of them. Under the MC, the client must consent to a fee–splitting arrangement, the fee must be reasonable, and the division must reflect the services performed and responsibilities assumed by each lawyer. DR 2–107. The MR don't require the last element; provided that the lawyers assume joint responsibility for the work, the fee is reasonable, and the client consents, it doesn't matter who actually did the work. MR 1.5(e). Thus, under *both* codes, what's missing in these facts is Plaintiff's consent. As a result, the fact that the fee is to be divided in proportion to the services performed and responsibilities assumed by each lawyer does not validate Alpha's conduct. Since option A doesn't recognize this, it's not the best response.

D isn't the best response, because the conduct it suggests won't make Alpha's conduct proper; instead, the problem with the Alpha–Beta arrangement is the lack of consent from Plaintiff.

If you chose option D, you were thinking of a requirement for contingent fee agreements under the Model Rules. Specifically, for a contingent fee agreement to be proper, it must have the following elements under the Model Rules: 1. it must be in writing; 2. the writing must state how the fee is determined (percentage to accrue in event of trial, appeal, settlement, what expenses will be deducted from recovery, and whether deductions occur before or after percentage is determined); and 3. after the matter is concluded, lawyer must provide a written statement of the outcome of the matter, and if there's recovery, he must show remittance to client and how it was determined. MR 1.5(c). As you can see, option D mirrors the third requirement. However, it doesn't apply to the facts here, where the propriety of Alpha's conduct hinges on whether it was proper to associate with Beta in the first place, and, if so, whether the fee–splitting deal is proper. In fact, the element that torpedoes both of these is the lack of consent from Plaintiff. Let's look at the association element first.

Under these facts, you learn that Alpha didn't think he could competently represent Plaintiff in every aspect of the representation. One of the courses of conduct proper under such circumstances is to associate with a lawyer competent in the matter, with the client's consent. DR 6–101(A)(1), MR 1.1 (the other proper courses are to withdraw, or study to become competent in the matter, at no unreasonable expense or delay to the client). What's missing here is Plaintiff's consent, and on this issue alone, Alpha's conduct was improper, since by disclosing Plaintiff's confidential information to Beta without Plaintiff's consent, Alpha violated his duty of confidentiality to Plaintiff. Even if that *had* been proper, the fee–splitting arrangement would have submarined Alpha. The rules differ slightly between the codes, although consent is necessary for each of them. Under the MC, the client must consent to a fee–splitting arrangement, the fee must be reasonable, and the division must reflect the services performed and responsibilities assumed by each lawyer. DR 2–107. The MR don't require the last element; provided that the lawyers assume joint responsibility for the work, the fee is reasonable, and the client consents, it doesn't matter who actually did the work. MR 1.5(e). Thus, under *both* codes, what's missing in these facts is Plaintiff's consent.

As to the fee–splitting deal, the problem there, too, is the lack of consent from Plaintiff. The standards under the two codes differ slightly. Under the Model Code, the client must consent to the arrangement, the fee must be reasonable, and the division must reflect the services performed and responsibilities assumed by each lawyer. DR 2–107. The Model Rules don't require the last element; as long as the lawyers assume joint responsibility for the work, the fee is reasonable, and the client consents, it doesn't matter who actually did the work (although if the fee division isn't proportional to the work performed, the client's consent must be in writing).

MR 1.5(e). Thus, *both* codes require client consent, which is lacking under these facts.

Since option D ignores the consent issue, and focuses instead on language from the rule on contingency fees in the Model Rules, it's not the best response.

Answer 39

D is the best response, because it correctly recognizes that the only way Attorney can properly accept the payment from Aunt is with Defendant's consent.

The central problem here is a conflict of interest, which arises whenever someone other than the client pay's the attorney's bill. The potential problem with such situations is the lawyer's loyalty; he may be tempted to divide his loyalty between his client and the one who's paying his fee. To avoid such problems, when someone other than the client is paying the lawyer's fee, the lawyer must:

1. obtain the client's consent after consultation;

2. believe that there's no interference with the lawyer's independent professional judgment or with the lawyer–client relationship; and

3. protect the client's confidences and secrets from the person paying the bill, as with any other client. MR 1.8(f), DR 5–107(A)(l).

Under these facts, you have Aunt offering to pay Defendant's bill. The only thing that makes this question tricky is that there really isn't a conflict of interest obvious from these facts; it's pretty obvious that Aunt is only trying to help out Defendant, and has no interest in influencing Attorney or learning Defendant's confidential information. However, the *potential* for this still remains, and so Defendant's consent would be necessary before Attorney could retain Aunt's money.

Note, incidentally, that option D uses the modifier "unless." In order for it to be correct, the reasoning must be the only way the result cannot occur. Here, the only way Attorney could act properly would be to obtain Defendant's consent to keep Aunt's money. Since option D recognizes that the propriety of Attorney's conduct is contingent on Defendant's consent, it's the best response.

A is not the best response, because Aunt's butting out of the case won't make Attorney's conduct proper.

The problem here is a conflict of interest, created by the payment of Defendant's attorney fees by someone other than Defendant. The potential problem with such situations is the lawyer's loyalty; he may be tempted to divide his loyalty between his client and the one who's paying his fee. To combat this, when someone other than the client is paying the lawyer's fee, the lawyer must:

1. obtain the client's consent after consultation;

2. believe that there's no interference with the lawyer's independent professional judgment or with the lawyer–client relationship; and

3. protect the client' s confidences and secrets from the person paying the bill, as with any other client. MR 1.8(f), DR 5–107(A)(1).

Note that for purposes of this rule it doesn't matter whether the person paying the bill *makes any attempt whatsoever* to influence the attorney; the rule exists because of the *potential* for this occurring. Under these facts, then, even if Aunt never calls Attorney again, it doesn't mean that his conduct in accepting the money is proper *unless he gets Defendant's consent first.*

Note that option A uses the modifier "if." This means that the reasoning must be plausible under the facts; the reasoning must address a central issue; and the result and the reasoning must agree. Here, the reasoning is plausible on the facts, because there's no indication that Aunt stuck her nose into the case. It's the second requirement that's the problem—the fact that she minded her own business doesn't change the fact that Defendant's consent is necessary in order for Attorney to keep the dough. Since option A doesn't recognize this, it's not the best response.

B is not the best response, because it doesn't address a central issue, even though it *is* correct.

The problem here is a conflict of interest, created by the payment of Defendant's attorney fees by someone other than Defendant. The potential problem with such situations is the lawyer's loyalty; he may be tempted to divide his loyalty between his client and the one who's paying his fee. To combat this, when someone other than the client is paying the lawyer's fee, the lawyer must:

1. obtain the client's consent after consultation;

2. believe that there's no interference with the lawyer's independent professional judgment or with the lawyer–client relationship; and

3. protect the client's confidences and secrets from the person paying the bill, as with any other client. MR 1.8(f), DR 5–107(A)(1).

The *most important* problem with these facts is that there's no indication that Attorney has gotten Defendant's consent to keep the money, which, as this rule indicates, is a prerequisite to retaining the payment from Aunt. It almost goes without saying that Attorney will have to reduce Defendant's bill accordingly, because if he didn't, he'd be charging an unreasonable fee, and would be subject to discipline on that basis. However, the issue under these facts is conflict of interest, and in that respect, the lack of consent is the missing element.

The best way to explain why the one issue is more important than the other is by analogy. Say you go to rent a car. The most important thing the rental company's going to be concerned about is how you're going to pay for the car. Of course, you also have to have a valid driver's license in order to rent a car, but that's taken for granted. The reduced fee to Defendant under these facts is the equivalent of the driver's license in the rental car situation.

Since option B doesn't address a central issue, although it's correct, it's not the best response.

C is not the best response, because it misstates the ethical rules.

Option C suggests that no one other than a party to a suit may pay the costs of the suit. This isn't true; for instance, one common situation where this is standard practice is when a lawyer represents a policyholder whose insurance company is paying the fee. What *is* true is that there are restrictions on payment of attorney fees by third parties, due to the possibility of a conflict of interest. The potential problem with such situations is the lawyer's loyalty; he may be tempted to divide his loyalty between his client and the one who's paying his fee. To combat this, when someone other than the client is paying the lawyer's fee, the lawyer must:

1. obtain the client's consent after consultation;

2. believe that there's no interference with the lawyer's independent professional judgment or with the lawyer–client relationship; and

3. protect the client's confidences and secrets from the person paying the bill, as with any other client. MR 1.8(f), DR 5–107(A)(1).

As long as these elements are satisfied, Aunt is free to pay *all* of Defendant's attorney's fees, if she so chooses. Thus, the fact that she's not a party to the litigation doesn't make the payment improper, and since option C doesn't recognize this, it's not the best response.

Answer 40

C is the best response, because it identifies the central reason Attorney won't be subject to discipline: Everything Attorney disclosed is in the record on the motion, which is a public record.

Both ethical codes place restrictions on trial publicity by lawyers. Under the Model Code, DR 7-107, a lawyer's public statements are proscribed if there's a "reasonable likelihood" of prejudicial impact on the proceedings. Under the Model Rules, MR 3.6(a), the state must show that the lawyer knows or should know that the extrajudicial statement will have a substantial likelihood of materially prejudicing an adjudicative proceeding (this is known as the "substantial likelihood" test, and it's more liberal than the

Model Code test). Both codes also list permissible and impermissible trial publicity. For instance, MR 3.6(c) lists permissible publicity statements:

1. the general nature of a claim or defense;

2. information in a public record (e.g., indictment, criminal complaint);

3. the existence, general scope, and nature (offense, claim or defense) of an investigation (as well as the identity of those involved, including officers and agencies, except where local law prohibits this);

4. the scheduling and result of any step in litigation;

5. a request to the public for help in obtaining evidence, or information about it;

6. a warning of danger concerning the behavior of anyone involved if it's reasonable to believe there's a likelihood of substantial harm to anyone or to the public interest; and

7. in a criminal case, the accused's identity, residence, occupation, and family status;

8. in a criminal case, if accused hasn't been apprehended, information necessary to aid in apprehension;

9. fact, time, and place of arrest.

As #2 above indicates, a lawyer may disclose publicly the contents of public records. That's all Attorney's statement contains, and so it's permissible.

Note that if the information had not been in a public record, Attorney would be subject to discipline for disclosing it, since a lawyer may not disclose publicly a witness's identity or expected testimony, for a civil matter triable by a jury, or a criminal matter. MR 3.6(b), DR 7–107(B), (G). Since the existence of the motion makes the statement permissible, and option C recognizes this, it's the best response.

A is not the best response, because it overlooks the fact that Repo's identity is disclosed in the motion.

Both ethical codes place restrictions on trial publicity by lawyers. Under the Model Code, DR 7-107, a lawyer's public statements are proscribed if there's a "reasonable likelihood" of prejudicial impact on the proceedings. Under the Model Rules, MR 3.6(a), the state must show that the lawyer knows or should know that the extrajudicial statement will have a substantial likelihood of materially prejudicing an adjudicative proceeding (this is known as the "substantial likelihood" test, and it's more liberal than the Model Code test). Both codes go on to list impermissible and permissible trial publicity. What makes option A tricky is that it's true that a lawyer cannot publicly disclose a witness's identity, MR 3.6(b), DR 7-107(B), (G), in a civil matter triable by a jury or a criminal matter. However, there's an *additional* fact that makes Attorney's statement proper, namely, that everything Attorney disclosed is in the record on the motion, which is a public record. Information in a public record (e.g., indictment, criminal complaint, or, as here, a motion), *may* be disclosed. MR 3.6(c). This only makes sense when you figure that anyone can find out the contents of public records, so there's no real reason to stop lawyers from disclosing what's in them. Since option A overlooks the existence of the motion, and arrives at the wrong result because of this, it's not the best response.

B is not the best response, because it fails to recognize that Attorney's statement will be permissible even if prospective jurors hear it.

What option B does is to focus on the rationale for restricting trial publicity; namely, to avoid prejudicial impact on the trial. Both codes contain such restrictions. Under the Model Code, DR 7–107, a lawyer's public statements are proscribed if there's a "reasonable likelihood" of prejudicial impact on the proceedings. Under the Model Rules, MR 3.6(a), the state must show that the lawyer knows or should know that the extrajudicial statement will have a substantial likelihood of materially prejudicing an adjudicative proceeding (this is known as the "substantial likelihood" test, and it's more liberal than the Model Code test). Both codes go on to list impermissible and permissible trial publicity. MR 3.6(c) lists information that is not considered unduly prejudicial. This list includes information contained in a public record (e.g., indictment, criminal complaint, motion). The fact that information is publicly available diminishes the possibility that it will influence the case, so it doesn't matter if the prospective jurors might hear Attorney's comments.

What's ironic about this option is that the *information itself*—namely, Repo's identity and her thoughts, which are likely to form part of her testimony—is exactly the kind of information both codes want to remain out of the public's eye (and away from the jurors), under MR 3.6(b) and DR 7–107(B) and (G). Nonetheless, the existence of the motion makes the information disclosable, and since option B doesn't recognize this, it's not the best response.

D is not the best response, because the "disclosability" of the information doesn't depend on whether or not the trial has commenced.

Both ethical codes place restrictions on trial publicity by lawyers; contrary to what option D states, these restrictions apply whether or not the trial has begun yet. Under the Model Code, DR 7–107, a lawyer's public statements are proscribed if there's a "reasonable likelihood" of prejudicial impact on the proceedings. Under the Model Rules, MR 3.6(a), the state must show that the lawyer knows or should know that the extrajudicial statement will have a substantial likelihood of materially prejudicing an adjudicative proceeding (this is known as the "substantial likelihood" test, and it's more liberal than the Model Code test). Both codes go on to list impermissible and permissible trial publicity. MR 3.6(c) lists information that is not considered unduly prejudicial. This list includes information contained in a public record (e.g., indictment, criminal complaint, motion). That's the case here, since the information was in a motion, so Attorney's statement was proper. (Note that had the statement not been in a motion, it would *not* have been disclosable, because a witness' s identity and expected testimony are considered prejudicial information, MR 3.6(b), DR 7 107(B), (G).)

If you chose this response, you may have been thinking about the restrictions on contact with jurors, which *do* vary depending on whether the time frame is pre–trial, trial, or post–trial, with the restrictions being most severe during the trial itself. However, that's not the issue here. Since option D mistakenly implies that the trial publicity rules vary depending on whether the trial has begun, it's not the best response.

Answer 41

D is the best response, because it recognizes why the representation is proper: Alpha was totally uninvolved with Deft's case when he worked for the government.

As a preliminary matter, the only way that Beta could be subject to discipline for representing Deft would be if Alpha couldn't represent Deft because of his former position at the district attorney's office, and that Beta's relationship with Alpha prohibits him from representing Deft, as well. The interesting thing about this question is that it *seems* like there ought to be a conflict of interest disqualification in it, but in fact there isn't one. All of the restrictions relating to former government lawyers only apply if the lawyer participated *personally and substantially* in the matter while working for the government. If this had been the case, Alpha couldn't represent Deft without the D.A.'s office's consent. However, as the facts state, "Alpha took no part in the investigation and had no knowledge of the facts other than those disclosed in the press." What this tells you is the rationale for the restrictions on former government lawyers—unfair advantage and disclosing secrets—doesn't apply, and so the restrictions don't apply. This means that Alpha would be free to represent Deft, and that therefore Beta can't be subject to imputed disqualification because of Alpha.

"Be that as it may," you're thinking. "But what if Alpha *did* take part in the case while he was assistant prosecutor?" In that case, he could not have anything to do with the case without consent from the appropriate government agency. MR 1.ll(a), DR 9–l0l(B). In addition, Beta would be subject to disqualification ("imputed" disqualification) unless the following two elements were met: 1. Alpha would have nothing to do with the case—no discussions, no access to files; and 2. the appropriate government agency would have to be given prompt written notice so that the government could ascertain the firm's compliance with screening procedures.

As this shows, the key fact here is that Alpha didn't have anything to do with the Deft case as assistant prosecutor, which makes it perfectly all right for Beta to represent Deft. Since option D recognizes this, it's the best response.

A is not the best response, because its reasoning, standing alone, would not prohibit Beta from representing Deft.

What option A does is to suggest that there is a conflict of interest problem with these facts, and that Beta is subject to imputed disqualification because Alpha worked in the district attorney's office while Deft's case was being prosecuted. This is only partially right; option A correctly identifies the problem, but misapplies the rule on disqualification. In fact, Alpha isn't even disqualified from representing Deft, so Beta couldn't possibly be disqualified because of Alpha's prior position. All of the restrictions relating to former government lawyers only apply if the lawyer participated *personally and substantially* in the matter while working for the government. As the facts state, "Alpha took no part in the investigation and had no knowledge of the facts other than those disclosed in the press." What this tells you is the rationale for the restrictions on former government lawyers—unfair advantage and disclosing secrets—doesn't apply, and so the restrictions don't apply. By stating that Alpha's mere presence in the D.A.'s office during Deft's investigation disqualifies him (and imputedly Beta) from representing Deft, option A overstates the actual restriction. The upshot is that Alpha would be free to represent Deft, and that therefore Beta can't be subject to imputed disqualification because of Alpha.

Note that even if Alpha *wasn't* free to represent Deft without the D.A.'s office's consent—namely, because he had participated personally and substantially in the Deft investigation—this wouldn't necessarily mean that Beta couldn't represent Deft, which is what option A suggests. Instead, as long as Alpha was screened from any participation in the case, *and* the D.A.'s office was notified so it could ascertain that Beta actually was screening Alpha from participation, then Beta could properly represent Deft. MR1.11(a)(DR 9–101(B) is interpreted similarly). In any case, since option A overstates the restrictions on former government lawyers, it's not the best response.

B is not the best response, because Beta is free to represent Deft without notifying the D.A.'s office or seeking consent.

What option B suggests is that these facts contain a conflict of interest due to Alpha's prior position with the D.A.'s office, that this conflict is "imputed" to Alpha's partner Beta, and that the only way to get around it is to seek the consent of the D.A.'s office. In fact, this isn't true. First, let's deal with Alpha's conflict. All of the restrictions relating to former government lawyers only apply if the lawyer participated *personally and substantially* in the matter while working for the government. As the facts state, "Alpha took no part in the investigation and had no knowledge of the facts other than those disclosed in the press." What this tells you is the rationale for the restrictions on former government lawyers—unfair advantage and disclosing secrets—doesn't apply, and so the restrictions don't apply. As a result, Alpha could represent Deft himself, and if he could, there's no conflict to impute to Beta, and Beta is free to represent Deft, as well.

If you chose this response, let's change the facts a little bit to pinpoint what you were thinking about. Say that Alpha had participated in the Deft case as assistant D.A., and that he subsequently wanted to represent Deft himself. The rule is that this would only be possible with consent from the D.A.'s office. MR 1.11(a), DR 9–101(B). That's where you got the "consent" language of option B. The "prompt notification" requirement would come into play if Alpha had participated personally and substantially in the Deft matter at the D.A.'s office, and *Beta* (not Alpha) was going to represent Deft. In *that* case, Alpha would have to be completely "screened" from representing Deft—no discussions, no access to files. In addition, the D.A.'s office would have to be given prompt written notice so it could ascertain that Alpha was, in fact, being properly screened from the case. The language in option B is a mishmash of these two rules. However, since Alpha didn't have any involvement with Deft's case on the government's behalf, these restrictions don't apply, and since option B doesn't recognize this, it's not the best response.

C is not the best response, because the representation is proper even if Alpha participates in the representation or shares the fee.

Option C implicitly recognizes that there's a conflict of interest issue in these facts, based on Alpha's prior position with the D.A.'s office. However, contrary to what option C states, Alpha doesn't have an impermissible conflict of interest, and so he needn't be screened from participation in the case. All of the restrictions relating to former government lawyer only apply if the lawyer participated *personally and substantially* in the matter while working for the government. If this had been the case, Alpha couldn't represent Deft without the D.A.'s office's consent. However, as the facts state, "Alpha took no part in the investigation and had no knowledge of the facts other than those disclosed in the press." What this tells you is the rationale for the restrictions on former government lawyers—unfair advantage and disclosing secrets—doesn't apply, and so the restrictions don't apply.

If you chose this response, you were thinking of the restrictions on former government lawyers as to *confidential governmental information* acquired while working for the government. The rule is that confidential government information a lawyer gains during public employment regarding a person, company, or other entity may not subsequently be used by the lawyer to the *material disadvantage* of that person or entity. MR 1.11(b). As to the other members of the firm, they may only represent clients where the potential of such "material disadvantage" is possible, i.e., if two conditions are met: (1) the former government lawyer must be completely screened from taking part in the case, and (2) the former government lawyer may not be directly allocated any portion of the fee from that client. As you can see, this is the rule you must have been thinking of. However, since Alpha doesn't *have* any confidential information about Deft, and even if he did, that information couldn't be used to Deft's disadvantage (since Beta will be representing Deft, not someone opposed to Deft), the rule doesn't apply to these facts. Since option C doesn't recognize this, it's not the best response.

Answer 42

D is the best response, because it correctly recognizes that there must be *certified* specialists in the office, in each of the specialties, in order for the ad to be proper.

By using the modifier "unless," option D states that the only proper way to advertise specialties is to have certified specialists in the firm. This is true, both under the facts of the problem and the ethics rules. Under both codes, a lawyer (or firm) cannot claim to be a specialist unless the state recognizes such specialties, for instance through a certification process. MR 7.4, DR 2–101(B). The facts here tell you that the state certifies legal specialists, and so in order for LAG to advertise specialists, they'd have to have lawyers who'd actually obtained certificates in each of the areas listed. Note that the *problem* with "specialty" advertising is that it denotes a special skill, and if a lawyer doesn't actually have that skill, the ad would be misleading.

Note, incidentally, that the name of the firm—Legal Associates Group—is one that would not be permitted under the Model Code! That's because the Model Code doesn't recognize trade names (although the Model Rules *do,* as long as they aren't misleading, and they don't imply a connection with a governmental agency or legal services organization. DR 2–102(B), MR 7.5(a). This isn't an issue under this problem at all, because you're expressly told that the trade name is permissible in the jurisdiction.

In any case, since option D recognizes that the propriety of the ad turns on having certified specialists at the firm, it's the best response.

A is not the best response, because it misapplies the code rules on advertising specialties.

Under both codes, a lawyer (or firm) cannot claim to be a specialist unless the state recognizes such specialties, for instance through a certification process. MR 7.4, DR 2–l0l(B). The reason for this restriction is that "specialty" advertising denotes a special skill, and if the lawyer doesn't actually *have* a special skill, the ad is misleading. Thus, what the codes are concerned with is the *perception* of special skill, not what the lawyer actually practices. A lawyer is free to practice in any specialty in which he's competent; however, if he wants to hold himself out as a specialist in any area, he must meet state guidelines for doing so. Under these facts, you're told that the state has a certification procedure. As a result, as long as LAG has lawyers in the firm who are certified in the areas listed, the specialty advertising will be proper. Note that this means it's all right if LAG has lawyers who practice anything else, as well—Dog Law, Household Appliance Product Liability Law, you name it.

If you chose this response, you probably confused the "limitation" and "specialization" language that's permissible in lawyer advertising. It's perfectly permissible for a lawyer to advertise the limitations on his practice (e.g., practice limited to Criminal Law), and presumably if he *did* so, then he would, in fact, have to limit his practice to Criminal Law in order for the ad to be true (which lawyer ads must be, under both codes). The *benefit* to claiming a limitation instead of a specialization is that it *implies* a special skill, but the lawyer doesn't have to comply with any state guidelines on specialties, like a certification procedure. Of course, by advertising specialties instead of limitations, LAG doesn't limit itself to those areas listed. Since option A doesn't recognize this, it's not the best response.

B is not the best response, because the fee information in the ad is proper regardless of whether an estimate is provided during the consultation.

DR 2–101(B) contains the limitations on fee information which may properly appear in lawyer ads (the MR only prohibit false and misleading ads, in general. MR 7.1). This list includes: The fee for an initial consultation ("free half–hour initial consultation"); availability of written fee schedule and/or estimate of fee for specific services; contingent fee rate, as long as it shows whether percentages are computed before or after costs ("Contingency fee = 30% of recovery, after costs"); range of fees (as long as it's stated that the specific fee within the range will vary depending on the particular matter to be handled for each client, and the client is entitled to an estimate of fee beforehand); hourly rate (as long as ad discloses that total fee will depend on number of hours devoted to a particular matter, and that the client is entitled to an estimate); fixed fees (as long as ad discloses that client is entitled to a free estimate).

As this list indicates, lawyers may advertise a fee for an initial consultation, without having to provide an estimate of the fee to be charged. *Other* kinds of fee advertising *do* have the "estimate" requirement, including range of fees, hourly rate, and fixed fees. The only limitation on the initial consultation fee here is that it must be true that LAG actually charges only

$15 for a first consultation. Since option B places restrictions on the consultation fee statement that don't exist, it's not the best response.

C is not the best response, because the fee information is properly included regardless of whether there is any other information about fees in the ad. DR 2–101(B) contains the limitations on fee information which may properly appear in lawyer ads (the MR only prohibit false and misleading ads, in general. MR 7.1). This list includes: The fee for an initial consultation ("free half–hour initial consultation"); availability of written fee schedule and/or estimate of fee for specific services; contingent fee rate, as long as it shows whether percentages are computed before or after costs ("Contingency fee = 30% of recovery, after costs"); range of fees (as long as it's stated that the specific fee within the range will vary depending on the particular matter to be handled for each client, and the client is entitled to an estimate of fee beforehand); hourly rate (as long as ad discloses that total fee will depend on number of hours devoted to a particular matter, and that the client is entitled to an estimate); fixed fees (as long as ad discloses that client is entitled to a free estimate).

As this list indicates, a fee for an initial consultation may properly be advertised without *any* mention of subsequent fees. If you chose option C, you were thinking of the ethics rules concerning when a lawyer should establish the *basis* of his fee. According to EC 2–19, the basis of the fee (e.g., hourly, contingent) should be established at the outset of the employment, to avoid misunderstandings later (under the MR, if the lawyer hasn't regularly represented a client, establishing the fee up front is mandatory. MR 1.5(b)). This rule addresses what happens when a client actually wants to be represented by LAG; the focus of this problem, instead, is the propriety of the ad. Since option C doesn't recognize that the fee information is proper, it's not the best response.

Answer 43

B is the best response, because it recognizes that none of Attorney's conduct is improper as long as the fee overall is reasonable.

The "reasonability" element is required by both codes. Note that there are really three separate aspects to the fee arrangement here. First, whether the fee itself is reasonable; second, whether it's proper to charge 50% of the fee up front; and finally, whether it's proper to finance the remainder of the fee with a promissory note. Let's look at each aspect separately.

There are eight elements that go into determining reasonability, according to DR 2–106(B) and MR 1.5(a): 1. the time, labor, and skill required, and the novelty and difficulty of the questions involved; 2. the opportunity cost—namely, the likelihood, from the client's point of view, that accepting this job will preclude the lawyer from accepting other jobs (e.g., due to a conflict of interest); 3. the customary fee in the locality for the services involved; 4. the amount at issue and the results obtained; 5. time limits imposed by the client or circumstances; 6. nature and length of the attorney–client relationship; 7. experience, reputation, and ability of lawyer; and 8. the nature of the fee—whether fixed or contingent.

Under these facts, Attorney bases her fee on the difficulty of the case and a reasonable hourly charge for the estimated time spent on it. While you aren't told any more about the reasonability of the fee, it's plausible that it's reasonable, and since option B uses the modifier "if," reasonability is all that's necessary. This is really the central issue here, because the other two aspects of Attorney's fee custom—charging 50% up front and financing the rest—are both proper. As to the prepayment, MR 1.5, Comment, provides that this is proper as long as any unearned part of the advance is refunded when the representation terminates (also, the advanced fee would have to go into Attorney's client trust account until it's earned). As to the financing, although this was traditionally frowned upon by the bar, it's now permissible for lawyers to finance legal fees in a variety of ways, including bank loans, personal notes, and even credit cards! By not mentioning Attorney's collection techniques, option B implicitly recognizes that they're proper, and since option B recognizes that the fee is proper as long as it's reasonable, it's the best response.

A is not the best response, because there's nothing wrong with establishing a fee before the attorney–client relationship begins, and beyond that, it's not clear that option A accurately reflects the facts.

As a general rule, a lawyer should establish the basis of his fee as soon as possible, whether or not the attorney–client relationship has been established. Under EC 2–19, the basis of the fee (e.g., hourly, contingent) should be established at the outset of the employment, to avoid misunderstandings later. Under the MR, this is *mandatory*, if the lawyer hasn't regularly represented the client. MR 1.5(b). Thus, Attorney is complying with the ethics rules by establishing her fee as soon as possible, contrary to what A states.

Option A also states conclusively that no attorney–client relationship has been formed when Attorney sets her fee. The facts don't really say this, for sure. Depending on which section of the codes you're considering, the relationship may begin when the potential client confides in the lawyer (which is when the lawyer's duty of confidentiality kicks in), when it becomes reasonable for the client to believe the lawyer is acting on his behalf (which is when the lawyer's duty of loyalty kicks in), and, naturally, when the lawyer and client agree to the representation. All you're told in these facts is that Attorney sets her fee when she's consulted, in advance of accepting employment. Since "accepting employment" determines the attorney–client relationship for every ethical duty, it's important not to look upon it as a watershed. Nonetheless, since Attorney can set her fee even before the attorney–client relationship exists, and A doesn't recognize this, it's not the best response.

C is not the best response, because it misstates the ethics rules.

There's nothing wrong with demanding pre-payment of legal fees. MR 1.5, Comment, provides that this is proper as long as any unearned part of the advance is refunded when the representation terminates (also, the advanced fee would have to go into Attorney's client trust account until it's earned). Of course, it may strike you as mean, strict, and money-grubbing, but that doesn't make it unethical. Since option C doesn't recognize this, it's not the best response.

D is not the best response, because acquiring such a security interest is proper.

Option D focuses on the propriety of taking a security interest in a client's property to secure payment of legal fees. There's nothing wrong with this, in that a lawyer may accept promissory notes, credit cards, personal guarantees, and virtually anything else to secure his fees (as long as it doesn't compromise his independent judgment).

If you chose this response, you may have been thinking there's a conflict of interest problem with Attorney taking a security interest in a client's property. The rule is that a lawyer must avoid acquiring property rights that might compromise his independent judgment, as part of his duty of unimpaired loyalty to his clients. One such prohibited interest is a proprietary interest in the subject matter of the litigation (except for reasonable contingent fees, permissible attorney's liens, certain costs of litigation advanced to the client by the lawyer), MR 1.8(j), DR 5–103(A). The reason this rule doesn't apply to these facts is that it's not the subject matter of the litigation that Attorney is taking a security interest in; all you're told is that she takes a note backed by full collateral, and since she only does *criminal* work, she couldn't realistically take a security interest in the subject matter of the representation.

Instead, as long as Attorney's fee is reasonable, her entire custom relating to fees is proper, since there's nothing wrong with the prepayment or the security interest. Since option D doesn't recognize that the security interest here is proper, it's not the best response.

Answer 44

D is the best response, because it correctly identifies that Prosecutor's stating his personal opinion makes his statement improper.

There are four specific items that a lawyer must avoid arguing or presenting as part of his duty not to state his personal opinions during a trial. Under DR 7–106(C)(4) and MR 3.4(e), these include: the justness of a cause, the credibility of a witness, the culpability of a civil litigant, or the guilt or innocence of the accused. The rationale for this is that the facts are to be determined by the fact finder (in this case, the jury); a lawyer for a party shouldn't supplement those facts with his personal opinions. Furthermore, if this prohibition *didn't* exist, and lawyers were allowed to express opinions, a lawyer's silence could be construed unfavorably to his client. ECC 7-24.

Under these facts, the statement that gets Prosecutor into trouble is *"I don't believe Wit was telling the truth."* By saying this, as option D states, Prosecutor is injecting his own interpretation of Wit's credibility, which the codes expressly forbid.

Note that everything else Prosecutor said was fine. By citing the testimony of the witnesses, Prosecutor was characterizing the evidence in a way favorable to the government, summarizing the evidence, and arguing that certain inferences may be drawn—namely, that because Wit's testimony is contradicted by every other witness, that Wit was lying. If Prosecutor had said, "The evidence as a whole tells you that Wit was lying" instead of "I don't believe Wit was telling the truth," there would be no problem; it's only when Prosecutor steps over the line and injects his own opinion that his conduct violates the ethics rules. Since D recognizes this, it's the best response.

A is not the best response, because stating the testimony correctly would not make Prosecutor's statement proper.

The problem here is that Prosecutor stated his personal opinion during a trial, by stating "I don't believe Wit was telling the truth." There are four specific items that a lawyer must avoid arguing or presenting as part of the duty not to state personal opinions during a trial. Under DR 7–106(C)(4) and MR 3.4(e), these include the justness of a cause, the credibility of a witness, the culpability of a civil litigant, or the guilt or innocence of the accused. The rationale for this is that the facts are to be determined by the fact finder (in this case, the jury); a lawyer for a party shouldn't supplement those facts with his personal opinions. Furthermore, if this prohibition *didn't* exist and lawyers were allowed to express opinions, a lawyer's silence could be construed unfavorably to his client. EC 7–24. Here, by stating that he didn't believe Wit, Prosecutor is offering his personal opinion as to the credibility of a witness, which violates both codes.

Note that what option A suggests—that a lawyer has a duty to accurately state the testimony in a case—isn't necessary true. Instead, a lawyer can characterize the evidence in a light favorable to his client, summarize the evidence, and argue that certain inferences may be drawn (under these facts, the inference is that since Wit's testimony is contradicted by every other witness, Wit was lying). As a result, as long as the lawyer doesn't *mischaracterize* what's been said in testimony, he can play with it to his client's advantage.

Note, incidentally, that option A uses the modifier "if." This means the reasoning must be plausible on the facts, it must resolve a central issue, and the result and the reasoning must agree. The second element is the problem here, since even if Prosecutor did accurately state the content of the testimony, his conduct would still be improper because he stated a personal opinion. Since A doesn't recognize this, it's not the best response.

B is not the best response, because Prosecutor's belief in the truth of his statement wouldn't make it proper. The problem here is that Prosecutor stated his personal opinion during a trial, by stating "I don't believe Wit was telling the truth." There are four specific items that a lawyer must avoid arguing or representing as part of the duty not to state personal opinions during a trial. Under DR 7–106(C)(4) and MR 3.4(e), these include the justness of a cause, the credibility of a witness, the culpability of a civil litigant, or the guilt or innocence of the accused. The rationale for this is that the facts are to be determined by the fact finder (in this case, the jury);

a lawyer for a party shouldn't supplement those facts with his personal opinions. Furthermore, if this prohibition *didn't* exist, and lawyers were allowed to express opinions, a lawyer's silence could be construed unfavorably to his client. EC 7–24. Here, by stating that he didn't believe Wit, Prosecutor is offering his personal opinion as to the credibility of a witness, which violates both codes.

Thus, what gets Prosecutor into trouble here is that he stated his opinion, *whether or not he believed it.* Of course, if he *didn't* believe Wit was lying, he'd also be making a misstatement, and that in and of itself is disciplinable. However, since stating an opinion is grounds for discipline, and option B doesn't recognize this, it's not the best response.

C is not the best response, because it doesn't identify the central problem with the statement: it's Prosecutor' s statement of his opinion.

The rule is that a lawyer's closing arguments may only refer to matters in evidence, or those fairly inferable from facts in evidence. Jurors' beliefs aren't admissible evidence nor may inferences be drawn from them, so that it's true, as option C states, that Prosecutor can't allude to the jurors' beliefs. But the problem with this is that it doesn't really reflect the facts; it's not the jurors' beliefs to which Prosecutor is alluding, but rather what *he thinks* the jurors' beliefs are: "... *I don't think* you believe him either." What's objectionable, as this indicates, is that it's Prosecutor's personal opinion that he's stating. The rule is that there are four specific items that a lawyer must avoid arguing or presenting as part of the duty not to state personal opinions during a trial. Under DR 7–106(C)(4) and MR 3.4(e), these include the justness of a cause, the credibility of a witness, the culpability of a civil litigant, or the guilt or innocence of the accused. The rationale for this is that the facts are to be determined by the fact finder (in this case, the jury); a lawyer for a party shouldn't supplement those facts with his personal opinions. Furthermore, if this prohibition *didn't* exist, and lawyers were allowed to express opinions, a lawyer's silence could be construed unfavorably to his client. EC 7–24. Here, by stating that he didn't believe Wit, Prosecutor is offering his personal opinion as to the credibility of a witness, which violates both codes.

If you chose this response, you may have been thinking of the "Golden Rule," which is that a lawyer cannot ask the jurors to put themselves in the shoes of his client. Although that rule also deals with the beliefs of jurors, it doesn't apply to these facts, since it's the *Prosecutor's* beliefs, not those of the jurors, which are objectionable. Since option C doesn't recognize this, it's not the best response.

Answer 45

A is the best response, because it recognizes that Judge is only required to report Attorney if Attorney acted incompetently.

The general rule is that when a judge becomes aware of unprofessional conduct by a lawyer, the judge should take appropriate disciplinary measures, which may include reporting the lawyer to the disciplinary authorities. CJC 3(B)(3). Thus, under these facts, the central issue is *why* Attorney didn't show up for the motion hearing. The facts don't tell you this, but option A, by using the qualifier "if," creates a condition under which Attorney would be subject to discipline—namely, incompetence. Lawyers have a duty to render competent service, and the failure to do so violates the ethics rules. DR 6–101, MR 1.1, 1.3. Since judges have a duty to report lawyers' ethical breaches, Judge should report Attorney.

This question points out something you should always keep in mind on the MPRE—namely, the importance at looking at *why* a lawyer did (or didn't do) something. It can frequently make the difference between proper and improper conduct. For instance, say Attorney's failure to show was because he was in a serious car accident, and was in intensive care during the motion hearing. If he had a one–man office, it's possible that there was no way for him to notify the court that he wouldn't be showing up. Say instead that Defendant bound and gagged Attorney and held him hostage, and *that's* why he didn't show up. We could go on, but you get the idea—what determines the unethical nature of Attorney's conduct is the reason for his failure to show. Because it conditions Judge's duty to report Attorney on conduct that would clearly be unethical, A is the best response.

B is not the best response, because Judge's duty to report Attorney doesn't depend on the *result* of the failure to show up.

The general rule is that when a judge becomes aware of unprofessional conduct by a lawyer, the judge should take appropriate disciplinary measures, which may include reporting the lawyer to the disciplinary authorities. CJC 3(B)(3). Thus, under these facts, if Attorney's conduct in failing to show up for the motion hearing was unethical, then Judge has a duty to report him, whether or not Attorney's failure to show resulted in Plaintiff's case being dismissed. For instance, if Attorney's failure to show was due to the fact that he was in a coma for a few months—or any other valid excuse—his conduct wouldn't be disciplinable *even if* Plaintiff's case was dismissed. In fact, on these facts, you aren't given enough to determine whether or not Judge should report Attorney, because you aren't told *why* Attorney didn't show up. What this means is that *no* answer option with the modifier "because" can be the best response, because that would mean that the facts indicating whether or not Attorney's conduct was unethical are clear in the question itself, and for this question, this simply isn't true.

If you chose this response, you may have been thinking of the rule on malpractice, since that's the only time in all of legal ethics that *results count.* That is, a lawyer can't be subject to malpractice if the client wasn't adversely impacted by his misconduct. Thus, if Plaintiff were suing Attorney for malpractice based on the conduct here, then Plaintiff would in part *have* to prove what option B suggests—that Plaintiff was adversely impacted by Attorney's conduct (of course, he'd also have to prove Attorney's misconduct as well, and there isn't enough in these facts to support such a claim, since you don't know why Attorney failed to show up).

In any case, since option B focuses on the results of Attorney's conduct instead of the conduct itself, it's not the best response.

C is not the best response, because Judge's duty to report Attorney doesn't turn on whether or not Plaintiff would have prevailed at trial.

The general rule is that when a judge becomes aware of unprofessional conduct by a lawyer, the judge should take appropriate disciplinary measures, which may include reporting the lawyer to the disciplinary authorities. CJC 3(B)(3). Thus, under these facts, if attorney's conduct in failing to show up for the motion hearing was unethical, then Judge has a duty to report him, *regardless* of whether Plaintiff would have prevailed at trial. This highlights the real problem with these facts, which is identifying *why* Attorney was a no–show for the motion hearing. If it was because of unethical conduct (e.g., incompetence), then Judge *should* report Attorney; if it was not, then he shouldn't. You simply can't tell on the facts as given.

If you chose this response, you were thinking of the rule on malpractice. For negligence–based malpractice claims (which most malpractice claims are), the client must prove *two* cases: one, the lawyer's negligence in handling the representation, and the other, that but for the lawyer's errors or omissions, the representation would have resulted in a vastly different, and more advantageous, outcome. Thus, under these facts, if Plaintiff sued Attorney for malpractice, he'd have to prove Attorney was negligent in failing to show up for the motion hearing, *and* that but for this, Plaintiff would have prevailed at trial. You can see the similarity between the second element of a negligence based malpractice suit and the reasoning of option C, with the exception that C *understates* what Plaintiff would have to prove—Plaintiff would have to prove that he *would* have prevailed, not that there's a *reasonable certainty* that Plaintiff would have prevailed. Since option C doesn't apply the correct rule to these facts, it cannot be the best response.

D is not the best response, because Judge may have a duty to report Attorney *whether or not* Attorney's conduct constituted contempt.

Note that option D uses the modifier "if." What this means is that the reasoning must give the only circumstance under which the result cannot occur. In order for D to be correct, if you reverse the result and change the modifier to "if and only if," the resulting statement would have to be correct. Doing this, you wind up with the following statement: "Judge should report Attorney if and only if Attorney's conduct was a contempt of court." Stated this way, perhaps you can see why D isn't the best response. The rule is that when a judge becomes aware of unprofessional conduct by a lawyer, the judge should take appropriate disciplinary measures, which may include reporting the lawyer to the disciplinary authorities. CJC 3(B)(3). Thus, Judge's duty to report Attorney turns on *why* Attorney failed to show up. If his failure was unethical—e.g., incompetent—then Judge has a duty to report Attorney whether or not Attorney's conduct also constitutes a contempt of court. Since option D doesn't recognize this, it's not the best response.

Answer 46

C is the best response, because it recognizes that, by failing to act in the best interests of *all* his clients, Attorney's conduct was unethical.

Lawyers have a duty of zealous advocacy on behalf of their clients. That is, a lawyer cannot intentionally fail to pursue any lawful objectives of his client, by reasonably available means. Violating this duty is disciplinable under the Model Code, DR 7–101(A), and improper under the Model Rules, MR 1.3, Comment.

Under these facts, the duty of zealous advocacy would encompass *all* the landowners, since Attorney represents them all. By supporting a proposal that would increase the risk of flooding on their land, Attorney violated his duty to pursue their objectives, and acted improperly on that basis.

Note that the fact that Attorney let his duty to Baker impact his professional judgment on behalf of the landowners creates a conflict of interest problem, as well. The basic idea is that a lawyer must be free to exercise his professional judgment on behalf of his client, and if his other responsibilities or interests prevent him from doing so, there's an impermissible conflict of interest. There are two duties underlying conflict of interest principles—confidentiality and loyalty—and the one that Attorney violated under these facts is the duty of loyalty. He let a compromising influence, his duty to Baker, influence his professional judgment on behalf of the landowners.

Incidentally, note that there isn't anything wrong with Attorney's representing all the landowners before the Commission. The rule on multiple representation in a non–litigation situation is that it's only possible if the lawyer reasonably ascertains that he can represent all the clients without adverse effect; he must fully explain the potential conflicts to all clients, and give them an opportunity to retain other counsel; and the clients must consent after consultation. All of these requirements are apparently met under these facts, so the representation *itself* isn't objectionable. However, since Attorney violated his duty of zealous advocacy to the landowners once the representation got underway, and option C recognizes this, it's the best response.

A is not the best response, because it doesn't take into account Attorney's duties to the other landowners.

Lawyers have a duty of zealous advocacy on behalf of their clients. That is, a lawyer cannot intentionally fail to pursue any lawful objectives of his client, by reasonably available means. Violating this duty is disciplinable under the Model Code, DR 7–101(A), and improper under the Model Rules, MR 1.3, Comment. Under these facts, the duty of zealous advocacy would encompass all the landowners, since Attorney represents them all. By supporting a proposal that would increase the risk of flooding on their land, Attorney violated his duty to pursue their objectives, and acted improperly on that basis.

If you chose this response, you were thinking of the duties of lawyers who are also public officials. The rule is that if a lawyer holds a public office, he has a duty to act in the best interest of the public, and he can't engage in any activities where his own interests could foreseeably conflict with his official duties. EC 8–8. This rule would apply to these facts if Attorney were a public official. He couldn't then advocate a plan on straightening the river that would not be in the public interest. However, under these facts, Attorney *isn't* a public official, so he has a duty to act on behalf of his clients, not the public in general. Since option A doesn't recognize this, it's not the best response.

B is not the best response, because it isn't the *formation* of the plan that's at issue here, but rather the fact that Attorney *supported* it.

What option B suggests is that had Attorney created the plan, his conduct would be improper, but that it's not improper if he just supports a plan someone else created. In fact, Attorney's hands are just as dirty in supporting the plan as if he'd created it himself, since by supporting it, he's violating his duty of zealous advocacy on behalf of the other landowners. The rule is that a lawyer cannot intentionally fail to pursue any lawful objectives of his client, by reasonably available means. Violating the duty of zealous advocacy is disciplinable under the Model Code, DR 7–101(A), and improper under the Model Rules, MR 1.3, Comment. Under these facts, the duty of zealous advocacy would encompass all the landowners, since Attorney represents them all. The fact that he supported a proposal that would increase the risk of flooding on their land is sufficient to violate this duty, even if Attorney himself didn't come up with the idea. Since option B doesn't recognize this, it's not the best response.

D is not the best response, because Attorney's conduct is improper even if failing to support the plan would have worked a substantial hardship on Baker.

The problem with the situation here is that, in backing a plan that would increase the chance of flooding on the landowners' property, Attorney is not acting as a zealous advocate of their interests. The rule is that a lawyer cannot intentionally fail to pursue any lawful objectives of his client, by reasonably available means. Violating the duty of zealous advocacy is disciplinable under the Model Code, DR 7–101(A), and improper under the Model Rules, MR 1.3, Comment. What option D does is to play Devil's advocate, and say that Attorney's conduct was proper if and only if failing to support the plan would have hurt Baker; in other words, option D suggests that if Attorney had been faced with having to hurt someone he represents, he's free to choose the "victim." In fact, such a situation would be a conflict of interest which would require Attorney to withdraw from the representation all together, since he'd be in a position where he couldn't exercise his independent professional judgment on behalf of all his clients, and acting against any of them in the matter, even once he'd withdrawn from representation, would violate his duty of loyalty to them.

Note that option D uses the modifier "unless." This means that in order for D to be correct, the reasoning must provide the only way the result *cannot* occur. As the analysis in the last paragraph shows, Attorney's conduct is improper regardless of whether failing to support the plan would hurt Baker, so the reasoning doesn't show the only way Attorney's conduct could be proper. Since option D doesn't recognize this, it's not the best response.

Answer 47

C is the best response, because it recognizes that there is no ethical rule that would stop Attorney from conducting the investigation.

As a general rule, a lawyer has the duty of zealously pursuing his client's interests, within the bounds of the law, by all reasonably available means. Since overturning Deft's conviction due to perjured evidence is clearly in Deft's best interests, Attorney should pursue it within the bounds of the law. Thus, under these facts, you'd have to ask yourself what there is to stop Attorney from conducting the investigation of the witness. First, such investigations cannot be vexatious or harassing. There's nothing here to suggest that this one is. Second is the rule prohibiting a lawyer from taking action on behalf of his client, when it's obvious that the action would only harass or maliciously injure someone else. DR 7–102(A)(1), MR 4.4. This rule doesn't really apply here because there's more than mere harassment to this investigation—Attorney is looking for evidence that a prosecution witness perjured himself. Since Attorney has a duty to zealously advocate Deft's interests and there's no counterbalancing rule forbidding him from conducting the investigation, it's proper to do so. Since option C recognizes this, it's the best response.

A is not the best response, because Attorney can conduct the interview without notifying the court first.

A lawyer has a general duty to zealously pursue the goals of his client, within the bounds of the law, by all reasonably available means. Here, Attorney has evidence that the witness for the prosecution perjured himself. Since overturning Deft's conviction due to perjured evidence is clearly in

Deft's best interests, Attorney should pursue it within the bounds of the law. What option A suggests is that Attorney's conduct is only non–disciplinable if he tells the court first about the information he received. In fact, this isn't true. Attorney is free to conduct the investigation, as long as it isn't vexatious or harassing, without notifying the court.

If you chose this response, you were probably thinking of the rule concerning *juror* misconduct, not *witness* misconduct. Part of a lawyer's duty not to exercise improper influence over proceedings is a responsibility to *promptly* reveal to the court any improper conduct by or toward jurors, potential jurors, or their families. DR 7–108(G). (The promptness requirement is there to save lawyers from the temptation of hanging on to evidence of juror misconduct until the verdict is rendered, and if it's against the lawyer's client, report the misconduct as a challenge to the jury verdict.) Since Attorney is investigating a witness and not a juror, this rule doesn't apply here.

Note that option A uses the modifier "unless." In order for A to be correct, the reasoning would have to be the only way the result could not occur. Here, this would have to mean that Attorney could avoid discipline only by notifying the court of the perjury evidence before he conducts the investigation. Since Attorney is free to conduct the investigation without notifying the court, and option A doesn't recognize this, it's not the best response.

B is not the best response, because Attorney may interview the witness.

Option B suggests that defense counsel is not free to interview prosecution witnesses. In fact, this isn't true. Defense counsel is free to interview government witnesses (although, as with all such interviews, it can't be vexatious or harassing). In addition, the interview would be prohibited if the only purpose behind it was to harass or maliciously injure someone. DR 7–102(A)(1), MR 4.4. This doesn't apply here, because the reason for the interview isn't harassment, but rather to gather evidence of perjury. Since overturning the verdict would serve Deft's interests, and there's no countervailing reason why the investigation (including the interview) can't be conducted, it's proper.

If you chose this response, you may have been thinking of the rule concerning opposing *parties,* not witnesses; a lawyer cannot communicate (or cause anyone else to communicate) with an opposing party represented by counsel without that counsel's consent. DR 7–104(A)(1), MR 4.2. Since this rule doesn't apply to witnesses for the opposition, and B mistakenly comes to the conclusion that the conduct is disciplinable, it's not the best response.

D is not the best response, because personal contact with the witness has no impact on whether the conduct is disciplinable. Since option D uses the modifier "unless," what it's saying is that the only way Attorney is subject to discipline is if he personally contacts the witness. In fact, Attorney won't be subject to discipline *even if* he contacts the witness himself. That's because Attorney has a duty to pursue the evidence of perjury, and there's nothing in these facts to suggest a problem with the investigation. In favor of the investigation is the fact that it will help overturn Deft's conviction, and thus conducting it would be part of Attorney's duty of zealous advocacy. Even then, if there were something about the conduct that made it unethical, the investigation couldn't properly take place. Option D suggests that the element that would make the investigation unethical is personal contact from Attorney. In fact, this isn't true; as long as the investigation is not vexatious or harassing, it'll be permissible.

If you chose this response, something you'll want to keep in mind is that if a course of conduct is unethical, it's unethical whether the attorney does it himself or gets someone else to do it for him. Thus, in any of the communication–related restrictions on lawyer conduct (e.g., communication with jurors, judges, opposing parties), not only is a lawyer prohibited from personal contact, but he can't get someone else to contact the off–limits personnel, either.

Since option D places emphasis on the Attorney/Investigator distinction that in fact has no impact on the disciplinability of the conduct, it's not the best response.

Answer 48

A is the best response, because it correctly recognizes that, unless doing so prejudices Client, choosing the December trial date is Attorney's prerogative.

Decision–making authority between a client and his lawyer is split this way: the client makes major decisions (concerning the objectives of representation, affecting the merits of the case, and substantially prejudicing the client's rights). MR 1.2, EC 7–7. Procedural and strategic decisions—the means of effectuating the client's objectives—are made by the lawyer regardless of the client's wishes, except that the lawyer should defer to the client regarding costs incurred and concerns about the adverse effect of certain tactics on third parties. What this means is that whenever a decision will substantially prejudice a client's rights, the decision must be made by the client, not the lawyer.

Under these facts, you have a civil case that is already a year old. You're also told that Client has told Attorney he'd be available for trial any time October through December. This is a crucial fact, because it suggests to you implicitly that a December trial date won't substantially prejudice Client; beyond that, option A *conditions* the propriety of Attorney's accepting the December trial date on that date's not prejudicing Client. Without this prejudice, there's nothing in these facts to suggest that Attorney doesn't have the authority to choose the December trial date (e.g., there's no evidence of increased costs or adverse effect on third parties).

What makes this problem a little tricky is that, under some circumstances, a non–prejudicial delay can subject a lawyer to discipline for incompetence. Part of a lawyer's duty of professional competence is that he not "neglect" matters entrusted to him. If a delay in performing duties is unreasonable, it's disciplinable even if it doesn't prejudice the client's case! For instance, say Client approached Attorney with his claim a year before the statute of limitations was due to run out on the claim. Because Attorney's office is busy, complaints are not filed until they have to be, and Client's complaint isn't filed until a week before the statute of limitations runs out. Assuming this delay is considered unreasonable, it's disciplinable, the reasoning being that "unreasonable delay can cause a client needless anxiety and undermine confidence in the lawyer's trustworthiness." Comment, MR 1.3. The reason this doesn't apply here is that, for one thing, it's unlikely that a two month delay in setting a trial date would be considered unreasonable, especially in light of Client's willingness to go to trial in December. For another thing, there isn't an option that addresses the possibility of an unreasonable delay.

Since option A recognizes that, in the absence of prejudice to Client, Attorney is free to choose the December trial date, it's the best response.

B is not the best response, because it states an erroneous rule of legal ethics.

A lawyer owes his clients the duty of competent service, regardless of whether the client's matter is civil or criminal. While this will generally mean that a lawyer will have to prepare for trial more quickly in criminal cases than civil ones, it doesn't mean that his criminal clients take precedence over his civil clients.

Instead, for purposes of this problem, you have to look at the specific call of the question—whether Attorney had the authority to agree to the December trial date without Client's approval. What this tells you is that the issue here is one of *decision–making authority,* namely, who gets to decide matters like trial dates—the client or the attorney? The rule is that the client makes major decisions (concerning the objectives of representation, affecting the merits of the case, and substantially prejudicing the client's rights). MR 1.2, EC 7–7. Procedural and strategic decisions—the means of effectuating the client's objectives—are made by the lawyer regardless of the client's wishes, except that the lawyer should defer to the client regarding costs incurred and concerns about the adverse effect of certain tactics on third parties. Thus, under these facts, Attorney would have the power to set the December trial date in the absence of substantial prejudice to Client, since there's no indication of cost or adverse effect issues on these facts. *This* is what determines the propriety of Attorney's conduct, not the fact that Client's case is civil instead of criminal. Since option B doesn't recognize this, it's not the best response.

C is not the best response, because it misstates Attorney's duties concerning her workload.

Contrary to what option C states, a lawyer does not have a duty to manage his calendar so all his cases can be tried promptly; rather, as part of his duty of competent representation, a lawyer must act with *reasonable diligence.* DR 6–101(A)(3), MR 1.3. As a result, this wouldn't require that Attorney accept the first available trial date in every case. In fact, doing so might sometimes be bad for her clients, in that she may not have sufficient time to prepare for some trials if she is bound to accept the earliest trial date available.

This response is quite tricky—for reasons we'll discuss in a moment—but if you think about it in light of the specific call of the question, you can see that it can't be the best response. The call of the question asks you whether it was proper for Attorney to accept the December trial date *without Client's consent.* What this tells you is that the issue is decision–making authority, namely, whether Attorney had the right to decide to accept the December trial date—not whether she should have arranged her schedule so as to accept the October date. If you chose the latter response, you probably overlooked the call of the question by reading a bit too quickly. In any case, the rule on decision–making authority is that the client makes major decisions (concerning the objectives of representation, affecting the merits of the case, and substantially prejudicing the client's rights). MR 1.2, EC 7–7. Procedural and strategic decisions—the means of effectuating the client's objectives—are made by the lawyer regardless of the client's wishes, except that the lawyer should defer to the client regarding costs incurred and concerns about the adverse effect of certain tactics on third parties. Thus, under these facts, Attorney would have the power to set the December trial date in the absence of substantial prejudice to Client, since there's no indication of cost or adverse effect issues on these facts.

Now let's take a look at what makes option C tricky. You may have a nagging feeling that at some point putting off trial dates would get Attorney into trouble, and you're right. This happens when the delay becomes *unreasonable,* the reasoning being that "unreasonable delay can cause a client needless anxiety and undermine confidence in the lawyer's trustworthiness." Comment, MR 1.3. Even if the issue here were delay and not decision–making power, Attorney wouldn't be subject to discipline, because the fact that Client already OK'd a possible December trial date tells you that the extra two months isn't unreasonable. However, the central problem with option C remains that it doesn't recognize that the issue is decision–making, which is why option C isn't the best response.

D is not the best response, because it doesn't establish a basis on which Attorney's conduct could be improper.

The question here asks you whether Attorney acted properly in accepting the December trial date *without Client's consent.* This tells you that the issue must be who gets to choose the trial date—Attorney or Client. What option D does, by using the modifier "unless," is to make the decision–making authority dependent on whether or not Attorney was appointed to represent the criminal client. In effect, option D states, "Attorney was correct in choosing the December trial date without Client's consent if and only if Attorney was appointed to represent the client in the criminal case." In fact, this doesn't represent the rule on decision–making.

The rule on decision–making authority is that the client makes major decisions (concerning the objectives of representation, affecting the merits of the case, and substantially prejudicing the client's rights). MR 1.2, EC 7–7. Procedural and strategic decisions—the means of effectuating the client's objectives—are made by the lawyer regardless of the client's wishes, except that the lawyer should defer to the client regarding costs incurred and concerns about the adverse effect of certain tactics on third parties.

Applying the rule to these facts, you find that Attorney would have the power to set the December trial date in the absence of substantial prejudice to Client, since there's no indication of cost or adverse effect issues on these facts. Note that this has nothing to do with how Attorney came to represent her criminal client. What option D does is open up a whole can of worms as to how an attorney who is appointed to represent an indigent criminal client should juggle the rest of his workload. This goes far beyond the facts in this question, and, frankly, it's unlikely it could be tested on the MPRE, since the whole issue of court-appointed counsel is subject to much debate.

In any case, since option D conditions the propriety of Attorney's conduct on how she got her criminal client and not on decision–making authority, it's not the best response.

Answer 49

A is the best response, because the only proper thing for Attorney to do is seek to withdraw from the representation altogether.

In these facts, you have Attorney representing multiple defendants—Able and Baker—in a criminal case, with a conflict of interest arising *after* the representation begins, namely, Able's trying to rat on Baker to save his own hide, and thus making their defenses inconsistent. The problem at this point is that Attorney has confidential information from *both* Able and Baker, which would stop Attorney from representing *either one,* since a lawyer can't represent someone with adverse interests in a matter once he has confidential information from another client. What this means is that Attorney must seek to withdraw from representing *both* Able and Baker.

Note that the conflict of interest creates *mandatory* grounds for withdrawal, because continued representation will result in a legal or ethical violation, which is one of the grounds for mandatory withdrawal under DR 2–110(B) and MR 1 .16(a). (The other grounds for mandatory withdrawal are a physical or mental condition of the lawyer which materially impairs or makes it unreasonably difficult to continue effective representation; the client discharges the lawyer; or it's obvious that the client's purpose is harassment or materially injuring someone.) Option A also mentions that Attorney must not simply withdraw, but rather he must request court approval to do so, which is also correct, since once a matter is before a court, a lawyer cannot withdraw from representation without the court's permission. DR 2–110(B) and MR 1.16(c).

Incidentally, note that the facts here illustrate why, as a practical matter, a lawyer should ordinarily decline to represent more than one co–defendant in a criminal case. MR 1.7(b) and Comment, DR 5–105(B) and (C). Such representation is only possible if the risk of adverse effect is minimal, the lawyer reasonably believes his judgment won't be impaired as to anyone he's representing, and each defendant is fully consulted and consents to the multiple representation. From the outset, separate counsel is necessary for codefendants where their interests *may not* coincide. Glasser v. U.S. (1942). Since the possibility for conflict is so strong when one lawyer represents multiple defendants, in the vast majority of cases such representation would be unethical.

Since option A recognizes that the conflict of interest requires Attorney to seek to withdraw from representing *both* Able and Baker, it's the best response.

B is not the best response, because the conflict of interest here would be considered non–consentable.

Option B implicitly recognizes that there's a conflict of interest problem here—Able and Baker have inconsistent defenses, such that Attorney can't continue to pursue the best interests of either of them. Attorney can't exercise independent professional judgment on behalf of either client without hurting the other. It would be in Able's best interests to plea bargain and rat on Baker, but if Attorney helps Able do so, Attorney would be acting adversely to his other client's interests. Similarly, if Attorney *doesn't* pursue the plea bargain for Able, he'd be acting adversely to Able's interests. However, where B trips up is in suggesting that it's proper for Attorney to go on representing one of them, Baker, with Able's consent. Consent would not remedy the conflict here, making it possible for Attorney to represent Baker only.

Most conflicts of interest are waivable, if the following two conditions are met: 1. the lawyer must reasonably believe that other interests will not adversely affect the representation, MR 1.7, DR 5–105(C), and 2. the client must explicitly consent after consultation (which requires communication of reasonably sufficient information to permit the client to appreciate the significance of the matter in question, including causes of action foreclosed by the conflict, and the consequences of consent even though it is subsequently withdrawn), MR 1.7(a)(1) and (b)(1); DR 5–105(C). The key word here is "most," since the conflict here is considered unconsentable. Apart from certain non-consentable conflicts of former government lawyers, there are only two types of conflicts that are not, practically speaking, consentable: cases where the client is not fully informed or suffers from impaired judgment, or where the consent itself would be considered objectively unreasonable. The latter is the problem here; representing a co–defendant with competing interests would be considered such a direct conflict that consent to the representation would not be recognized.

Note that option B is correct in the sense that it states that court approval would be necessary for Attorney to withdraw as Able's lawyer. That's because once a matter is before a court, the lawyer can't withdraw from representation without court approval. DR 2–110(B) and MR 1.16(c).

Under these facts, Attorney's only proper course of action would be to seek to withdraw from representing *both* Able and Baker. The fact that he has confidential information from each one makes continuing to represent either one an ethical violation, and since consent isn't possible in this situation, withdrawal is the only alternative. Since option B doesn't recognize this, it's not the best response.

C is not the best response, because it overlooks the fact that any consent from Baker would be invalid.

Option C implicitly recognizes that there's a conflict of interest problem here—Able and Baker have inconsistent defenses, such that Attorney can't continue to pursue the best interests of both of them. Attorney can't exercise independent professional judgment on behalf of either client without hurting the other. It would be in Able's best interests to plea bargain and rat on Baker, but if Attorney helps Able do so, Attorney would be acting adversely to his other client's interests. Similarly, if Attorney *doesn't* pursue the plea bargain for Able, he'd be acting adversely to Able's interests. However, where C falters is in suggesting that it's proper for Attorney to go on representing one of them, Able, with Baker's consent. Consent would not remedy the conflict here, making it possible for Attorney to represent Able only.

Most conflicts of interest are waivable, if the following two conditions are met: 1. the lawyer must reasonably believe that other interests will not adversely affect the representation, MR 1.7, DR 5–105(C), and 2. the client must explicitly consent after consultation (which requires communication of reasonably sufficient information to permit the client to appreciate the significance of the matter in question, including causes of action fore-closed by the conflict, and the consequences of consent even though it is subsequently withdrawn), MR 1.7(a)(1) and (b)(1); DR 5–105(C). The key word here is "most," since the conflict here is considered unconsentable. Apart from certain non-consentable conflicts of former government law-yers, there are only two types of conflicts that are not, practically speaking, consentable: cases where the client is not fully informed or suffers from impaired judgment, or where the consent itself would be considered objec-tively unreasonable. The latter is the problem here; representing a co–de-fendant with competing interests would be considered such a direct conflict that consent to the representation would not be recognized.

Note that option C is correct in the sense that it states that court approval would be necessary for Attorney to withdraw as Baker's lawyer. That's be-cause once a matter is before a court, the lawyer can't withdraw from rep-resentation without court approval. DR 2–110(B) and MR 1.16(c).

Under these facts, Attorney's only proper course of action would be to seek to withdraw from representing *both* Able and Baker. The fact that he has confidential information from each one makes continuing to represent either one an ethical violation, and since consent isn't possible in this sit-uation, withdrawal is the only alternative. Since option C doesn't recog-nize this, it's not the best response.

D is not the best response, because there's a conflict of interest in these facts that can only be remedied by Attorney's seeking to withdraw from the representation altogether.

Under these facts, you have one lawyer, Attorney, representing two crim-inal defendants, Able and Baker. The problem is that there's a conflict in the representation, such that Attorney can't exercise independent profes-sional judgment on behalf of either client without hurting the other. It would be in Able's best interests to plea bargain and rat on Baker, but if Attorney helps Able do so, Attorney would be acting adversely to his other client's interests. Similarly, if Attorney *doesn't* pursue the plea bargain for Able, he'd be acting adversely to Able's interests. Thus, contrary to what option D states, Attorney cannot continue to represent Able and Baker, even if, as D suggests, he doesn't call Able as a witness. It's not Able's ac-tually testifying against Baker that's a problem, but the fact that he can't zealously pursue the goals of both clients.

Instead, since Attorney has confidential information from both Able and Baker, the only proper course is to seek the court's permission to withdraw from representing both of them. (Court permission for withdrawal is always required if the matter is before a court.) In fact, the facts here are a clear illustration of why it's almost never advisable for a lawyer to take on multiple defendants in a criminal case. Since option D doesn't recognize that Attorney cannot go on representing both Able and Baker—nor, in fact, either one of them—it's not the best response.

Answer 50

C is the best response, because it recognizes the additional elements that must be met in order for Judge's *ex parte* contact with Attorney to be proper.

As a general rule, a judge cannot have *ex parte* communications regarding a pending or impending proceeding not authorized by law, except he *can* seek the advice of disinterested legal experts. Canon 3(A)(4). The exception is what's at work here. In order for the "disinterested legal expert" exception to insulate Judge from discipline for relying on Attorney's letter, Judge would have to fulfill two additional requirements:

1. he'd have to notify all the parties as to who was consulted, and the substance of the advice given; and

2. he'd have to give all parties a reasonable opportunity to respond to the advice.

Note, as a threshold matter, that option C uses the modifier "unless." This means that in order for it to be the best response, the reasoning must be the only way the result *cannot* occur. Applying the rule from 3(A)(4) to the facts, you can see that this is true. If Judge doesn't communicate the contents of the letter to the parties, through their counsel, and give them an opportunity to respond, he will have acted improperly.

Note that option C states that Judge need only notify the lawyers in the case about Attorney's letter before he renders his decision. This is an important point to remember about the "disinterested legal expert" rule; namely, the judge doesn't have to seek the parties' *consent* before consulting a legal expert, he need only notify them of the contact. Furthermore, the notice needn't come before the judge consults the expert; they may be told afterward, as long as they have an opportunity to respond to the advice given.

Note also that the point at which the disinterested legal expert rule "kicked in" under these facts was when Judge decided to use Attorney's explanation of the law rather than that of the lawyers in the case. Until then, Judge was free to read and file anything about law.

Since option C correctly applies the disinterested legal expert rule to these facts, it's the best response.

A is not the best response, because the initiator of the communication doesn't determine its propriety.

Option A suggests that the communication here would only be impermissible if Judge initiated it. In fact, this misstates the rule on judge's *ex parte* communications about a pending or impending matter. The rule is that a judge cannot have *ex parte* communications regarding a pending or impending proceeding not authorized by law, except that he *can* seek the advice of disinterested legal experts. Canon 3(A)(4). The exception is what's at work here. In order for the "disinterested legal expert" exception to insulate Judge from discipline for relying on Attorney's letter, Judge would have to fulfill two additional requirements:

1. he'd have to notify all the parties as to who was consulted, and the substance of the advice given; and

2. he'd have to give all parties a reasonable opportunity to respond to the advice.

Note that this rule applies regardless of who initiated the contact. In fact, it's important to keep in mind that if *any* ethical rule prevents a certain kind of communication—e.g., *ex parte* contact with jurors, contact with an opposing party represented by counsel—it doesn't matter who initiates it. Here, as soon as Judge concludes that he's going to rely on Attorney's advice, his duty to notify the lawyers in the case kicks in. Since option A doesn't recognize this, it's not the best response.

B is not the best response, because the fact that Attorney isn't connected with the case doesn't of itself make the contact with him proper.

Option B uses the modifier "if." This means the reasoning must be plausible on the facts, it must resolve a central issue, and the result and the reasoning must agree. Here, it's plausible that Attorney doesn't have any clients who'll be affected by ABCO v. DEFO. The problem is that this doesn't make contact with him permissible. Under these facts, Judge is involved with *ex parte* communications about a pending or impending matter. The rule is that a judge cannot have such communications not authorized by law, except he *can* seek the advice of disinterested legal experts. Canon 3(A)(4). The exception is what's at work here. In order for the "disinterested legal expert" exception to insulate Judge from discipline for relying on Attorney's letter, Judge would have to fulfill two additional requirements:

1. he'd have to notify all the parties as to who was consulted, and the substance of the advice given; and

2. he'd have to give all parties a reasonable opportunity to respond to the advice.

Thus, the only way Judge could properly rely on Attorney's advice is by notifying the parties and giving them a chance to respond to the advice. Since Attorney's lack of contact with the case doesn't make the communication proper, and option B doesn't recognize this, it's not the best response.

D is not the best response, because Judge may, if certain conditions are satisfied, accept Attorney's advice even if he has no connection with the case whatsoever.

Option D suggests that a judge is confined to the trial briefs of counsel in the case for interpretation of the law. In fact, this isn't true. If a judge wants additional legal advice in a case, the *typical* course is to seek *amicus curiae* briefs from lawyers not connected with the case. The specific problem under these facts is the possibility that Judge may violate the rule against *ex parte* communications about a pending or impending matter. The rule is that a judge cannot have such communications not authorized by law, except that he *can* seek the advice of disinterested legal experts. Canon 3(A)(4). The exception is what's at work here. In order for the "disinterested legal expert" exception to insulate Judge from discipline for relying on Attorney's letter, Judge would have to fulfill two additional requirements:

1. he'd have to notify all the parties as to who was consulted, and the substance of the advice given; and

2. he'd have to give all parties a reasonable opportunity to respond to the advice.

If Judge satisfies these additional elements—and there's nothing in these facts to say that he couldn't—he can properly rely on Attorney's reasoning even though Attorney is not on record as counsel in the case, contrary to what option D states. (Note, incidentally, that the rule against *ex parte* communication doesn't stop a judge from consulting with "court personnel whose function is to aid the judge in carrying out his adjudicative responsibilities" (e.g.,law clerks), or with other judges. CJC Canon 3(A)(4), Commentary.) Since Judge can potentially properly rely on Attorney's advice even though he doesn't represent a party in the case, and D doesn't recognize this, it's not the best response.